I0884867

Routledge Revivals

Gulliver and the Gentle Reader

Originally published in 1973, *Gulliver and the Gentle Reader* critically examines the writing of Jonathan Swift. The book is predominately concerned with what Rawson coins 'the "unofficial" energies' which work below the surface of Swift's conscious themes. Alongside this discussion, Rawson provides detailed studies on historical, cultural and psychological relationships, and the connections that exist between these areas, and the more extreme writers of the later period such as Breton, Mailer, and Yeats, as well as the connections with the writers such as his contemporary Pope, and those that followed such as Johnson, and Sterne. This book will be of interest to students of literature, as well as those researching in the area of literature.

Routledge Revivals

Gulliver and the Gentle Reader

Studies in Swift and Our Time

Claude Rawson

Routledge
Taylor & Francis Group

First published in 1973
by Routledge and Kegan Paul
Republished in 1991
by Humanities Press International Inc.

This edition first published in 2017 by Routledge
2 Park Square, Milton Park, Abingdon, Oxon, OX14 4RN
and by Routledge
711 Third Avenue, New York, NY 10017

Routledge is an imprint of the Taylor & Francis Group, an informa business

Publisher's Note
The publisher has gone to great lengths to ensure the quality of this reprint but points out that some imperfections in the original copies may be apparent.

Disclaimer
The publisher has made every effort to trace copyright holders and welcomes correspondence from those they have been unable to contact.

A Library of Congress record exists under ISBN: 91016181

ISBN 13: 978-1-138-55879-3 (hbk)
ISBN 13: 978-0-203-71344-0 (ebk)
ISBN 13: 978-1-138-55884-7 (pbk)

GULLIVER AND THE GENTLE READER

GULLIVER AND THE GENTLE READER

Studies in Swift and our Time

Claude Rawson

HUMANITIES PRESS INTERNATIONAL, INC.
NEW JERSEY AND LONDON

First published in 1973
by Routledge & Kegan Paul Ltd

This paperback edition first published,
with a new preface, in 1991 by
Humanities Press International, Inc.
Atlantic Highlands, NJ 07716, and
3 Henrietta Street, Covent Garden, London WC2E 8LU

Library of Congress Cataloging-in-Publication Data

Rawson, Claude Julien.
Gulliver and the gentle reader : studies in Swift and
our time / Claude Rawson.
p. cm.
Reprint. Originally published:
London ; Boston : Routledge & K. Paul, 1973.
Includes bibliographical references and index.
ISBN 0-391-03710-2
1. Swift, Jonathan, 1667–1745—Criticism and
interpretation. I. Title.
[PR3727.R28 1991]
828'.509—dc20 91–16181
CIP

British Library Cataloguing in Publication Data

Rawson, Claude
Gulliver and the gentle reader.
I. Title
823.5

ISBN 0391037102

CONTENTS

FOR MY PARENTS

PREFACE TO THE PAPERBACK EDITION

This book, like *Henry Fielding and the Augustan Ideal under Stress*, which is being simultaneously reissued, was written on the following general assumptions: that what has traditionally passed for an 'Augustan world picture' is not a useful concept; that the aspirations to order and stability visible in some leading writers were undercut by energies of misrule, both personal and cultural; that (contrary to the assumptions of traditional literary history) the thought and writings of the period, like those of any period, always exist under pressure and display loose ends and inconsistencies which are as powerful and important as the notional structures ('spirit of the age', 'providence of wit', 'great chain of being', 'peace of the Augustans') through which literary historians have sought to understand or contain them; that 'periods' are not sealed units; and that literary texts are best understood in a total context which includes not only their contemporaneous setting but also comparable texts from earlier and later (including modern) times.

These assumptions, and their application to individual writers (chiefly Swift and Fielding, but also Pope, Johnson and some others) were controversial in the 1970s, when the books first appeared, and they continue to challenge some orthodoxies. The passage of time has shown them to have provoked a good deal of debate and to have had an impact on the study of my two principal authors.

Two features of this book to which I attach special importance—its focus on some aspects of author-reader relations and on the self-implication or even self-subversiveness of Swift's satire—were early forays into territory now occupied by some theorists with whose current work I do not often feel in accord. There is now, I believe, a greater readiness than before to understand the other aspects of Swift's work explored in this book. I am thinking especially of his deep and in some ways prophetic inwardness with certain modes of the modern imagination which he would have repudiated: the posturing Shandean self-consciousness, for example, which runs from Sterne to Norman Mailer and which he might be said to have parodied in advance; the eruptive violences and the play of 'black humour' which link him to the surrealists and the literature of 'cruelty'; his extraordinary influence on writers whose adversarial or disruptive outlooks might seem the antithesis of his authoritarian commitment to tradition and rule.

This book, like its companion volume, has been out of print for some time, and it gives me pleasure that both are again being made available to readers.

Yale University
October 1990

PREFACE TO THE FIRST EDITION AND ACKNOWLEDGMENTS

The studies in this book were written over the same period of years as those which form my recent volume, *Henry Fielding and the Augustan Ideal Under Stress* (Routledge & Kegan Paul, 1972). The two books are related by various common themes and ideas, most notably by their preoccupation with authorial temperaments and styles which reflect a tension between Augustan ideals of correctness and 'polite' civilization on the one hand, and inner and outer forces of misrule on the other. From this point of view, my two central figures, Fielding and Swift, throw light on one another, both in their resemblances and their differences, to an extent which made it seem undesirable and perhaps impossible to write about either without frequently referring to the other, and a certain amount of overlap will be found between the two books, including, in a few cases, brief passages nearly identical with one another. These have been kept to the minimum, and occur only where it seemed to me that a difficult or complex line of argument would otherwise come through less clearly.

There are also similarities of method between the two books. I have not attempted to provide a progressive account of Swift's development, and, as with Fielding in the previous book, I discuss a late work (here *Gulliver's Travels*) early in the book, and concentrate increasingly on an early work (here *A Tale of a Tub*) as the book progresses. It seemed to me that some of my principal themes were better deployed in this way: the order of the chapters is in fact roughly my order of composition, and records the unfolding of my own present conception of Swift. I imagine that the first essay will seem closest to orthodox readings of Swift, if there are such things, and that the later ones will seem, as they are meant to seem, increasingly exploratory. One thread of argument to which I attach importance is that Swift's satire reveals itself not primarily as a Satire on Man in some impersonal or third-person sense which leaves the reader and the author out, but that some of its most powerful energies attack the reader (or 'second person') and finally implicate the author himself (or 'first person') in various ways, 'official' and 'unofficial'.

Some of the 'unofficial' energies of Swift's writing move further still, beyond satire to some kind of indulgence of the things mimicked or satirized. These energies seem to me to connect Swift with certain extremist or violent writers of later times, despite the fact that he would have disavowed the various kinds of 'modernity' they stood for. I have also been concerned to indicate certain paradoxes, which are related to this, in his relations with some writers of his own century. One such paradox is Swift's radical difference from Pope, the major writer with whom he had the closest ties of friendship and with whom he shared so many consciously formulated attitudes on moral and cultural matters. Another paradox is that of Swift's important *similarities* with Johnson, who disliked his work, and Sterne, whose work he would have disliked.

My method has been to explore these themes with a degree of deliberate circularity, to return in different contexts to the same crucial passages, and to examine them from what may sometimes seem overlapping or conflicting points of view. As in the book on Fielding, this method seemed to me likelier to reflect the many-sided complexity of the works discussed than a more logically ordered arrangement.

Chapter I was first published, in a slightly different form, in *Imagined Worlds: Essays on Some English Novels and Novelists in Honour of John Butt*, ed. Maynard Mack and Ian Gregor (Methuen, 1968), pp. 51-90. Chapter II and part of chapter III appeared, also in a slightly different form, in *Essays in Criticism*, xx (1970), 24-56, and xxii (1972), 161-81, and are reprinted by kind permission of the editors.

Chapter II grew out of a paper read at the Annual Convention of the Modern Language Association of America in New York in 1968. To Max Novak, who invited me to do this, I owe debts of gratitude which go well beyond the specific occasion. He has been a warm friend and a valued intellectual stimulus for many years. To many scholars at the Convention with whom I had the privilege to exchange views I owe many points of information, and much clarification of ideas. The Pope and Johnson sections of chapter II were read as a paper to G. S. Rousseau's Eighteenth-Century Seminar at the University of California, Los Angeles, and I owe much to the searching discussion which followed.

Other parts of this book were read as papers at the Universities of

Newcastle upon Tyne and Warwick, where many colleagues and students helped me to form my ideas.

The following persons read parts of the book, made corrections, answered questions and suggested ideas: T. C. Cave, Richard N. Coe, Ian Donaldson, G. K. Hunter, J. C. Maxwell, Jenny Mezciems, my wife Judy Rawson, Arthur H. Scouten, Martin Wright.

To Joyce Pemberton and Ann Griffin I am deeply indebted for many kinds of secretarial assistance, always accomplished with generosity, patience and skill.

To the University of Warwick Library, and especially to Audrey Cooper, I owe a great and continuing debt for many kinds of help. The University's generous sabbatical leave facilities enabled me to complete the book in freedom from teaching and from administrative duties, and for this I am grateful.

C. J. Rawson
University of Warwick

NOTE ON TEXTS AND ABBREVIATIONS

The following abbreviations have been used throughout in references to Swift's writings:

Correspondence: ed. Harold Williams, 5 vols (Oxford, 1963-5)
Journal to Stella: ed. Harold Williams, 2 vols (Oxford, 1948)
Poems: ed. Harold Williams, 2nd edn, 3 vols (Oxford, 1958)
Works: The Prose Writings of Jonathan Swift, ed. Herbert Davis and others, 14 vols (Oxford [Blackwell], 1939-68).

All quotations are from these editions, unless otherwise noted. I normally give volume and page references in the notes, but chapter, section or line of individual works, where convenient, in brackets in the text. A special exception for *Gulliver's Travels* in my first chapter is explained at chapter I, n.18.

All quotations from Pope's poems use the Twickenham texts and lineation.

CHAPTER I

GULLIVER AND THE GENTLE READER

JILL You put me in the wrong
JACK I am not putting you in the wrong
JILL You put me in the wrong for thinking you put me in the wrong.

(R. D. Laing, *Knots*)

''Tis a great Ease to my Conscience that I have writ so elaborate and useful a Discourse without one grain of Satyr intermixt':[1] this, from the Preface to *A Tale of a Tub*, outdoes even Gulliver's claims to veracity in its cheeky outrageousness. That 'provocative display of indirectness'[2] which Herbert Read (in a fine though somewhat unfriendly phrase) saw in *Gulliver* governs also the mad parodic word of the *Tale*. The seven prefatory items followed by an Introduction, the signposted chapters of digression (one of them in praise of digressions), the pseudo-scholarly annotation (with the 'commentator' sometimes at odds with the 'author'), the triumphant assimilation into the notes of Wotton's hostile exegesis, the asterisks and gaps in the MS., the promise of such forthcoming publications as *A Panegyrick upon the World* and *A General History of Ears*, have an exuberance which transcends mere parody and mere playfulness. In such a context, the posturing denial of satiric intention draws a provoking and almost unsettling attention to itself. We have not yet reached the sudden violences, and the more radical underminings, of the religious allegory or the Digression on Madness, but we are made curiously insecure as to how, exactly, to take the joke.

Nor can we comfortably separate, in our minds, the silly geniality of the putative 'author' from Swift's own more astringent presence. Typically, we become aware of a strange interplay of astringency and exuberance, in which it is not always easy to distinguish between narrator and real author. The narrator, or mock-author, is a creature of mad and monstrous egotism, who confides his private problems and draws garrulous attention to his literary techniques. But the *Tale*'s whole marathon of self-posturing cannot be entirely accounted for by its ostensible purpose, which is to mock those modern authors, 'L'estrange, Dryden, *and some others*' (*Tale*, 1),[3] who write this sort of book straight. For the *Tale* has at the same time a vitality of sheer performance which suggests that a strong self-conscious pressure of primary self-display on Swift's own part is also at work; the almost 'romantic' assertion of an immense (though edgy, oblique, and agressively self-concealing) egocentricity. Swift's descendants in the old game of parodic self-consciousness are Romantics of a special sort, like Sterne and (after him) the Byron of *Don Juan*. If the *Tale*'s 'Digression in Praise of Digressions' looks back to, and mocks, things like L'Estrange's 'Preface upon a Preface',[4] it also looks forward to Sterne's 'chapter upon chapters', and it is not for nothing that Tristram thinks his book will 'swim down the gutter of Time' in the company of Swift's.[5]

Whatever the ancestry of the technical devices as such, the parodic intrusions of Swift's 'authors' have a centrality and importance, and are made by Swift to carry a strength of personal charge, which seem to be new.[6] In Sterne and Byron, and in the Norman Mailer of *Advertisements for Myself*, self-conscious forms of parody and self-parody openly become a solipsistic exercise, an oblique mode of self-exploration and self-display much more radical and far-reaching than the playful posturings of Cervantes or Burton, or even Rabelais. Compare the fact that Swift's *Tale* is a satire of advertisements for oneself not only with the title of Mailer's book, but with the fact that Mailer's 'advertisements' are exactly the kind of prefatory note and solipsistic digression which Swift parodies. Mailer's coy description of his practice and motives might almost be taken from the *Tale*, with its 'admirable desire to please his readers', its typographic self-consciousness, its acknowledgment of the superior attraction of prefaces over the books themselves:[7]

> The author, taken with an admirable desire to please his readers, has also added a set of advertisements, printed in italics, which surround all of these writings with his present tastes, preferences, apologies, prides, and occasional confessions. Like many another literary fraud, the writer has been known on occasion

to read the Preface of a book instead of a book, and bearing
this vice in mind, he tried to make the advertisements more
readable than the rest of his pages.

It might be argued that Mailer has reached a point where irony, or at least any very fundamental degree of self-mockery, has largely disappeared, and that he provides an impure comparison. Perhaps this fact shows *a fortiori* the special potential of Swiftian parody for turning into a primary self-assertion, and more will be said about Mailer later.[8] In Sterne, where the outward forms of mockery and self-mockery are still almost as prominent as in Swift, and where the style looks back to Swift most directly and avowedly, there is a more immediate guide to certain 'unofficial' aspects of Swift's manner.

Swift has in common with Sterne, against most pre-Swiftian practitioners of 'self-conscious narration', the imposition of an exceptional immediacy of involvement with the reader. The narrators are not, of course, the equivalents of Swift or even Sterne: but each is an 'I' of whose existence and temperament we are kept unremittingly aware, who talks to the reader and seems to be writing the book, and through whom the real author projects a very distinctive presence of his own. Swift and Sterne also share a kind of intimate, inward-looking obliquity which sets them off, say, from their master Rabelais, who like them projects a formidable presence, but whose boozy companionable exhibitionism amounts to an altogether different (and more 'open') manner. This obliquity (more or less instinctive in Swift, more coyly self-aware in Sterne) perhaps takes the place of an overt self-expression which Augustan decorum, and whatever personal inhibitions, discouraged.[9]

There are, however, important differences also. When Swift's 'author' declares in his Dedication to Prince Posterity that 'what I am going to say is literally true this Minute I am writing: What Revolutions may happen before it shall be ready for your Perusal, I can by no means warrant',[10] Swift is exposing the trivial ephemerality of modern writers. Similar remarks from Sterne (or, without any ironic admixture, from Richardson) proudly proclaim the immediacy of their method of writing '*to the Moment*'.[11] Swift's mimicry repudiates that intimacy between author and reader which Sterne and Richardson celebrate, but it does not *cancel* such intimacy, as I shall hope to show. Again, when Swift's 'author' proclaims in the Preface his determination 'to assist the diligent Reader' in 'putting himself into the Circumstances and Postures of Life, that the Writer was in, upon every important Passage as it flow'd from his Pen', so that there may be 'a Parity and strict Correspondence of

Idea's between the Reader and the Author',[12] Swift is attacking modern garrulities of self-revelation which for him amount to indecent exposure. In Sterne such remarks, however fraught with all manner of Shandean indirection, are genially proffered tokens of relationship. Tristram wants to tell you everything about himself, because he and Sterne enjoy his character (including the irony injected into it by Sterne, and of which Sterne's parodic performance is a part) as a rich fact of human nature. Both want to get the reader intimately involved:[13]

> As you proceed farther with me, the slight acquaintance, which is now beginning betwixt us, will grow into familiarity; and that, unless one of us is in fault, will terminate in friendship.—*O diem praeclarum!*—then nothing which has touched me will be thought trifling in its nature or tedious in its telling.

The difference is not simply a matter of parody, for that exists in Sterne too. Swift's 'author', like Sterne's, often addresses the reader and invokes 'all the Friendship that hath passed between Us'. At the end of the *Tale*, he has no more to say but thinks of experimenting on how to go on writing '*upon Nothing*', 'to let' (in a phrase Sterne might have used) 'the Pen still move on':[14]

> By the Time that an Author has writ out a Book, he and his Readers are become old Acquaintance, and grow very loth to part: So that I have sometimes known it to be in Writing, as in Visiting, where the Ceremony of taking Leave, has employ'd more Time than the whole Conversation before.

Neither this, nor Sterne's passage, is quite straight. That both are in some sense ironic need not be laboured. But Sterne's irony is of that puppyish, clinging sort which prods, cajoles, sometimes irritates the reader into a participation which may be reluctant and grudging, but which is also primary, direct and real. Swift's words assert the same intimacy, but the actual effect of the Swiftian acidity at the end of the 'author's' innocent sentence would *appear* to be to sever the link, to achieve not intimacy but an alienation. Sterne's irony is one of fond permissive indulgence; the egotism, though mocked, is freely played with, and the reader offered hospitality within it. In Swift's characteristic sting, the friendly egotism freezes into a stark reminder of the fact of mockery or parody of egotism, and (more than parody though by way of it) the claim to friendship with the reader becomes a kind of insulting denial.

But this denial is not an effacement of Swift, nor a suspension of the reader's close sense of his presence. The parody is charged with a peculiarly personal quality of tart defiance (that 'self-assertion' of which Leavis speaks in his essay on Swift),[15] which seems to differentiate it from more normal modes of parody, whose formal business it is to mock books. It is a truism that Swiftian parody, like that of many writers who choose to make their most serious statements about life through the medium of allusions to books, is usually more than parody in that, in various directions, it transcends parody's limiting relation to the works parodied. *A Modest Proposal* is both more and other than a mockery of those economic proposals whose form it adopts. The real concern is with matters with which the parodic element as such has no necessary connection: the state of Ireland (rather than economic projectors) in the *Modest Proposal*, human pride (rather than popular travel-writing) in *Gulliver*. The problem sometimes arises of just where the dominant focus lies: a parodic energy may blur a more central intention, and there may be a hiatus between a local parodic effect and the main drift of the discourse. An aspect of this, to which I shall return briefly, is that teasing fluctuation, or bewildering uncertainty, of *genre* which critics have noted in some of Swift's works, and which gives a curious precariousness to the reader's grasp of what is going on. This has an undermining effect which is, in some ways, closely related to the more definite acts of authorial aggression. Beyond the truism that the satire's principal concerns transcend parody stands a further, more disturbing truth: that the nonparodic concerns are themselves transcended by energies which are much less easy to pin down, because they are not 'official' or overt.

The *Tale* differs in a formal sense from the *Modest Proposal* and *Gulliver* in that the 'modernity' which it attacks finds one of its main symptoms in the kind of book that is being parodied, so that the congruence between parody and the 'real' subject is particularly close. Even so, it would be wrong to suggest that this 'real' subject is merely a matter of silly or offensive stylistic habits, like garrulousness or digressiveness. The cumulative effect of the *Tale*'s formidable parodic array is to convey a sense of intellectual and cultural breakdown so massive and so compelling that the parodied objects, as such, come to seem a minor detail. This in no case makes the parody expendable. The manner of the hack-author, bland proposer, or truthful boneheaded traveller are essential to the effects Swift is creating, and not merely as means of highlighting satiric intensities through disarming naïvetics of style. My last example from the *Tale* shows how parody of friendly gestures from author to reader not only mocks modern garrulousness and all the intellectual slovenliness that goes with it (as well as capturing incidentally a typical social absurdity), but puts the reader himself under attack. This 'Satire of the Second Person', in H. W. Sams's useful phrase,[16] is not primarily a matter of *satirizing* the reader, but of making him uncomfortable in another sense, as a person we are rude to is made uncomfortable. Swift, as much as Sterne, is reaching out to the reader, and the alienation I spoke of does not in fact eliminate intimacy, though it destroys 'friendship'. There is something in Swift's relations with his reader that can be described approximately in terms of the edgy intimacy of a personal quarrel that does not quite come out into the open, with gratuitous-seeming sarcasms on one side and a defensive embarrassment on the other. Such a description can only be a half-truth. And, like many of the examples I shall be discussing, the passage is much lighter than any account of it can be. It is a joke (a good one), and playful. But it is attacking play, and its peculiar aggressiveness is a quality which I believe to be not merely incidental but pervasive in Swift's major satires.

This aggressiveness towards the reader is what chiefly distinguishes Swift from the later writers to whom he can be compared, and who imitate him or are prefigured in his work. It takes many forms, and is not confined to contexts of parody. In the *Tale*, however, parody cannot help being closely involved, and Swift's determined and naked hostility to the targets of his parody has several immediate consequences which differentiate his effects from those of similar passages in Sterne or Mailer. The primacy of the parodic element diverts formal attention (as distinct from our informal sense of Swift's teasing and often explosive presence) away from Swift to his satiric victims. The parody prevents by this means that unSwiftian note of self-cherishing which sometimes creeps into Sterne's, or Mailer's, use of 'self-conscious' mannerisms and other 'modern' postures, and correspondingly discourages easy complicities in the reader, without freeing the reader from an awkward sense of relationship. But whether parody is present or not, the aggression I speak of is usually quite inescapable in Swift's satire. What is involved is not necessarily a 'rhetoric' or thought-out strategy, so much as an atmosphere or perhaps an instinctive tone. This is not to mistake Swift for his masks, but to say that behind the screen of indirections, ironies, and putative authors a central Swiftian personality is always actively present, and makes itself felt.

Consider a scatological passage in *Gulliver*. I do not wish to add here to the available theories about the scatology and body-disgust as such.

Psychoanalysts have examined it; C. S. Lewis says, sturdily, that it is 'much better understood by schoolboys than by psychoanalysts'; another critic says the 'simplest answer is that as a conscientious priest [Swift] wished to discourage fornication';[17] others say that Swift was just advocating cleanliness, mocking the over-particularity of travel-writers, or doing no more any way than other writers in this or that literary tradition. But most people agree that there is a lot of it, and it has been a sore point from the start. Swift knew it, and knew that people knew, and early in book I he has a characteristic way of letting us know he knows we know (I.ii.29).[18] Gulliver had not relieved himself for two days, and tells us how in his urgency he now did so inside his Lilliputian house. But he assures us that on future occasions he always did 'that Business in open Air', and that the 'offensive Matter' was disposed of 'every Morning before Company came' by two Lilliputian servants.[19] Gulliver thinks the 'candid Reader' needs an explanation, so he tells us why he tells us this:

> I would not have dwelt so long upon a Circumstance, that perhaps at first Sight may appear not very momentous; if I had not thought it necessary to justify my Character in Point of Cleanliness to the World; which I am told, some of my Maligners have been pleased, upon this and other Occasions, to call in Question.

It is Gulliver and not Swift who is speaking, but it is Swift and not Gulliver who (in any sense that is active at this moment) has had maligners. Gulliver does have enemies in Lilliput, notably after urinating on the palace-fire, but the reader does not know this yet, and it is difficult not to sense behind Gulliver's self-apology a small egocentric defiance from the real author. This would be true whether one knew him to be Swift or not: but it comes naturally from the Swift whose writings, and especially *A Tale of a Tub*, had been accused of 'Filthiness', 'Lewdness', 'Immodesty', and of using 'the Language of the Stews' (Swift called it being 'battered with Dirt-Pellets' from 'envenom'd ... Mouths'.)[20] Swift's trick consists of doing what he implies people accuse him of, and saying that this proves he isn't like that really: the openly implausible denial becomes a cheeky flaunting of the thing denied, a tortuously barefaced challenge. This self-conscious sniping at the reader's poise occurs more than once: a variant instance of mock-friendly rubbing-in, for the 'gentle Reader's' benefit, occurs at the end of II.i, where the particularity of travel-writers is part of the joke.[21]

A related non-scatological passage, which Thackeray praised as 'the best stroke of humour, if there be a best in that abounding book',[22] is Gulliver's final farewell to his Houyhnhnm master, whose hoof he offers to kiss, as in the papal ceremony.[23] (Gulliver seems to have leanings that way: he also wanted to kiss the Queen of Brobdingnag's foot, but she just held out her little finger—II.iii.101.) 'But as I was going to prostrate myself to kiss his Hoof, he did me the Honour to raise it gently to my Mouth. I am not ignorant how much I have been censured for mentioning this last Particular' (IV.x.282). Since the passage occurs in the first edition, Gulliver or Swift could hardly have been censured for mentioning this before. 'Detractors' would be presumed by the reader to object that human dignity was being outraged, and Swift was of course right that many people would feel this about his book in general. But this is not Gulliver's meaning at all, and the typical Swiftian betrayal that follows gains its real force less from mere surprise than from its cool poker-faced fanning of a reader's hostility which Swift obviously anticipated and actually seemed on the point of trying to allay: 'Detractors are pleased to think it improbable, that so illustrious a Person should descend to give so great a Mark of Distinction to a Creature so inferior as I. Neither have I forgot, how apt some Travellers are to boast of extraordinary Favours they have received. But...' Thackeray's praise ('audacity', 'astounding gravity', 'truth topsy-turvy, entirely logical and absurd') comes just before the famous 'filthy in word, filthy in thought, furious, raging, obscene' passage:[24] it is perhaps appropriate that such coarse over-reaction should be the counterpart to a cheerful complacency in the face of the subtler energies of Swift's style.

The mention of travellers in the hoof-kissing passage brings us back to parody, but emphasizes again how readily Swiftian parody serves attacking purposes which are themselves non-parodic. Edward Stone's view that this reference is proof that Swift is merely joking at the expense of boastful travellers misses most of the flavour of the passage.[25] (One might as easily say that the main or only point of the passage is to guy a papal rite. I do not, of course, deny these secondary jokes, or their piquancy.) But parody is important, almost as much in its way as in the *Tale*. Gulliver is an author, who announces forthcoming publications about Lilliput (I.iv.47-8; I.vi.57) and Houyhnhnmland (IV.ix.275)—which is a common enough device—and whose putative authorship of the work we are actually reading, as well as being the source of many of its most central ironies, enables Swift to flaunt his own self-concealment in some amusing and disconcerting ways.[26] A portrait of Gulliver was prefixed to the early editions, and in 1735 this acquired the teasing caption 'Splendide Mendax'.[27] The elaborate claims to veracity in 'The

Publisher to the Reader' and in the text itself gain an additional piquancy from this. The 1735 edition also prints for the first time Gulliver's letter to Sympson, which, as prefatory epistles go, is a notably unbalanced document, providing advance notice of Gulliver's later anti-social state and by the same token giving a disturbing or at least confusing dimension to the sober opening pages of the narrative. Gulliver's announcement in the letter that *Brobdingnag* should have been spelt *Brobdingrag* (p. 8) belongs to a familiar kind of authenticating pretence in both fiction and prose satire, but in so far as we remember it later it does make it slightly unsettling to read *Brobdingnag* with an *n* every time it occurs in the book. It is clear that these devices, though not meant to be believed, are not bids for verisimilitude in the manner, say, of Richardson's 'editorial' pretence or the countless other tricks of fiction-writers before and after Swift (the correcting footnote, the manuscript partly missing or lost, the discovered diary, the pseudo-biography). Nor are they quite a matter of pure hearty fun, as in Rabelais, meant to be enjoyed *precisely as* too outrageous to be believed. For one thing, Swift's celebrated 'conciseness' is too astringent. It is also too close to the idiom of sober factuality, and some people were literally taken in.

We are hardly expected to take *Gulliver's Travels* as a straight (even if possibly mendacious) travel story. But the sea captain who claimed to be 'very well acquainted with Gulliver, but that the printer had Mistaken, that he livd in Wapping, & not in Rotherhith', the old gentleman who searched for Lilliput on the map, the Irish Bishop who said the 'Book was full of improbable lies, and for his part, he hardly believed a word of it'[28] (though some of these readers may have been more *ben trovati* than real) do tell a kind of truth about the work. Swift's whole ironic programme depends on our not being taken in by the travel-book element, but it does require us to be infected with a residual uncertainty about it; and these instances of an over-successful hoax fulfil, extremely, a potential in the work to which all readers must uneasily respond. This is not to accept the simpler accounts of Swiftian betrayal, which suggest that the plain traveller's, or modest proposer's, factuality lulls the reader into a false credulity, and then springs a trap. With Swift, we are always on our guard from the beginning (I believe this is true of sensitive *first* readings as well as later ones), and what surprises us is not the fact of betrayal but its particular form in each case. But if we are on our guard, we do not know what we are guarding against. The travel-book factuality, to which we return at least at the beginning and end of each book (even the end of book IV, in its strange way, sustains and elaborates the pretence), is so insistent, and at its purest so lacking in obvious pointers to a parodic intention, that we really do not know *exactly* how to take it. What saves the ordinary reader from being totally taken in is, obviously, the surrounding context. (The very opening of the narrative, from the 1735 edition onwards, is coloured by the letter to Sympson: but even before 1735 one would have needed to be exceptionally obtuse to think, by the end of the first chapter, that one was still reading a travel-book.) But not being taken in, and knowing the plain style to be parodic, do not save us from being unsure of what is being mocked: travel-books, fictions posing as travel-books, philosophic tales (like *Gulliver* itself) posing as fictions posing as travel-books.[29] Bewilderment is increased by the uncertainty of how much weight to give, moment by moment, to the fact of parody as such and to whatever the style may be mocking, since the parody as we have seen is continuously impregnated with satiric purposes which transcend or exist outside it, but which may still feed on it in subtle ways. And we cannot be sure that some of the plainness is not meant to be taken straight, not certainly as factual truth, but (in spite of everything) momentarily as realistic fictional trimmings: at least, the style helps to establish the 'character' of the narrator, though this 'character' in turn has more life as the basis of various ironies than as a vivid fictional personality. No accurate account can exhaust the matter, or escape an element of giddy circularity. The proper focus for Swift's precise sober narrative links is paradoxically a blurred focus, because we do not know what to make of all the precision. The accumulation of unresolved doubt that we carry into our reading of more central parts of *Gulliver's Travels* creates, then, not a credulity ripe for betrayal, but a more continuous defensive uneasiness. This undermining of our nervous poise makes us peculiarly vulnerable, in more than the obvious sense, to the more central satiric onslaughts.

The parodic element, though not primary, is never abandoned. At the end of book IV, when any live interest in travel-writers may be thought to have totally receded in the face of more overwhelming concerns, Gulliver keeps the subject alive with some tart reminders of his truthfulness and the mendacity of other travellers. The practice is commonplace, but again there is nothing here either of Rabelais's friendly outrageousness as he refers to his 'histoire tant veridicque', or his or Lucian's corresponding frank admission that they are telling monstrous lies, or the honest workmanlike concern with verisimilitude that we find in, say, *Erewhon*.[30] Gulliver says:

Thus, gentle Reader, I have given thee a faithful History of my

> Travels for Sixteen Years, and above Seven Months; wherein I have not been so studious of Ornament as of Truth. I could perhaps like others have astonished thee with strange improbable Tales; but I rather chose to relate plain Matter of Fact in the simplest Manner and Style; because my principal Design was to inform, and not to amuse thee (IV.xii.291).

This passage, which belongs with the well-known (and perhaps somewhat more light-hearted) remark to Pope about vexing the world rather than diverting it, emphasizes Swift's fundamental unfriendliness by a characteristic astringency (that tone is partly Swift's though Gulliver may overdo it), and by a use of the second person singular which is aggressively contemptuous. This probably parodies or inverts the common use of 'thee' and 'thou' in addresses to 'gentle readers', where, so far as the pronoun is not merely neutral, intimacy or familiarity is the point. But one can also compare places where an author treats his reader with mild aggressiveness, as when Burton opens his long preface to *The Anatomy of Melancholy* by proclaiming his freedom to tell or withhold information which the reader wants: in fact, the passage hardly has a Swiftian tang, and Burton ends the preface by earnestly requesting 'every private man ... not to take offence' and by presuming 'of thy good favour, and gracious acceptance (gentle reader)'.[31] Fielding's usages range from warm friendliness (*Tom Jones*, XVIII.i), through a more ruggedly admonishing but still friendly tone (IX.vii), to a partial identification of the reader with 'a little reptile of a critic' (X.i): but even here there is an initial comic relaxation (the comparison with Shakespeare and his editors), and the later concession to the reader that perhaps 'thy heart may be better than thy head'; and when Fielding takes stock of his relations with the reader in XVIII.i he warmly disclaims any intention to give offence.[32]

But Swift's use of 'thee' is the hostile one ('thou' and 'thee' were also often addressed to inferiors),[33] where familiarity, so to speak, has bred contempt. And what we sense in Swift's attack is not the grand public voice of the Satirist, which is, for example, Pope's voice. When Pope uses the hostile 'thee' in the *Essay on Man* (e.g. III.27ff., 'Has God, thou fool! work'd solely for thy good, ... Is it for thee the lark ascends and sings? ...'), it is Man he is addressing, not the reader. Swift's refusal of the 'lofty Stile' in the *Epistle to a Lady* rests on an old notion that ridicule is more effective than lambasting ('Switches better guide than Cudgels'), but he has a significant way of describing what the raillery does: it 'nettles', 'Sets the Spirits all a working'. 'Alecto's Whip' makes the victims (here specifically 'the Nation's Representers') 'wriggle, howl, and skip': the satirist makes clear that the whip is to be applied to 'their Bums', and that he will not be deterred by the smell.[34] Nothing could make clearer the note of quarrelsome intimacy that is the hall-mark of Swift's satire. It may not be very attractive, but it is not meant to be: and it has a unique disturbing effectiveness.

Gulliver's angers (whether nagging tartness, as in the passage under discussion, or ranting fury) reflect a cooler needling offensiveness from the Swift who manipulates the 'switch'. The chapter, and the volume, end with Gulliver's onslaught on Pride, and his petulant instruction to all English Yahoos 'who have any Tincture of this absurd Vice, that they will not presume to appear in my Sight'. It is Gulliver and not Swift who is speaking (here it is important not to confuse the two: saying this has almost become a nervous tic among critics), but there is really no sufficiently vivid alternative point of view that we can hang on to at this final moment. I shall return to this, and to what Gulliver actually says, later. What I want to stress here is that the final chapter begins with a needling defiance and the openly unfriendly intimacy of a petty insult, and ends with quarrelsome hysteria. The hysteria is Gulliver's and Swift seems in control. But the quarrel with the reader is one which Swift has been conducting through Gulliver, even though, when Gulliver becomes acutely unbalanced, there is an incomplete (at least a not quite literal) Swiftian commitment to what the quarrel has come to.

Gulliver is sometimes called a gay book. Arbuthnot seems to have started this when he said, 'Gulliver is a happy man that at his age can write such a merry work'.[35] His letter is joyful about the success of *Gulliver*, and tells of the Captain who claimed to know Gulliver, and the old man who looked up his map. Arbuthnot loved 'mischief the best of any Good natured man in England',[36] and is full of happy complicity in Swift's success and the bonus of a hoax. Pope and Gay were also 'diverted' by the reception of the book.[37] Part of the 'merry' seems more Scriblerian in-joke than sober description. But the book really can be merry: one thinks of witty fantastications like the joke about the handwriting of ladies in England (I.vi.57),[38] or the charming comedy of the Lilliputian speculations about Gulliver's watch (I.ii.35), which Johnson praised.[39] Such things are very funny, with mild satiric overtones, but without being unduly charged with needling obliquities or any blistering intensity. This is true even in some cases where we should expect Swift to be very hostile. Much of the folly of scientists in book III is treated thus, the flappers, the substitution of things for words, the mathematical obsession which makes the Laputians describe 'the Beauty of a Woman ... by Rhombs, Circles, Parallelograms, Ellipses, and other Geometrical Terms' (III.ii.163) (a joke which is not without bearing on our own habit of reducing women's shapes to 'vital statistics'). *Gulliver* has a notably unbuttoned way of giving itself over to local eruptions of mood, but it may be that the very fluctuations of tone invite us (though it will not do to be too solemn) to reconsider the whole nature of the 'merriment'. Swift obviously enjoyed the comedy of incongruity that runs right through the work (the Lilliputian troop on Gulliver's handkerchief, various Houyhnhnm postures, the She-Yahoo embracing Gulliver): this comes through plainly in his letter to Motte discussing illustrations to the book.[40] But a good deal of this grotesque comedy, notably in Brobdingnag, is close to being rather painful. The hailstones as big as tennis-balls, the huge frog, the monkey which takes Gulliver for one of its own (II.v.116ff.) have an undeniable science-fiction humour, but Gulliver is throughout in peril of his life. This is even truer of the slapstick comedy of the bowl of cream (II.iii.108): not only is it fraught with painful possibilities for Gulliver, but it reflects a crude and bitter malevolence in the court dwarf. J. M. Bullitt speaks well of Swift's 'seeming merriment' as reflecting 'an almost compulsive desire to separate himself from the intensity of his own feelings',[41] and the margin between high-spirited fun and more disturbing purposes is sometimes a thin one. If notions of the jest as a breaker of tensions, a disguised means of attack, or a showy (*vive la bagatelle!*) shrugging-off of painful feeling seem too ponderous to impose on some (not all) of these passages, they are not foreign to Swift's manner as a whole, and come into his thinking about satire:[42]

> All their Madness makes me merry:
>
> . . . .
>
> Like the ever-laughing Sage,
> In a Jest I spend my Rage:
> (Tho' it must be understood,
> I would hang them if I cou'd).

And if the self-humour in these verses forbids us to take the passage at its literal intensity (as it forbids us to take at *their* literal intensity the 'hate and detest' and 'Drown the World' passages in the letters to Pope expressing the 'misanthropy' behind the *Travels*),[43] yet the self-humour is plainly not of the kind that cancels what is said. I imagine, indeed, that the self-humour may in some ways be more disturbing than the plain uncompromising statement would have been without it. In dissociating the thing said from the full violence of the saying, the ironist both unsettles the reader and covers himself. Since we have here no firm alternative viewpoint to give us our bearings, we can only know that the ironist means part of what he says, but not exactly how large, or quite what sort of, a part; and so do not know what defences are called for. More important, obviously half-meant self-undercutting statements of this kind ('I would hang them if I cou'd', 'I hate and detest that animal called man') are more uncomfortable than if they had been wholly meant, for then we might have the luxury of dismissing them as ranting folly. In just this way, our consciousness of Gulliver's folly makes us paradoxically more, not less, vulnerable to the onslaughts on our self-esteem in book iv. Had Gulliver been presented as sane, we should (since again there is no real alternative voice, and no firm norm is indicated) have had to identify him with the satirist behind the mask, and so have been enabled to reject both as totally outrageous. As it is, we reject what comes from Gulliver, and are left with that disturbingly uncertain proportion of it which comes from Swift. It is precisely Gulliver's distance from Swift that permits the Swiftian attack to look plausible. Much of the humour of *Gulliver's Travels* has this effect, not really of attenuating (still less of belying) the Swiftian attack, as some critics hold, but of lending it that self-defensive distancing which makes it viable. Gulliver's solemn habit of trotting and neighing, fully aware of and undeterred by people's ridicule (iv.x.279), releases the whole situation from any possibility of Swift himself seeming solemn.

The same may be said, the opposite way round, of those jokes at the expense of the Houyhnhnms, which are sometimes said to prove that *Gulliver's Travels* has an anti-Houyhnhnm message: their perplexed 'Gestures, not unlike those of a Philosopher' (iv.i.226) when they try to understand Gulliver's shoes and stockings, their language which sounds like High Dutch (iv.iii.234), their way of building houses, threading needles and milking cows (iv.ix.274). The first thing I would note is that humour about the Houyhnhnms is never of a destructive tartness: contrast some of the anti-Lilliputian jokes. It also makes the Houyhnhnms (otherwise somewhat stiffly remote, or so some readers feel) seem engagingly awkward and 'human', and Swift has a note of real tenderness in some of the passages, the description of the Houyhnhnm dinner-party for example (iv.ii.231-2). Irvin Ehrenpreis, in a fine account of this humour, says that Swift is smiling at his own 'whole project of bestowing concrete life upon unattainable abstractions' and 'warning the sophisticated reader that [he], unlike Gulliver, appreciates the comical aspect of his own didacticism'.[44] The concession conforms to the normal method of the work: one of its effects is to make it more difficult for the reader to answer back.

But the humour has other resonances too. One Houyhnhnm absurdity that some critics make much of is their complacent notion that man's physical shape is preposterous and inefficient for the purposes of life. This is a nice joke when we think of a Houyhnhnm mare threading a needle. But it turns to a cruel irony not at the Houyhnhnms', but at mankind's, expense, when Gulliver's Houyhnhnm master assumes that men are anatomically incapable (despite their impulses) of fighting the destructive wars Gulliver tells him about. Gulliver replies with an exuberant assertion to the contrary that displays a moral fatuity which also has its comic side:

> I could not forbear shaking my Head and smiling a little at his Ignorance. And, being no Stranger to the Art of War, I gave him a Description of Cannons, Culverins, Muskets, Carabines, Pistols, Bullets, Powder, Swords, Bayonets, Sieges, Retreats, Attacks, Undermines, Countermines, Bombardments, Sea-fights; Ships sunk with a Thousand Men; twenty Thousand killed on each Side; dying Groans, Limbs flying in the Air: Smoak, Noise, Confusion, trampling to Death under Horses Feet: Flight, Pursuit, Victory; Fields strewed with Carcases left for Food to Dogs, and Wolves, and Birds of Prey; Plundering, Stripping, Ravishing, Burning and Destroying. And, to set forth the Valour of my own dear Countrymen, I assured him, that I had seen them blow up a Hundred Enemies at once in a Siege, and as many in a Ship; and beheld the dead Bodies drop down in Pieces from the Clouds, to the great Diversion of all the Spectators (IV.v.247).

This enthusiastic fit is obviously funny. It is funny partly because of the concreteness with which Gulliver generalizes, the entranced particularity with which he evokes not a real battle which happened but some sort of common denominator of war.[45] The effect is instructively different from that of a scene in *Nineteen Eighty-Four* which seems to make some of the same points, and which (like other things in that novel) may have been distantly modelled on Swift.[46] An entry in Winston Smith's diary describes a war-film with a ship full of refugees being bombed, and a 'wonderful shot of a child's arm going up up up right into the air', and a greatly diverted audience applauding and 'shouting with laughter'. Smith says the film is very good, and talks of 'wonderful' scenes as Gulliver might. To this extent he is conditioned by the awful world of 1984, but he is struggling for his mental freedom (writing the diary is itself punishable by death), and he suddenly breaks off to think of his account as a 'stream of rubbish'. The scene does not become funny, because Smith is, in a deeper and partly unconscious sense, disturbed and pained by it, instead of being in Gulliver's fatuous trance of grotesque delight. Orwell drives the painfulness home by having Smith say that there was in the audience a prole woman who 'suddenly started kicking up a fuss and shouting they didnt oughter of showed it not in front of kids they didnt'. That there should be, within the situation itself, this glimpse of a hurt and protesting normality does not offer much reassurance: but it reaches out to the reader in a kind of complicity of despair. Neither Orwell nor the reader can stand apart from the narrator, or from the rest of the humanity described, and there can be no question of laughing anything off.

The incident in Orwell, however representative (it is in its way as representative as Swift's passage, and of similar things), is a vivid specific occurrence (though only a film), to which a pained immediacy of reaction on Smith's and on the reader's part is natural and appropriate. In Gulliver's account, even when, as at the end, he seems to turn to specific occurrences, there is a comic lack of distinction between the general and the particular, and Gulliver's all embracing celebration has a callous yet oddly innocent absurdity. The comic note, and the fact that the horror is so diffused, ensure that no immediacy of participation by the reader in the things described is possible, or expected. For obvious reasons there is no complicity between the reader and either Gulliver or any member of the applauding crowds. Nor is the grim high-spirited comedy a congenial idiom for any complicity between the reader and Swift: the reader has, rather uncomfortably, to laugh *at* Gulliver, without having anyone very much to laugh *with*. We may speculate whether the exuberance of Gulliver's speech belongs to the moral folly of his original complacent acceptance of mankind; or is an ironic mimicry, after disenchantment, of this early complacent acceptance; or is an exuberant repudiation, proceeding either from righteous indignation or from what some critics might call the *medical* rather than moral folly of Gulliver's final state of misanthropy. On the question of such choices, I shall have more to say.[47] But if we do wish to insist on Gulliver's folly, in *any* sense, in this particular speech, it is clear that there can be no question of such folly, or of Swift's comic sense, cancelling or seriously attenuating the point about war and attitudes to war which the passage makes: one of their effects, as with other examples of Swift's humour, is to remove Swift's angry attack from the plane of rant. Yet we are not, I think, very actively horrified at Gulliver's *feelings*, as we should have been if they had been Winston Smith's. In a novel, or in life, we should be revolted by his callousness. But we cannot, here or elsewhere, respond to him as a 'character'. He is too absurd and two-dimensional. There is a detachment of the character from what he reveals to us which is part of the whole satiric formula of *Gulliver's Travels*, and which the humour here reinforces. We think less about Gulliver than about war, and what Swift is telling us about our attitudes to it. The message is disturbing, and for all the fun, Swift is not, anymore than elsewhere, being very friendly.

The tense hovering between laughter and something else, the structural indefiniteness of genre and the incessantly shifting status and function of the parodic element, the ironic twists and countertwists, and the endless flickering uncertainties of local effect suggest that one of Swift's most active satiric weapons is *bewilderment*. It is perhaps not surprising that this weapon should have backfired, and that there should have been so much doubt and disagreement both about the unity of the work, and the meaning of its final section. One of the risks, but also rewards, of the attacking self-concealments of irony is that they draw out their Irish bishops. But we are all, inevitably, Irish bishops in some degree: and the Swift who sought to vex the world may well be deriving a wry satisfaction from our failures to pin him down, although he might not consent to know us in Glubbdubdrib (III.viii.197). What one means by 'unity' is too often rather arbitrary, but there is perhaps a broad overall coherence in the consistency and progression of *Gulliver*'s onslaught on the reader's bearings and self-esteem. But it is a tense and rugged coherence, and no neatly chartable matter, and any more 'external' unities of formal pattern or ideology seem ultimately inseparable from, and possibly secondary to, those satiric procedures and tones which create the commanding impact of the Swiftian voice. An attachment to schematic patterns *per se*, of the kind for which books I and II provide such a brilliant model, seems to have had two results. One has been a tendency to wish either or both the other books away. The other has been a quest to discover in the work as a whole something of the geometrical shapeliness that exists between the first two books. The exercise easily becomes disembodied even when its limitations are partially recognized: 'it hardly seems to matter much that books I and III deal with bad governments, while books II and IV, in alternating pattern, deal with good governments.[48]

There are of course some broad structural facts of considerable significance, such as that we are led through three books of allegorical societies which are in principle translatable into real life (with a mixture, as Thomas Sheridan put it, of good and bad qualities 'as they are to be found in life'),[49] and which provide a solid background of 'realistic' evidence of human vice, into the stark world of moral absolutes of book IV; and that the Struldbrugs at the end of book III are a horrifying climax which prepares us for this. The specific fact that the Struldbrugs give a terrifying retrospective deepening to the Houyhnhnms' fearlessness of death is only one aspect of their disturbing importance: their chief force, at first meeting, is to put the concerns of the narrative once and for all on an entirely new plane. Again, the fact, noted by Case and others,[50] that the incidental persons in the narrative links between the four main episodes tend to become nastier and nastier, provides an important progression, not perhaps because the reader senses it as a progression (unless it happens to be pointed out), but because the evil of sailors and others (the 'real' men) in books III and IV provides a relevantly documented and depressing background to the main preoccupations of those books. (The Portuguese Captain and his crew are an exception to which I shall come later.) The point about these patterns is not that they are neat and flawlessly progressive (they are not), and not merely that they fit in with the 'themes' (though they do): it is that they have an effect *as we read*, without our necessarily being aware of them *as patterns*. After all, the real point about even the special relationship between books I and II is not the series of arithmetical piquancies, but the unfolding irony about human self-importance.

This self-importance, or pride, is at the centre of the work's concerns. A principle that is sometimes overlooked in discussions not only of structural shape but of ideological themes is that these things make themselves felt, if at all, through the reader's continuous submission to *local* effects, which means in this case exposure to the Swiftian presence at close quarters. Ideologically, *Gulliver's Travels* revolves round the familiar Augustan group of concepts, Nature, Reason and Pride. Its position is basically a commonplace one, but it bears some restating because some ironies of characteristic force and stinging elusiveness proceed from it. Nature and Reason ideally coalesce. Nature is ideal order, in all spheres of life: moral, social, political, aesthetic. Deviations from this are unnatural, as murder or any gross misdeed might, in our own idiom, be called an unnatural act. If one said that the deed came naturally to one, one would be using the term in a different sense. Such other meanings were also of course available to Swift, and I shall argue that the interplay between ideal and less ideal senses provides an important irony. Reason is the faculty which makes one behave naturally (in the high sense), makes one follow Nature and frame one's judgment (and behaviour) by her just and unerring standard. So More's Utopians (in some ways ancestors of the Houyhnhnms) 'define virtue to be life ordered according to nature, and that we be hereunto ordained of God. And that he doth follow the course of nature, which in desiring and refusing things is ruled by reason',[51] and the Houyhnhnms believe a somewhat secularized version of the same thing (IV.v.248). The terms Nature and Reason are often in fact interchangeable. Where this is not so, they may complete one another: Nature teaches the Houyhnhnms 'to love the whole Species', Reason to distinguish between persons on merit (IV.viii.268). The Houyhnhnms, etymologically '*the Perfection of Nature*' (IV.iii.235), combine Nature and Reason in the highest sense. Their virtues are friendship, benevolence, decency, civility, but they have no ceremony or foolish fondness (IV.viii.268). This means that they have both emotions and propriety, but that neither is misdirected or excessive. They would have understood Pope's phrase in *The Temple of Fame* (l. 108) about 'that useful Science, to be *good*'. Their morality is pervaded by an uncompromisingly high (and instinctive) common-sense and utilitarianism, and what might be called an absolute standard of congruity or *fittingness*. Thus they cannot understand lying, because speech was made to communicate (IV.iv.240), or opinion, because there is only one truth and speculation is idle (IV.viii.267). It follows that behaviour which offends against this unerring standard is readily seen as deviation or perversion. (This is a suggestion which Swift exploits very fully and painfully.) Even physically, the Houyhnhnms are rational-natural, for (thanks partly to their simple diet, Nature being, as Gulliver knows from some 'insipid' meals, 'easily ... satisfied'—IV.ii.232) they are never ill, illness being a deviation from the natural state of the body. For a comic boiling-down of this mind–body ideal, one might cite Fielding's deist Square, who 'held human nature to be the perfection of all virtue, and that vice was a deviation from our nature, in the same manner as deformity of body is'.[52] Swift has his tongue in his cheek about some Houyhnhnm notions of the 'natural' standard of mind–body integration, as when the Houyhnhnm master, in a passage of not very flattering but entirely delightful comedy, considers our physical shape unsuited for the employment of Reason in 'the common Offices of Life' (IV.iv.242): but Swift *is* seriously suggesting that luxurious eating habits are a cause of human physical degeneracy, so that morality and physical health are causally related and not only (as apparently for Square) by analogy. Nature ideally is one, and her laws pervasive.

In *Gulliver's Travels*, however, there is a gap between Nature and 'human nature', in an actual sense, which would make Square's complacency untenable, though his *rationale* is perfectly applicable to the Houyhnhnms. The Houyhnhnms are not complacent in Square's sense because in them the ideal and the actuality are fully matched. Actually, Square's remarks also concern an ideal and, like other forms of philosophical 'optimism', logically allow for an uglier reality: but, given the ugly facts, Swift (and Fielding) would see a monstrous impropriety in putting the matter that way at all. Mankind is guilty of a collective deviation from Nature and Reason at every level, and this Unreason, by the familiar buried pun, becomes in *Gulliver* (as in *A Tale of a Tub* or the *Dunciad*) a vast and wicked madness: the congruence between madness and moral turpitude is one of the most vivid and inventively resourceful themes of Augustan satire. Scientists, or those of a certain sort, are one of the traditional examples. They delve into what Nature keeps hidden, and they seek to pervert Nature (in such cases the word slides easily from an ideal sense to something approaching 'things as they are') into something other than it is, 'condensing Air into a dry tangible Substance', 'softening Marble for Pillows and Pin-Cushions', arresting the growth of wool on sheep (III.v.182).[53] The phrase 'natural philosophy' provides an exploitable pun (Fielding said in *Tom Jones*, XIII.v, that natural philosophy knew 'nothing of Nature, except her monsters and imperfections'), and when Gulliver explained to the Houyhnhnm master 'our several Systems of *Natural Philosophy*, he would laugh that a Creature pretending to *Reason*, should value itself upon the Knowledge of other Peoples Conjectures, and in Things, where that Knowledge, if it were certain, could be of no Use' (IV.viii. 267-8). Science becomes divorced from usefulness and good sense. The Laputians are 'dextrous' mathematicians on paper but have no idea of 'practical Geometry' (III.ii.163). Natural philosophy is thus at least doubly unnatural, in that it variously violates Nature, and in that it is the irrational pastime of creatures who pretend to Reason. This is routine perversion, built-in to the situation. It exercised Swift, and Pope, *as* perversion. But there are further perversities. One is the encroachment of science on government. The Brobdingnagians stand out from the 'Wits of *Europe*' in not having 'reduced *Politicks* into a *Science*'. Unlike us, they have no books on 'the *Art of Government*', and despise mystery, refinement (a term which, as in many other satires of Swift and Pope, has familiar suggestions of dishonesty and other vices, as well as folly: 'heads refin'd from Reason')[54] and intrigue (II.vii.135). The Laputians, on the other hand, like our Mathematicians, have a 'strong Disposition' to politics (III.ii.164), and the Academy of Lagado has a school of political projectors (though that, by some characteristic reversals, has crazed professors trying to do genuine political good, as well as schemes which hover uncertainly between outright folly and a sort of mad good sense—III.vi.187ff.) What, Gulliver asks, is the connection between mathematics and politics? Perhaps it is that 'the smallest Circle hath as many Degrees as the largest', so that it might be thought that managing the world requires 'no more Abilities than the handling and turning of a Globe'. But he thinks the real explanation is 'a very common Infirmity of human Nature, inclining us to be more curious and conceited in Matters where we have least Concern, and for which we are least adapted either by Study or Nature' (III.ii.164). This professional perversion or unnaturalness has connections with a whole series of ironies about perversity in the professions and occupations of men. The Yahoos are of a 'perverse, restive Disposition' (IV.viii.266), and Swift seems to see human perversity as a thing of almost unending coils of self-complication. But before coming to this, the main outline may be summarized thus.

In this Nature-Reason system at its simplest and purest, every vice is readily resolved into a violation of nature, and therefore into a peculiarly culpable form of unreason. The greed, quarrelsomeness, ambition, treachery, and lust of men, as we encounter them throughout the *Travels*, are in an elementary sense unnatural by definition. This unnaturalness is prone to almost infinite refinements, and therefore as we shall see open to a painful and varied series of ironic expositions. But the overriding unnaturalness, which becomes unbearable to Gulliver at the end, is that the 'Lump of Deformity, and Diseases both in Body and Mind' called man, should be 'smitten with *Pride*': pride, in the assumption itself, in the face of so much folly, that man is a rational animal, the pride of having any self-esteem at all (as Gulliver, though perhaps not Swift, might more extremely put it), and (in the special case of scientists and their like) the pride of impiously tampering with God's creation and the normal state of things. Pride, which governs the mad scientists of book III (and the philosopher experts in the earlier books, I.ii.37, II.ii.103-4); the puny self-importance of the Lilliputians in book I, who play at men; and that of men, which emerges by extension in book II, is the most deeply unnatural of all the vices because, as the other vices prove, there is nothing to be proud of.

This diagnosis of mankind is an Augustan commonplace, and many important elements of it may be found not only in an earlier humanism but also in various old traditions of classical and Christian thought. But Swift refines on it by a number of characteristic ironies which serve to undermine any comfort we might derive from having to contend with a simple categorical indictment of mankind, however damaging. Whichever way we interpret book IV, man is placed, in it, somewhere between the rational Houyhnhnms and the bestial Yahoos. He has less reason than the former, more than the latter. The Houyhnhnms recognize this in Gulliver, though they think of him, and he eventually thinks of himself, as basically of the Yahoo kind. A Houyhnhnm state may be unattainable to man, but there are norms of acceptable, though flawed, humanity which do not seem, in the same way, beyond the realm of moral aspiration: one-time Lilliput (I.vi.57ff.), modern Brobdingnag, the '*English* Yeomen of the old Stamp' (III.viii.201), the Portuguese Captain. These positives must be taken gingerly. Ancient Lilliput and the old Yeomen are no more, Brobdingnag is hardly a European reality, there are not many like the Portuguese Captain and his crew, although some other decent people make fleeting unremarkable appearances. Still, they are there, and at worst, we reflect, we are still better than the Yahoos. But in conceding this assurance, Swift also takes it away. This is not just in the dramatic strength of the parallels between them and us, which culminate in the 'objective' test of the female Yahoo's sexual craving for Gulliver (IV.viii.266-7). There are qualities in which Gulliver is actually inferior: 'Strength, Speed and Activity, the Shortness of my Claws, and some other Particulars where Nature had no Part' (IV.vii.260). Swift can be more or less playful with those 'usual Topicks of *European* Moralists' (II.vii.137) about man's physical inferiority to animals, and an earlier speech of the Houyhnhnm master, already referred to, has its rich comic side (IV.iv.242-3). But it is a point meant to be taken note of, and recurs with some insistence. There is no mistaking the tartness with which we are told, in a further twist, that the Yahoos (to whom men are physically inferior!) are superior in agility to asses, though less comely and less useful in other respects (IV.ix.272-3). This is a Houyhnhnm view, but we need not suppose that Swift meant it literally in order to sense that he is having another snipe at the human form divine.

But more important is the assertion that man's portion of Reason, which theoretically raises him above Yahoos in non-physical matters, is in fact something 'whereof we made no other Use than by its Assistance to aggravate our *natural* Corruptions, and to acquire new ones which Nature had not given us' (IV.vii.259). The notion that men use their reason to make themselves worse rather than better was not invented by Swift,[55] but it disturbingly weakens the contrary assurance that it is after all by virtue of our reason that we are better than the Yahoos. It is a Houyhnhnm comment, but so are the contrary ones (IV.iii.234; IV.vi. 256; IV.ix.272). No one else tells us much either way. It recurs in various forms. Gulliver comes to realize that men use Reason 'to improve and multiply those Vices, whereof their Brethren in this Country had only the Share that Nature allotted them' (IV.x.278). When men are under discussion, linguistic usage on the subject of Reason and Nature tends to change: Reason multiplies vices, Nature allots them. In an earlier passage there is even an unsettling doubt as to whether Reason in this case really *is* Reason. It occurs after the cruel irony in which the Houyhnhnm master supposes that, odious as men are, Nature has created their anatomy in such a way as to make them 'utterly uncapable of doing much Mischief' (IV.v.247), to which Gulliver replies with the account of war which I discussed earlier. The master then says he hates Yahoos but cannot *blame* them any more than he would blame 'a *Gnnayh* (a Bird of Prey) for its Cruelty',[56] but as to man,

> when a Creature pretending to Reason, could be capable of such Enormities, he dreaded lest the Corruption of that Faculty might be worse than Brutality itself. He seemed therefore confident, that instead of Reason, we were only possessed of some Quality fitted to increase our natural Vices (IV.v.248).

This possibility, that man's Reason is not Reason, is not entertained. It goes against the run of the book's argument. But it is characteristic of Swift to place it before us, as an alternative (if only momentarily viable) affront. Either we have no Reason, or what we have is worse than not having it. The irresolution saps our defences, for we need to answer on two fronts.[57] At the same time, neither point is true to the book, which does concede (notably through several comments of the Houyhnhnm master himself) that Gulliver is both better and more rational than the Yahoos. Swift is needling us with offensive undermining possibilities even while a moderately comforting certainty is being grudgingly established. Of the two negative, undermining streams of argument, the dominant one is that which says we do have Reason, but that it makes us worse. Its most intense manifestation occurs with Gulliver's description of the Yahoos' horrible smelly sexuality. The passage incidentally shows how germane the term Reason is, in ways we might not automatically expect, not merely to the concept 'good morals' but also to the concept 'virtuous passions'. It drives home how the most unlikely vices tend to equal unreason (or, in the perverted human sense, not *unreason* but Reason):

> I expected every Moment, that my Master would accuse the *Yahoos* of those unnatural Appetites in both Sexes, so common among us. But Nature it seems hath not been so expert a Schoolmistress; and these politer Pleasures are entirely the Productions of Art and Reason, on our Side of the Globe (IV.vii.264).

Though this has special resonances in the context of *Gulliver's Travels*, and a true Swiftian tang, it is also the classic language of primitivism, which is in fact a minor theme of the work. The Houyhnhnms are in some respects prelapsarian innocents, ignorant of at least some forms of evil, and with no bodily shame or any idea of why Gulliver wears clothes. They also have no literature, but a high oral tradition in poetry and knowledge (IV.iii.235; IV.ix.273-4). Utopian Lilliput and the old English Yeomen are idealized pre-degenerate societies, and Swift's concern with the idea of the degeneration of societies has often been noted. But there is the contrary example of Brobdingnag, an advanced and largely good society which, by a shaming and pointed contrast with Lilliput and England, has emerged from an earlier turpitude (II.vii. 138).[58] The Yahoos prove that there is no idealization of the noble savage: and though the Houyhnhnms do have a primitivist element, the high ideal of Nature associated with them embodies some key-values of civilized Augustan aspiration. This may partly proceed from a not fully resolved duality in the conception of Reason both as civilized achievement and as corrupting force, not to mention the sense, perhaps tending against both others, of a spontaneous rightness which 'strikes... with immediate Conviction' (IV.viii.267).

But, if so, the confusion is not really Swift's. The fact is that both the language of ideas on these matters, and ordinary English idiom, make available these various senses. Nature and Reason were all-purpose terms, and Swift, who was not writing a logical treatise (although it has been shown that he was, in a manner, refuting logical treatises),[59] was only too ready, as we have seen, to exploit the ironic possibilities offered him by the language. His whole style in this work thrives on what from a strictly logical point of view is a defiant (and transparent) linguistic sleight of hand. The textbook definition of man as *animal rationale* simply refers to that reasoning faculty which was supposed to distinguish men from beasts. Swift's 'disproof' consists of tacitly translating a descriptive definition into a high ethical and intellectual ideal, and then saying that man's claim to Reason is fatuously and insufferably arrogant.[60] The often-quoted formulation in the sermon 'On the Trinity' that '*Reason* itself is true and just, but the *Reason* of every particular

Man is weak and wavering, perpetually swayed and turned by his Interests, his Passions, and his Vices'[61] shows that Swift is perfectly aware of semantic distinctions when he wants to be. It can also stand as an acceptable boiling-down of much that is said about human unreason in *Gulliver's Travels*. Swift's concern here, however, is not to boil the issue down to its commonplace propositional content, but to exploit the damaging ironies by all the verbal means which the language puts at his disposal.

The double standard by which the words Nature and Reason tend to be used in a debased sense when they refer to men, and an ideal sense when they refer to Houyhnhnms, lies at the heart of this. The dreadful thing is that man is neither natural in the high sense, nor (like the Yahoos, as the quotation about 'politer Pleasures' showed) in the low. If we then grant that this double unnaturalness is itself natural to man, we find him becoming unnatural even to this nature. Suggestions of multiple self-complicating perversity exist in the accounts of all men's occupations and professional activities. One might instance the Laputian reasoners, who are 'vehemently given to Opposition, unless when they happen to be of the right Opinion, which is seldom their Case' (III.ii.163); the Admiral who 'for want of proper Intelligence ... beat the Enemy to whom he intended to betray the Fleet' (III.viii.199); the kings who protested to Gulliver in Glubbdubdrib

> that in their whole Reigns they did never once prefer any Person of Merit, unless by Mistake or Treachery of some Minister in whom they confided: Neither would they do it if they were to live again; and they shewed with great Strength of Reason, that the Royal Throne could not be supported without Corruption (III.viii.199);

the politician who 'never tells a *Truth*, but with an Intent that you should take it for a *Lye*', and vice versa (IV.vi.255).[62] Most elaborate is the chain of ironies about the unnaturalness of the law. It is unnatural that laws should exist at all, since Nature and Reason should be sufficient guides for a rational creature. Other related perversities are: that while meant for men's protection, the law causes their ruin; that (for a variety of discreditably tortuous reasons) one is always at a disadvantage if one's cause is just; that lawyers use irrelevant evidence, and a jargon which no one can understand (which among other things runs against the reiterated principle that speech is only for communication); that lawyers, who are expected to be wise and learned, are in reality 'the most ignorant and stupid' of men (IV.v.248-50). A major irony running through this is that man is unnatural even to his own natural unnaturalness. Assuming that moral perversion is natural to the species, it becomes, in this sense, natural for judges to accept bribes. But it is even more natural for judges to be unjust, so that 'I have known some of them to have refused a large Bribe from the Side where Justice lay, rather than injure the *Faculty*, by doing any thing unbecoming their Nature or their Office' (IV.v.249).

One becomes unnatural to one's lesser natural iniquities when a deeper iniquity competes with them. The concept of Nature is debased by an ever-declining spiral into whatever depths mankind might perversely sink to. Whatever these depths, Gulliver can follow the spiral downwards and (both in his naïve complacent phase and in his later disenchanted misanthropy) accept them as natural. The spiral has almost endless possibilities, and the reader for much of the time has not even the comfort of feeling that there is a rock-bottom. But there is, at the end, something like rock-bottom, a final insult to the nature of things which Gulliver finds completely unbearable:

> My Reconcilement to the *Yahoo*-kind in general might not be so difficult, if they would be content with those Vices and Follies only which Nature hath entitled them to. I am not in the least provoked at the Sight of a Lawyer, a Pick-pocket, a Colonel, a Fool, a Lord, a Gamester, a Politician, a Whoremunger, a Physician, an Evidence, a Suborner, an Attorney, a Traytor, or the like: This is all according to the due Course of Things: But, when I behold a Lump of Deformity, and Diseases both in Body and Mind, smitten with *Pride*, it immediately breaks all the Measures of my Patience; neither shall I be ever able to comprehend how such an Animal and such a Vice could tally together. The wise and virtuous *Houyhnhnms*, who abound in all Excellencies that can adorn a rational Creature, have no Name for this Vice in their Language, which hath no Terms to express any thing that is evil, except those whereby they describe the detestable Qualities of their *Yahoos*; among which they were not able to distinguish this of Pride, for want of thoroughly understanding Human Nature, as it sheweth it self in other Countries, where that Animal presides. But I, who had more Experience, could plainly observe some Rudiments of it among the wild *Yahoos* (IV.xii.296).

Pride, the complacency of thinking that man is a rational animal, now becomes the 'absurd Vice' which is the final aggravation of all our iniquities, the ultimate offence to Nature. Yet even Pride, the ultimate unnaturalness, is itself part of 'Human Nature' ('for so they have still the Confidence to stile it',[63] says Gulliver to Sympson, p. 7), so that we may wonder whether we really have after all reached rock-bottom, or whether there is yet another opening for still deeper unnaturalness to be revealed. The suspicion arises that if things do stop here, it is only because the book must close somewhere, rather than because the subject is exhausted. And in this final impasse the only possible response, dramatically, is Gulliver's mixture of insane hatred and impotent petulance as he forbids any English Yahoo with 'any Tincture of this absurd Vice' ever to appear in his sight.

The book ends here, with Gulliver a monomaniac and his last outburst a defiant, and silly, petulance. We are not, I am sure, invited to share his attitudes literally, to accept as valid his fainting at the touch of his wife (IV.xi.289) and his strange nostalgic preference for his horses. He has become insane or unbalanced, judged by standards of ordinary social living, and I have already suggested one reason why, in the whole design of the work, this is appropriate: it makes his rant viable by dissociating Swift from the taint of excess, without really undermining the attack from Swift that the rant stands for. It is Gulliver's manner, not Swift's, which is Timon's manner, as critics are fond of noting, which means that he (like Lucian's or Plutarch's or Shakespeare's Timon),[64] and not Swift, is the raging recluse. But his are the final words, which produce the taste Swift chose to leave behind: it is no great comfort or compliment to the reader to be assaulted with a mean hysteria that he cannot shrug off because, when all is said, it tells what the whole volume has insisted to be the truth.

It is wrong, I think, to take Gulliver as a novel-character who suffers a tragic alienation, and for whom therefore we feel pity or some kind of contempt, largely because we do not, as I suggested, think of him as a 'character' at all in more than a very attenuated sense: the emphasis is so preponderantly on what can be shown through him (including what he says and thinks) than on his person in its own right, that we are never allowed to accustom ourselves to him as a real personality despite all the rudimentary local colour about his early career, family life and professional doings. An aspect of this are Swift's ironic exploitations of the Gulliver-figure, which to the very end flout our most elementary expectations of character consistency: the praise of English colonialism in the last chapter, which startlingly returns to Gulliver's earlier boneheaded manner, is an example. The treatment of Gulliver is essentially *external*, as, according to Wyndham Lewis, satire ought to be.[65] Nor is Gulliver sufficiently independent from Swift: he is not identical with Swift, nor even similar to him, but Swift's presence behind him is always too close to ignore. This is not because Swift approves or disapproves of what Gulliver says at any given time, but because Swift is always saying something *through* it.

Gulliver in his unbalanced state, then, seems less a character than (in a view which has much truth but needs qualifying) a protesting gesture of impotent rage, a satirist's stance of ultimate exasperation. Through him, as through the modest proposer (who once offered sensible and decent suggestions which were ignored), Swift is pointing, in a favourite irony, to the lonely madness of trying to mend the world, a visionary absurdity which, in more than a shallow rhetorical sense, Swift saw as his own. At the time of finishing *Gulliver*, Swift told Pope, in a wry joke, that he wished there were a 'Hospital' for the world's despisers.[66] (If Gulliver, incidentally, unlike the proposer, does not preach cannibalism, he does ask for clothes of Yahoo-skin—IV.iii.236—and uses this material for his boat and sails—IV.x.281). But Gulliver does not quite project the noble rage or righteous pride of the outraged satirist. The exasperated petulance of the last speech keeps the quarrel on an altogether less majestic and more intimate footing, where it has, in my view, been all along. Common sense tells us that Swift would not talk like that in his own voice, but we know disturbingly (and there has been no strong competing voice) that this is the voice he chose to leave in our ears.

Still, Gulliver's view is out of touch with a daily reality about which Swift also knew, and which includes the good Portuguese Captain. Gulliver's response to the Captain is plainly unworthy, and we should note that he has not learnt such bad manners (or his later hysterical tone) from the Houyhnhnms' example. But we should also remember that the Captain is a rarity,[67] who appears only briefly; that just before Gulliver meets him the horrible mutiny with which book IV began is twice remembered (IV.x.281; IV.xi.283); that the first men Gulliver meets after leaving Houyhnhnmland are hostile savages (IV.xi.284); and that just after the excellent Portuguese sailors there is a hint of the Portuguese Inquisition (IV.xi.288). The Captain does have a function. As John Traugott says, he emphasizes Gulliver's alienation and 'allows Gulliver to make Swift's point that even good Yahoos are Yahoos'.[68] But above all perhaps he serves as a reasonable concession to reality (as if Swift were saying there *are* some good men, but the case is unaltered), without which the onslaughts on mankind might be open to a too easy repudiation from the reader. In this respect, he complements the other disarming concessions, the humour and self-irony, the physical comicality of the Houyhnhnms, Gulliver's folly, and the rest.

Even if Swift is making a more moderate attack on mankind than Gulliver, Gulliver's view hovers damagingly over it all; in the same way that, though the book says we are better than the Yahoos, it does not allow us to be too sure of the fact. (The bad smell of the Portuguese Captain, or of Gulliver's wife, are presumably 'objective' tokens of physical identity, like the She-Yahoo's sexual desire for Gulliver.) This indirection unsettles the reader, by denying him the solace of definite categories. It forbids the luxury of a well-defined stand, whether of resistance or assent, and offers none of the comforts of that author-reader complicity on which much satiric rhetoric depends. It is an ironic procedure, mocking, elusive, immensely resourceful and agile, which talks at the reader with a unique quarrelsome intimacy, but which is so hedged with aggressive defences that it is impossible for him to answer back.

Finally, a word about the Houyhnhnms. It is sometimes said that Swift is satirizing them as absurd or nasty embodiments of extreme rationalism. Apart from the element of humour, discussed earlier, with which they are presented, they are, it is said, conceited and obtuse in disbelieving the existence or the physical viability of the human creature. But, within the logic of the fiction, this disbelief seems natural enough. The Lilliputians also doubted the existence of men of Gulliver's size (I.vi.49), and Gulliver also needed explaining in Brobdingnag (II.iii. 103-4). In both these cases the philosophers are characteristically silly, but everybody is intrigued, and we could hardly expect otherwise. Moreover, Gulliver tells Sympson that some human beings have doubted the existence of Houyhnhnms (p. 8), which, within the terms of the story (if one is really going to take this sort of evidence solemnly), is just as arrogant. More important, the related Houyhnhnm doubt as to the anatomical viability or efficiency of the human shape (apart from being no more smug than some of Gulliver's complacencies *in favour* of mankind) turns to a biting sarcasm at man's, not at the Houyhnhnms', expense when, as we have seen, the Houyhnhnm master supposes that man is not capable of making war (IV.v.247).

The Houyhnhnms' proposal to castrate some younger Yahoos (IV.ix. 272-3) has also shocked critics. But again this follows the simple narrative logic: it is no more than humans do to horses. Our shock should be no more than the 'noble Resentment' of the Houyhnhnm master when he hears of the custom among us (IV.iv.242). To the extent that we *are* shocked, Swift seems to me to be meaning mildly to outrage our 'healthy' sensibilities, as he does in the hoof-kissing episode. But in any event, the Houyhnhnms get the idea *from* Gulliver's account of what men do to horses, so that either way the force of the fable is not on man's side. The fiction throughout reverses the man–horse relationship: horses are degenerate in England (p. 8 and IV.xii.295), as men are in Houyhnhnmland. Again, I think man comes out of it badly both ways: the Yahoos of Houyhnhnmland make their obvious point, but the suggestion in reverse seems to be that English horses are poor specimens (though to Gulliver better than men) because they live in a bad human world. At least, a kind of irrational sense of guilt by association is generated. We need not suppose that Swift is endorsing Gulliver's preference of his horses to his family in order to feel offended about it. At many (sometimes indefinable) points on a complex scale of effects, Swift is getting at us.

The Houyhnhnms' expulsion of Gulliver belongs to the same group of objections. It seems to me that some of the sympathy showered on Gulliver by critics comes from a misfocused response to him as a full character in whom we are very involved as a person. The Houyhnhnm master and the sorrel nag are in fact very sorry to lose Gulliver, but the logic of the fable is inexorable: Gulliver is of the Yahoo kind, and his privileged position in Houyhnhnmland was offensive to some, while his rudiments of Reason threaten (not without plausibility, from all we learn of man's use of that faculty) to make him a danger to the state as leader of the wild Yahoos (IV.x.279). The expulsion of Gulliver is like Gulliver's treatment of Don Pedro: both episodes have been sentimentalized, but they are a harsh reminder that even good Yahoos are Yahoos.

The main charge is that the Houyhnhnms are cold, passionless, inhuman, unattractive to us and therefore an inappropriate positive model. The fact that we may not like them does not mean that Swift is disowning them: it is consistent with his whole style to nettle us with a positive we might find insulting and rebarbative. The older critics who disliked the Houyhnhnms but felt that Swift meant them as a positive were surely nearer the mark than some recent ones who translate their own dislikes into the meaning of the book. But one must agree that the Houyhnhnms, though they are a positive, are not a *model*, there being no question of our being able to imitate them. So far as it has not been grossly exaggerated, their 'inhumanity' may well, like their literal *non*-humanity (which tells us that the only really rational animal is not man), be part of the satiric point: this is a matter of 'passions'.

They are, of course, not totally passionless.[69] They treat Gulliver, in all personal contacts, with mildness, tenderness and friendly dignity (IV.i.224ff.). Gulliver receives special gentleness and affection from his master, and still warmer tenderness from the sorrel nag (IV.xi.283). Their language, which has no term for lying or opinion, 'expressed the Passions very well', which may mean no more than 'emotions' but does mean that they have them (IV.i.226). In contrast to the Laputians, who have no 'Imagination, Fancy and Invention' (III.ii.163), but like the Brobdingnagians (II.vii.136), they excel in poetry (IV.ix.273-4), though their poems sound as if they might be rather unreadable and are certainly not of a very rapturous kind.

But their personal lives differ from ours in a kind of lofty tranquillity, and an absence of personal intimacy and emotional entanglement. In some aspects of this, they parallel Utopian Lilliput (I.vi.60ff.), and when Gulliver is describing such things as their conversational habits ('Where there was no Interruption, Tediousness, Heat, or Difference of Sentiments'), a note of undisguised wishfulness comes into the writing (see the whole passage, IV.x.277). W. B. Carnochan has shown, in a well-taken point, that such freedom from the 'tyrant-passions' corresponds to a genuine longing of Swift himself.[70] I do not wish, and have no ability, to be psychoanalytical. But in a work which, in addition to much routine and sometimes rather self-conscious scatology (however 'traditional'), contains the disturbing anatomy of Brobdingnagian ladies, the account of the Struldbrugs, the reeking sexuality of the Yahoos and the She-Yahoo's attempt on Gulliver, the horrible three-year-old Yahoo brat (IV.viii.265-6), the smell of Don Pedro and of Gulliver's family and Gulliver's strange relations with his wife, one might well expect to find aspirations for a society which practised eugenics and had an educational system in which personal and family intimacies were reduced to a minimum. Gulliver may be mocked, but the cumulative effect of these things is inescapable, and within the atmosphere of the work itself the longing for a world uncontaminated as far as possible by the vagaries of emotion might seem to us an unattractive, but surely not a surprising, phenomenon.

But it is more important still to say that the Houyhnhnms are not a statement of what man ought to be so much as a statement of what he is not. Man thinks he is *animal rationale*, and the Houyhnhnms are a demonstration (which might, as we saw, be logically unacceptable, but is imaginatively powerful), for man to compare himself with, of what an *animal rationale* really is. R. S. Crane has shown that in the logic textbooks which commonly purveyed the old definition of man as a rational animal, the beast traditionally and most frequently named as a specific example of the opposite, the non-rational, was the horse.[71] Thus Hudibras, who 'was in *Logick* a great Critick', would[72]

> undertake to prove by force
> Of Argument, a Man's no Horse.

The choice of horses thus becomes an insulting exercise in 'logical' refutation. The Yahoos are certainly an opposite extreme, and real man lies somewhere between them. But it is no simple comforting matter of a golden mean. Man is dramatically closer to the Yahoos in many ways, and with all manner of insistence. While the Houyhnhnms are an insulting impossibility, the Yahoos, though not a reality, are an equally insulting *poss*ibility. Swift's strategy of the undermining doubt is nowhere more evident than here, for though we are made to fear the worst, we are not given the comfort of knowing the worst. 'The chief end I propose to my self in all my labors is to vex the world rather than divert it': and whatever grains of salt we may choose for our comfort to see in these words, 'the world', gentle reader, includes *thee*.

CHAPTER II

ORDER AND CRUELTY

Swift, Pope and Johnson

HAMM ... you're on earth, there's no cure for that!

(Samuel Beckett, *Endgame*)

Swift's satire often suggests an impasse, a blocking of escape routes and saving possibilities. This feeling presses on the reader for reasons which do not necessarily follow from the satiric topic as such, from the specific wickedness Swift is castigating, or any outright assertion that the wickedness is incurable. Incurability is certainly often implied, and the sense of an impasse is (by a paradox which is only apparent) related to a complementary vision of unending paths of vicious self-complication, bottomless spirals of human perversity. This is less a matter of Swift's official ideological views than of mental atmosphere and ironic manipulation: that is, of a more informal, yet very active, interplay between deliberate attacking purposes (and tactics), and certain tense spontaneities of self-expression. My concern is with the stylistic results of this interplay, though I do not pretend that the deliberate purposes can be clearly distinguished from the more shadowy ones. It may be that in Swift such dividing lines *need* to be unclear. I begin with Swift's most frequently discussed passage, the mock-argument[1]

> that in most Corporeal Beings, which have fallen under my Cognizance, the *Outside* hath been infinitely preferable to the *In*: Whereof I have been farther convinced from some late Experiments. Last Week I saw a Woman *flay'd*, and you will hardly believe, how much it altered her Person for the worse. Yesterday I ordered the Carcass of a *Beau* to be stript in my Presence; when we were all

> amazed to find so many unsuspected Faults under one Suit of Cloaths: Then I laid open his *Brain*, his *Heart*, and his *Spleen*; But, I plainly perceived at every Operation, that the farther we proceeded, we found the Defects encrease upon us in Number and Bulk: from all which, I justly formed this Conclusion to my self; That ... He that can with *Epicurus* content his Ideas with the *Films* and *Images* that fly off upon his Senses from the *Superficies* of Things; Such a Man truly wise, creams off Nature, leaving the Sower and the Dregs, for Philosophy and Reason to lap up. This is the sublime and refined Point of Felicity, called, *the Possession of being well deceived*; The Serene Peaceful State of being a Fool among Knaves (*Tale*, IX).

Here, the example of the flayed woman supports an argument similar to that of *A Beautiful Young Nymph Going to Bed*: whores can look horrible when their finery is stripped off, conventional celebrations of female beauty gloss over some ugly facts, the *Outside* looks better than the *In* and creates inappropriate complacencies. The flayed woman is portrayed in less detail, and seems physically less shocking, than the nymph of the poem, with her artificial hair, eyes and teeth, and her 'Shankers, Issues, running Sores'.[2] But she is, in a sense, more 'gratuitous'. In the poem, however horrible the details, the main proposition is sustained by them in a manner essentially straightforward, formulaic, and indeed conventional.[3] The account is a nightmare fantastication, but it is also simply a *donnée*: the poem asks us to imagine such a woman, and the point is made. The nymph is entirely subordinated to obvious formulaic purposes, even though 'subordination', in another sense, ill describes the vitality of the grotesquerie.

The flayed woman (and stripped beau), on the other hand, are momentary intensities which do not merely *serve* the argument they are meant to illustrate, but actually *spill over* it. They take us suddenly, and with devastating brevity, outside the expectations of the immediate logic, into a surprising and 'cruel' domain of fantasy. 'Cruel' is here used in something like Artaud's sense, as lying outside or beyond ordinary moral motivations, and Swift's brevity is essential to the effect. For this brevity, and the astringent blandness of the language, arrest the play of fantasy sufficiently to prevent it from developing into a moral allegory in its own right. The point is important, because brevity is not a necessary feature of what we nowadays think of as the literature of cruelty, that is, of such writers as Sade, Jarry, the followers of Artaud in the theatre, the authors included in Breton's *Anthologie de l'Humour Noir* and allied literary explorers of the black joke and the 'gratuitous' shock. When Breton placed Swift at the head of his anthology, as *véritable initiateur* of a black humour emancipated from the 'degrading influence' of satire and moralising,[4] he told a real truth, for Swift has (I believe) a temperamental tendency in this direction. But the tendency is powerfully held in check by conscious moral purposes which harness it to their own use. Hence his gratuitous cruelties are usually brief eruptions, only as long (so to speak) as the Super-Ego takes to catch up, and any extensive development of a grim joke normally dovetails into a fully-fledged moral demonstration or argument, as in the *Beautiful Young Nymph* or the *Modest Proposal*. Brief quasi-cannibalistic frissons in *Gulliver* (Gulliver using the skins of Yahoos for making clothes or sails, *G.T.*, IV.iii and x)[5] are more gratuitous than the *Modest Proposal*, as the flayed woman is more gratuitous than the *Beautiful Young Nymph*. The *Gulliver* passages are extremely minor comic assaults on our 'healthy' sensibilities, lacking the intensity of the passage from the *Tale*; but in one paradoxical sense they also are more unsettling than the more extended use of the cannibal image, precisely because in the *Proposal* the image is the direct sustaining principle of a moral argument. To this extent Breton seems off the mark when he follows his Swift section (which includes a substantial portion of the *Proposal*) with an elaborate cannibal extravaganza from Sade.[6]

This is not to say that the briefer passages have no moral implication (nor that the extended ones lack the power to shock, or have no local and subsidiary intensities of their own). Presumably the clothes of Yahoo-skin are also a reminder of the animality of man, while the flayed woman purports to illustrate the notion that appearances are more agreeable than reality. But it would take a perverse reader to feel that these moral implications provide the dominant effect. The gruesomeness of the flayed woman is so shockingly and absurdly *over*-appropriate to the ostensible logic as to be, by any normal standards, inappropriate. Critics who recognize this sometimes sentimentalize the issue by arguing that the flayed woman overspills the immediate moral not into an amoral gratuitousness, but into a different and more powerful moral significance: that she represents, for example, Swift's pained protest at this treatment of whores.[7] This seems as wrong as William Burroughs's notion that the *Modest Proposal* is 'a tract against Capital Punishment'.[8] I doubt Swift's opposition to either oppression, and if anything the allusion to flaying invites comparison with this sudden *re-direction* of the cannibal irony in the *Modest Proposal*:[9]

Neither indeed can I deny, that if the same Use were made of several plump young girls in this Town, who, without one single Groat to their Fortunes, cannot stir Abroad without a Chair, and appear at the *Play-house*, and *Assemblies* in foreign Fineries, which they never will pay for; the Kingdom would not be the worse.

In both cases the black joke suggests, if not literal endorsement of the hideous punishment, a distinct animus against the victim. The presence of this animus indicates that the irony is not, after all, gratuitous in the strictest Gide-ian sense. No human act can be entirely gratuitous (that is, absolutely motiveless), as Gide himself admitted:[10] it can only be disconnected from its normal *external* functions, in this case the moral implications expected of the satire. If in both cases the animus is transferred suddenly away from the official paths of the formula (truth vs. delusion; eating people is wrong), yet still carries a redirected moral charge (against whores, or foolish girls whose vanity is crippling Ireland's economy), there is an explosive overplus in the sheer wilful suddenness of the act of redirection as such. A haze of *extra* hostility hangs in the air, unaccounted for, dissolving the satire's clean logic into murkier and more unpredictable precisions, spreading uneasiness into areas of feeling difficult to rationalize, and difficult for the reader to escape. Part of Swift's answer to the dilemma posed for the satirist by his own belief that '*Satyr is a sort of* Glass, *wherein Beholders do generally discover every body's Face but their own*' (*Battle of the Books*, Preface)[11] is thus to counter, by a strategy of unease, the reader's natural tendency to exclude himself from the explicit condemnation: his escape into 'Serene Peaceful States' is blocked off even when he is innocent of the specific charge.

Often in such cases, moreover, the irony is manipulated in such a way as to suggest that the reader cannot be wholly unimplicated even in the specific charge. It is not only through unexpectedness or diversionary violence that the flayed woman and stripped beau spill over the logical frame. They also have an absurd tendency to generalize or extend the guilt to the rest of mankind, through a tangle of implications which act in irrational defiance of any mere logic. If the argument had been overridingly concerned to demonstrate that appearances can be fraudulent, superficial views inadequate, and vanity misplaced, the notion that people look ugly when stripped of their clothes or cosmetics would have been a sufficient, and a logically disciplined, support to it. To specify whores and beaux would be a perfectly legitimate singling out of social types who trade disreputably on appearances, and are otherwise open to moral censure. These didactic reasonings, and the larger-scale exposure of mad 'moderns', obviously remain present. But, in the wording as it stands, they are also, characteristically, subverted; as though the several wires crossed, making an explosive short-circuit. Flayed or dissected bodies hardly produce the most morally persuasive evidence of the delusiveness of appearances; nor do they as such prove a moral turpitude. If a whore's body alters for the worse when flayed, or a beau's innards look unsavoury when laid open, so would anyone else's, and the fact does not obviously demonstrate anybody's wickedness. The images, which begin as specific tokens of guilt aimed at certain human types, teasingly turn into general signs of the human condition. The images' strong charge of undifferentiated blame is thus left to play over undefined turpitudes attributable to the whole of mankind. The beau's innards recall an earlier statement by the *Tale*'s 'author', about having 'dissected the Carcass of *Humane Nature*, and read many useful Lectures upon the several Parts, both *Containing and Contained*; till at last it smelt so strong, I could preserve it no longer' (*Tale*, v).[12]

The passage parodies Wotton and others,[13] but, as often with Swiftian parody, transcends its immediate object. And the imagery's characteristic oscillation between moral turpitude and bodily corruption irrationally suggests a damaging equivalence between the two, placing on *Humane Nature* a freewheeling load of moral guilt which is inescapable and which yet attaches itself to faults outside the moral domain.

For if satire that is 'levelled at all' (i.e. 'general' rather than 'personal') 'is never resented for an offence by any, since every individual Person makes bold to understand it of others, and very wisely removes his particular Part of the Burthen upon the shoulders of the World, which are broad enough, and able to bear it' (*Tale*, Preface),[14] this is only likely to be true of a 'general' satire of *specific* vices. Where the aggression turns indistinct, and overspills the area of specifiable moral guilt, no opportunity is given for complacent self-exculpation on a specific front, and the reader becomes implicated. Instead of permitting the individual to shift his load on to the world's shoulders, Swift forces the reader to carry the world's load on *his*. The result, second time round, is that even the specific charges begin to stick: we become identified with whores, beaux, moderns. We cannot shrug this off by saying that it is Swift's 'author' who is speaking and not Swift. The intensities are Swift's, and depend on the blandness and even friendliness of the 'author'. The 'author' is saying in effect *hypocrite lecteur*, *mon semblable, mon frère*, and saying it kindly and welcomingly; but it is Swift who is making him say it, and the reader must decide whether he likes the thought of such a brother.

The cumulative sense of impasse (all mankind becoming implicated in the attack, the attack surviving any dismissal of specific charges, the curious revalidation of these charges by that fact, the miscellaneous blocking of the reader's escape-routes) depends, then, on energies which exceed the legitimate logical implications of the discourse. These energies cannot be accounted for by a mere retranslation of the mock-logic into its non-ironic 'equivalent', and part of their force depends on the violation of whatever consequential quality exists either in the hack's zany reasoning or its sober didactic counterpart. The carefully and extensively prepared polarity between the mad values of the modern hack, and the sanity of the non-singular, traditionalist, rational, unsuperficial man of sense, may seem for a while, in the Digression on Madness, solid and definite enough to provide at least limited reassurance against the more unsettling stylistic tremors. The reassurance is undermined but perhaps not eliminated by the flayed woman and stripped beau. But in the final sentence of the paragraph, the bad and good cease to function in lines that are parallel and opposite: the lines collapse, and cross. The comforting opposition is brought to a head, and then shattered, against the whole direction of the argument, by the suggestion that the alternative to being a fool is to be not a wise man but a knave.[15]

Critics often assume some form of 'diametrical opposition' between putative and real authors at this point. Either Swift's voice suddenly erupts, nakedly, from the other's vacuous chatter, or at best 'fools' and 'knaves' have simultaneously one clear value for Swift and an opposite one for his 'author'. I suggest that the relationship is at all times more elusive, and that the rigidities of mask-criticism (even in its more sophisticated forms) tend to compartmentalize what needs to remain a more fluid and indistinct interaction. (The theoretically clear opposition, in the preceding part of the Digression, between mad and sane, or bad and good, is a different thing: a temporary build-up, created for demolition.) The notion that in the 'Fool among Knaves' we suddenly hear Swift's own voice makes a kind of sense: but it runs the danger of suggesting quite improperly both that we have not actively been hearing this voice throughout, and that we now hear nothing else. In actual fact, the phrase trades simultaneously on our feeling that the sudden intensity comes straight from Swift, and on our reluctance to identify Swift even momentarily with an 'author' whom the work as a whole relentlessly ridicules. The paradox of that 'author' is that he has enormous vitality, a 'presence' almost as insistent as Swift's, without having much definable *identity* as a 'character'. He needs to be distinguished from Swift, but hardly as a separate and autonomous being. He is an ebullient embodiment of many of Swift's dislikes, but the ebullience is Swift's, and the 'author' remains an amorphous mass of disreputable energies, whose vitality belongs less to any independent status (whether as clear-cut allegory or full-fledged personality) than to an endlessly opportunistic subservience to the satirist's needs. Unduly simplifying or systematic speculation as to when Swift is talking and when his 'persona', or about their 'diametrically opposite' meanings if both are talking at once, often turns masks into persons, and induces in some critics the most absurd expectations of coherently developed characterization. Thus W. B. Ewald's classic work on Swift's 'masks' footnotes its discussion of the fools-knaves passage with the astonishing statement that 'The author's interest in observing and performing anatomical dissections is a characteristic which remains undeveloped in the *Tale* and which does not fit very convincingly the sort of *persona* Swift has set up.'[16]

It is, of course, true that the 'author' uses 'fool' as a term of praise, as Cibber in the *Dunciad* praises Dulness. The Digression on Madness is a 'praise of folly', and the 'author' proudly declares himself 'a Person, whose Imaginations are hard-mouth'd, and exceedingly disposed to run away with his *Reason*'.[17] The *Tale* presents, in its way, quite as much of an upside-down world as Pope's poem, but relies much less systematically on any single or dominant *verbal* formula. I do not mean that the *Dunciad* lacks that rudimentary two-way traffic between terms of praise and blame which we see in the *Tale* when, for example, the 'author' praises his 'Fool' as 'a Man truly wise', although it may be true that even at this level the *Tale*'s ironic postures are more teasingly unstable (indeed the 'author' seems not only to be scrambling simple valuations of wisdom and folly, but also perverting the 'true' paradox that 'folly is wisdom'). But the poem's mock-exaltation of fools rests essentially on a few strongly signposted terms (*dunce*, *dull*, etc.), which advertise the main ironic formula, and guarantee its fundamental predictability. When we feel uneasy or embarrassed in the *Dunciad*, it is because the main irony is *too* consistently sustained, rather than not enough. When Cibber praises Dulness ('whose good old cause I yet defend', 'O! ever gracious...', I. 165, 173, etc.), we may feel that Pope's blame by praise becomes awkward, not because the formula threatens to slip, but because it strains belief through overdoing. The implausibility may be no greater in itself than the hack's celebration of 'Serene Peaceful States'. But Cibber's praise has the slow unemphatic stateliness of a rooted conviction, while the hack's occurs in a context full of redirections, 'Fool' being disturbed by 'Knaves', as indeed the paragraph's happy style is disturbed throughout by alien intensities (flayed woman, beau's innards). Cibber at such moments fails to take off into the freer air of Pope's satiric fantasy, and solidifies instead into an improbably oversimplified 'character'. His heavy 'consistency' embarrasses differently from the 'inconsistencies' of Swift's hack, who, being in a sense no character at all, obeys no laws but those of his creator's anarchic inventiveness. The embarrassments in Pope are rare, but damaging. They are unintended, and disturb that poise and certainty of tone essential to Pope's verse. In Swift's satiric ambience, embarrassment is radical: it is a moral rather than an aesthetic thing, and is the due response to the rough edges and subversions of a style whose whole nature it is to undermine certainties, including the certainties it consciously proclaims.

Such blurred and shocking interchange (rather than sharp ironic opposition) between speaker and satirist is not confined to unruly works like the *Tale*. It occurs even in the *Modest Proposal*, that most astringent and tautly formulaic of Swift's writings. When the proposer uses the famous phrase, 'a Child, *just dropt from its Dam*',[18] a shock occurs because the style has hitherto given no unmistakable indication of its potential nastiness. Swift means the phrase to erupt in all its cruel violence, yet it is formally spoken by the proposer, and we are not to suppose *him* to be a violent, or an unkind man. Is the nasty phrase 'inconsistent' with his character? In a way, yes. On the other hand, part of Swift's irony is that prevailing values are so inhumane, that a gentle and moderate man will take all the horror for granted. If he can sincerely assert his humanity while advocating monstrous schemes, may he not also be expected to use a nasty phrase calmly and innocently? In which case, the usage might be 'consistent' with his character, thus indicating 'diametrical' opposition between him and Swift. But inhumane propaganda which claims, or believes itself, to be humane (say that of a 'sincere' defender of apartheid), does not use inhumane language; and we should have to imagine the speaker as incredibly insensitive to English usage, if he really wanted himself and his scheme to seem as humane as he believed they were. Such discussion of the 'character' and his 'consistency' leads to deserts of circularity. But the problem hardly poses itself in the reading (as it poses itself, down to the question of insensitivity to usage, over Cibber's praise of Dulness), and what becomes apparent is the irrelevance, rather than the truth or untruth, of the terms. The violent phrase is not an 'inconsistency' but a dislocation, among other dislocations. It has nothing to say about character, but breaks up a formula (the formula of a calm, kindly advocacy of horrible deeds), within a style which both includes such formulas and is given to breaking them up. Thus, when (in contrast to the *Dunciad*'s blame-by-praise, where it is easy to translate one set of terms into its opposite) Swift's speakers praise fools, or proclaim their humanity in brutal language, our reaction is to oscillate nervously between speaker and satirist. If we bring this oscillation into the open by asking (as critics are always asking) whether a bad speaker is using bad terms in a good sense, or whether Swift himself is making some form of explosive intervention, we find no meaningful answer. But there is a sense in which it is a meaningful *question*, for it brings into the open an uncertainty which is essential to the style.

The uncertainty is most strikingly illustrated in the Digression's 'Knaves'. For it is this electrifying term, with all its appearance of simplifying finality, which most resists tidy-minded schematisms of parallel-and-opposite valuation and the rest. If 'Fool' was good to the 'author' and bad to Swift, are 'Knaves' bad to the 'author' and good to Swift? Does the sentence's impact really reside in our feeling that 'Knave' is the fool's word for a quality Swift would name more pleasantly? If so, which quality? The answer is deliberately indistinct. Perhaps the 'Knaves' are those 'Betters' who, in the Preface to the *Battle of the Books*, are said to threaten the serenity of fools (the Preface too is 'of the Author', though an 'author' at that moment more similar than opposite to Swift).[19] But if this points to a partial explanation, it does so *ex post facto*, and is not experienced in the reading. To the extent that we are, in context, permitted to escape the suggestion that the world is absolutely divided into fools and knaves, we confront alternatives that are elusive, unclear. If we do not take 'Knaves' as Swift's word, literally meant, we cannot simply dismiss it as coming from the 'author' and being therefore translatable into something less damaging. We cannot be sure of the nature of any saving alternative, and may even uneasily suspect that we are in a fool's 'Serene Peaceful State' for imagining that such alternatives exist. The style's aggressive indistinctness thus leaves damaging possibilities in the air, without pinning Swift down to an assertion definite enough to be open to rebuttal. And so it seems more appropriate to note the imprisoning rhetorical effect of 'Fool among Knaves' than to determine too precisely who means what by those words. A rhetorical turn which wittily blocks off any respectable alternative to being a fool, is reinforced by those either-way uncertainties which the whole style induces in the reader. The reader is thus poised between the guilt of being merely human, and an exculpation which is as doubtful as the charges are unclear. The apparent definiteness of the epigram, and the reader's cloudy insecurity, mirror and complete each other in an overriding effect of impasse.

Fools and knaves go proverbially together, balancing one another in a variety of traditional sayings, a familiar source of more or less ready ironies for the witty phrase-maker. Swift's mot tends towards the most universalizing of fool-knave proverbs ('Knaves and fools divide the world'). But part of its flavour lies outside the grimmer implications, in the stylistic bravura which makes an established phrase complete itself in defiance of contextual expectations. The sudden appearance of 'Knaves' at the end of the sentence has a delighted rightness. It is a witty and exhilarating idiomatic homecoming. The wit gives pleasure in itself, and playfully suggests the survival of linguistic order within a certain mental anarchy.

Wit (in the high as well as the restricted sense) knows its enemies well: 'By *Fools* 'tis *hated*, and by *Knaves undone*',[20] and the erection of symmetries of style as a means of maintaining order among life's unruly energies is a familiar function of Augustan wit. Such symmetries have their effect more as acts of authorial presence, authorial defiances of chaos, than necessarily as embodiments of a widespread or active faith in stability or harmony. If the witty completeness of Swift's 'Fool among Knaves' holds together a world of unruly energies, the joke is also, by its qualities of surprise and shock, an unruly energy in its own right. The idiomatic homecoming is achieved with such tear-away unpredictability, that it leaves equally open the possibility of a fresh engulfment in the hack author's chaos, or of further victorious but unexpected versatilities from the satirist. The sudden poise seems more like a tense individual triumph, uncertain to be repeated and wholly dependent on our momentarily vivid sense of the satirist's mastery, than like the revelation of a serenely ordered structure on which we may henceforth depend.

Even the more predictable symmetries of Augustan style, the parallelism, antithesis, balance, the patternings which complete a formula or satisfy an expectation (idiomatic, syntactical, metrical, or logical), do not always evoke harmonious parterres of order, stability and ease. Pope's couplets are full of the kind of symmetry in which damaging alternatives are so starkly paired as to suggest not the comforting boundaries of a fixed and ordered world, but closed systems of vice or unhappiness from which there is no apparent release. Many thumbnail characterizations in the *Epistle to a Lady*, for example, contain such imprisoning paradoxes as 'A fool to Pleasure, and a slave to Fame', 'The Pleasure miss'd her, and the Scandal hit', 'Young without Lovers, old without a

Friend' (ll. 62, 128, 246). These perhaps have a brevity of the ready-made, and certainly an external quality. Pope's concern is psychological, to define character, but his subjects here are either placed in predicaments mainly circumstantial ('Young without Lovers'), or described in very generalized psychological terms ('A fool to Pleasure') which suggest rapid and sketchy inference from outward behaviour. If the stylistic patterns evoke certain forms of impasse, rather than an easy sense of order, the impasse hardly becomes total or absolute. One is free to feel that circumstances might change or behaviour improve, whereas prisons of the mind will seem correspondingly inescapable because (as Milton's Satan discovered when he saw that hell was partly a mental state)[21] they are carried everywhere within us. The typical impasse in Swift rests on a psychological factor, a perpetual perverse restlessness (madness close to badness) similar to what Johnson more compassionately saw as 'that hunger of imagination which preys incessantly upon life'.[22] The fact that Satan's '"my self am Hell"' is immediately followed by a 'geographical' glimpse of bottomlessness, or infinite regression, 'And in the lowest deep a lower deep/Still threatning to devour me',[23] bears a suggestive relation to the endless coils of perverse self-complication of Swift's vision of man on earth, and to the ever-unsatisfied cravings of Johnson's passage. Such an impasse, especially in ages unused to the idea of a psychiatric 'cure', is capable only of a religious solution, an annihilation of the self and its prisons within a greater imprisonment:[24]

> Take mee to you, imprison mee, for I
> Except you' enthrall mee, never shall be free.

Swift and Johnson were not, like Milton's Satan, blocked off from the possibility of a saving 'submission' ('that word/Disdain forbids me, and my dread of shame'),[25] and both looked devoutly to 'things eternal',[26] but they normally thought of submission in less transcendent terms than those of Donne's prayer. They speak not of cures or liberations, but of disciplines and palliatives, of a superimposition of moral solidities more practical than spiritually complete, of a concealment or silencing (not elimination) of doubts.[27]

For Pope, such rescue operations seemed less necessary. His mental processes were less prone to residual discomfort, less likely than Swift's or Johnson's to abut in a subversive dissatisfaction. He could thus more readily accommodate them into a system complete and intricate enough to absorb inner subversiveness instead of crushing it. The *Essay on Man* imagines a world where there can ultimately be no imprisoning loose ends, because it holds all the answers: 'All Discord, Harmony, not understood' (1.291). There is no sentimental denial of Discord, and Pope's satires give it due acknowledgment. But the world of the *Essay*, with its fresh, infectious delight in the conventional coherences of a theodicy, has no relevance for minds to whom Discord was a psychological condition rather than a philosophical problem, and neither Johnson nor Swift could have committed themselves to such a world, even as an imaginative abstraction or game. Johnson disliked the poem, but approved of the line 'Man never Is, but always To be blest' (1.96). Johnson's comment is significant. It secularizes and psychologizes the line into meaning that no *present moment* can be happy, 'but that, as every part of life, of which we are conscious, was at some point of time a period yet to come, in which felicity was expected, there was some happiness produced by hope'.[28] Pope's implication is very different. He is not so much concerned with the doomed unhappiness of present moments, as talking about an afterlife in which the devout and humble man may hope to find a happiness of whose nature he at present remains ignorant. The emphasis of Pope's preceding line, 'Hope springs eternal in the human breast', is expansive and positive, not tiredly cynical in the way popular quotation often assumes, nor 'realistically' earth-bound in Johnson's way. For in Johnson's reading, hope becomes a useful if necessarily delusive alleviation, not cure, of an incurable human dissatisfaction. Like alcohol: pressed further as to whether 'a man was not sometimes happy in the moment that was present, he answered, "Never, but when he is drunk"'.

If those ordered stylistic dispositions characteristic of much Augustan writing can express, in Pope, states of vicious inextricability and impasse, the point is *a fortiori* true of Johnson, in both verse and prose: 'wav'ring man ... Shuns fancied ills, or chases airy good'; 'Human life is every where a state in which much is to be endured, and little to be enjoyed'; 'Marriage has many pains, but celibacy has no pleasures'; 'the more we enquire, the less we can resolve'.[29] Such configurations are sometimes (in *Rasselas*) undercut by a mild humour, and we may often dissociate the statements, in a formal sense, from the writer, who frequently does not speak in his own person. Johnson, and Swift, differ from Pope in the kind and degree of their authorial commitment to configurations of impasse. In Johnson, the commitment is most *direct* (not necessarily *closer* than Swift's, whose tense self-involvement with his absurd and satirized speakers is extremely intimate, though endlessly oblique; and whose subversive brilliance exists in a kind of mirror-opposition to his hack's subversive folly). This is true even when he speaks through fictional characters, for these often recognizably embody views, and styles of thought and expression, also found in the more formally Johnsonian voices of the *Rambler* or the conversations in Boswell's *Life*. Johnson's wit is the most subdued of the three writers', and the undercutting in *Rasselas* is mild, suggesting not dissociation but a ruefully avuncular endorsement. Johnson's eloquent literalness, and the emphasis which he places on the psychological factor in the human condition, contribute an impression of laboured introspective involvement far removed from the confident externalized precisions of Pope. Certain twists and countertwists of the human mind, which Swift renders through feats of ironic mimicry, Johnson can *state* with an astonishing and compassionate baldness:[30]

> Then say how hope and fear, desire and hate,
> O'erspread with snares the clouded maze of fate,
> Where wav'ring man, betray'd by vent'rous pride,
> To tread the dreary paths without a guide,
> As treach'rous phantoms in the mist delude,
> Shuns fancied ills, or chases airy good.

The last line does not confine itself to implying the vanity of man's pursuit of good and avoidance of ills, but says that the good and ills on which his energies are spent are themselves unreal, compulsively imaginary: the ironic completeness of the human impasse, and its essentially *psychological* root, are simultaneously made vivid.

The completeness, indeed, depends on the psychological nature, and Pope is a good deal less emphatic on both points than either Johnson or Swift. Even when his examples of mental imprisonment have relatively little tendency to shift to a circumstantial or a behavioural plane, and instead dwell (as in the portrait of Flavia) on a self-entrapped mental *constitution*,[31]

> Wise Wretch! with Pleasures too refin'd to please,
> With too much Spirit to be e'er at ease,
> With too much Quickness ever to be taught,
> With too much Thinking to have common Thought:
> Who purchase Pain with all that Joy can give,
> And die of nothing but a Rage to live,

Pope is still, as in the other examples, offering what defines itself as an individual case. The poem's informing generalizations ('"Most Women have no Characters at all"', 'Ladies, like variegated Tulips, show', 'Woman's at best a Contradiction still')[32] are so much window-dressing for the individual set-pieces. Unlike Johnson's individual 'characters' in the *Vanity*, which are a long painful illustration of the opening lines, implicating the whole of mankind, Pope's have a buoyant autonomy which reduces the universalizing frameworks to relative insignificance. If the portrait of Flavia is 'general' and not merely 'personal' satire (and it may indeed be 'personal' in the most specific sense, as well as having wider applicability), it is general of the type, not comprehensive. Of the dozen-odd fool-knave passages listed in Abbott's *Concordance* of Pope, not one has the globally imprisoning reach of Swift's mot. When, indeed, a Popeian character seeks to involve large sections of mankind into one or other of the two alternatives (Sir Gilbert, who 'holds it for a rule,/ That "every man in want is knave or fool" ', or Atossa, who 'Shines, in exposing Knaves, and painting Fools,/ Yet is, whate'er she hates and ridicules'),[33] it is on the slanderer and not his many victims that Pope lets the trap fall. Such firm delimiting of the attack permits a confident self-exclusion for both poet and reader. Pope is more cleanly dissociated than either Swift or Johnson from his speakers and characters, not only in upside-down works like the *Dunciad*, but (thanks to formalized rhetorical postures) even when the damaging statements are *spoken* not by the characters, but by the poet about them. Swift's wider and more damaging comprehensiveness implicates both himself and his reader, and permits neither to stand outside; in this way, as well as through the tense intimacies of the style, Swift's satire is so general that it becomes personal—and of the second and first, not only of the third, person.[34]

The buoyancy of Pope's categorizations may be due to an active feeling that there exist not just saving possibilities, but actual worlds of order and decency, outside them. But there is certainly a quite individual delight in creating little fictions of order around cases of inconsistency and contradiction. The lines in which Flavia becomes immured within her own self-contradictions convey the poet's systematizing triumph more strongly than they oppress us with her impasse. His rhetoric here, as in other places, very strongly advertises its dominating stabilities. Each finality, each climax, even each shocking anti-climax, take their place in a well signposted pattern which is actually *style-induced*. There may be startling reversals, but they are always part of a visible rhythm of rising and falling, inflation and bathos, deception and undeception, and there is nothing which erupts in such sudden defiance of all expectation or pattern as Swift's 'Fool among Knaves'. 'Inconsistency' yields special satisfactions, not (as in Swift) of mimicry, but of organization. Hence not only the crisp buoyancies of single-line epigrams, but the relaxed, lingering amplitude, the easy metrical sweep that savours itself as it prepares sudden quickenings to conclusiveness, of such lines as these:

> Rufa, whose eye quick-glancing o'er the Park,
> Attracts each light gay meteor of a Spark,
> Agrees as ill with Rufa studying Locke,
> As Sappho's diamonds with her dirty smock.[35]

Whenever 'Order in Variety we see',[36] in the world of Pope's poems, we become aware not so much of the 'universal harmony' in itself, as of the creative delight of the poet in inventing it. Even the *real* landscape in *Windsor-Forest* to which these words particularly refer seems (if the word may be imagined in a favourable sense) 'staged'. And those generalizations which impute a widespread and disreputable human variousness may oddly carry more pleasure than pain. Pope's couplet about women being like the 'variegated Tulips'[37] is itself ironic, and prefaces some accounts of strange and perverse states, but there is a pleasure, turning to gallantry, in the image's momentary power to systematize, so that a combined elegance, in the women and in Pope's ordering of their variety, survives the sarcasm: ''Tis to their Changes that their charms they owe'. Contrast the ending of *The Lady's Dressing Room*, where Swift combines women, tulips and ideas of order: 'Such Order from Confusion sprung,/Such gaudy Tulips rais'd from Dung.'[38]

But Pope's usual way with damaging generalizations is to turn quickly to particulars, which are more amenable to the sort of enclosed definition which lets the rest of humanity out. 'Characters' overwhelm their universalizing contexts. In the *Epistle to Cobham*, the generalizing lip-service to human nature's 'puzzling Contraries' (l. 124) is even greater than in *To a Lady*: 'Our depths who fathoms, or our shallows finds,/ Quick whirls, and shifting eddies, of our minds?' (ll. 29-30). The corresponding stress on triumphs of individual categorization is also greater. The 'ruling passion' seems a convenient formula less because it is a particularly good means to psychological insights than because of the pleasures of conclusive definition which it yields:

> Search then the Ruling Passion: There, alone,
> The Wild are constant, and the Cunning known (ll. 174ff.).

The satisfactions are largely aesthetic. The lengthy portrait of Wharton which follows this couplet is full of vivid debating triumphs:

> This clue once found, unravels all the rest,
> The prospect clears, and Wharton stands confest.
> . . . .

Ask you why Wharton broke thro' ev'ry rule?
'Twas all for fear the Knaves should call him Fool.
    Nature well known, no prodigies remain,
Comets are regular, and Wharton plain.

If the concept of a 'ruling passion' is something whose ramifying completeness imprisons the satiric victim, and if Pope's play of paradox and antithesis reinforces this imprisonment, there is nevertheless in the poem a feeling not of imprisonment but of release. 'The prospect clears': such manifest delights of the controlling intellect have at least as much vitality as the turpitudes of Wharton and the rest. Contrast the very different finality of Swift's famous mot about Wharton's father, where the witty energy is entirely devoted to closing-in on the victim, and where the astringency of the prose-rhythms makes Pope's verse seem almost jaunty: 'He is a Presbyterian in Politics, and an Atheist in Religion; but he chuseth at present to whore with a Papist'.[39]

This astringency is revealing. It is often found where Swift practises what we may call couplet-rhetoric, that style in both verse and prose whose qualities of balance, antithesis, and pointedness mirror (ironically or not) Augustan ideals of coherence, regularity and decorous interchange, as well as paradoxes of enclosed self-contradiction.[40] He seldom wrote heroic couplets, perhaps resisting the almost institutionalized sense of order which the form seemingly aspires to proclaim, and preferring more informal verse styles. His more exuberant effects, unlike Pope's, occur in more open-ended or unpredictable styles, and the patternings of a pointed or epigrammatic manner frequently freeze in his hands to a slow harsh deliberateness. The fact that such patternings occur mostly in his prose may have something to do with the greater amplitude of the prose medium, which makes possible longer, slower units of sense. But there is no Popeian buoyancy in Johnson's verse, and plenty in Fielding's prose, as the following passage shows:[41]

> Master Blifil fell very short of his companion in the amiable quality of mercy; but he as greatly exceeded him in one of a much higher kind, namely, in justice: in which he followed both the precepts and example of Thwackum and Square; for tho' they would both make frequent use of the word *mercy*, yet it was plain, that in reality Square held it to be inconsistent with the rule of right; and Thwackum was for doing justice, and leaving mercy to Heaven. The two gentlemen did indeed somewhat differ in opinion concerning the objects of this sublime virtue; by which Thwackum would

> probably have destroyed one half of mankind, and Square the other half.

This may recall some of the passages from Pope's *Epistle to a Lady*: balance, contrast, a tremendous display of powers of summation, an obvious delight in the feats of style which so memorably and satisfyingly categorize some unsavoury facts. There is, too, the confident authorial presence, a decorous and gentlemanly self-projection, simplified but enormously alive, free of the vulnerabilities of undue intimacy with the reader or undue closeness to the material, yet proclaiming an assured and reassuring moral control. The categorizations point to a kind of vicious closed system, but unlike Swift's imprisoning paradoxes and like those of Pope, they deal with single persons or types, rather than with mankind at large or with wide and damagingly undefined portions of it. Moreover, the kind of exuberance found in Fielding as in Pope turns the closed systems into authorial triumphs of definition, instead of allowing them to generate an oppressive feeling of impasse. When Swift is exuberant on Fielding's or Pope's scale, he does not produce a finality towards which the preceding rhetoric has been visibly tending, but assaults us with sudden shocks of *re*definition, turning us into knaves if we refuse to be fools. Fielding, like Pope, rounds his paradoxes to a conclusiveness which, being both prepared-for and specific, limits their applicability and creates a feeling of release. If the buoyant brevities of Pope's couplets are absent in Fielding's passage, the amplitude of the prose medium in his case permits versatilities of elaboration, of weaving and interweaving, which are their counterpart in exuberant definition.

Prose, then, does not in itself make couplet-rhetoric astringent. Here, however, is Gulliver on prime ministers:[42]

> he never tells a *Truth*, but with an Intent that you should take it for a *Lye*; nor a *Lye*, but with a Design that you should take it for a *Truth* ... (IV.vi);

and on the causes of war:[43]

> Sometimes one Prince quarrelleth with another, for fear the other should quarrel with him. Sometimes a War is entered upon, because the Enemy is too *strong*, and sometimes because he is too *weak*. Sometimes our Neighbours *want* the *Things* which we *have*, or *have* the Things which we want ... (IV.v).

These passages create little 'anti-systems', absurdly self-consistent worlds of perverse motivation, whose complete disconnection from humane and rational purposes gives them an air of unreality, of disembodied vacancy. (The vision is partly a satiric counterpart to Johnson's tragic sense of man, shunning 'fancied ills' and chasing 'airy good'.) Such satiric systematizations are not uncommon in Augustan literature, and Pope's *Moral Essays* also occasionally turn excesses of vice and irrationality into paradoxical pseudo-systems. Pope does not, however, allow them to take on so much crazy autonomy, but often refers them to an all-explaining ruling passion. Because Swift deliberately withholds explanations at this level, we have to fall back on some absolute notion of the ingrained perversity of the human species, which alone can account for such ghoulishly self-sustaining perversity.

Above all, where the epigrammatic summations of Pope or Fielding suggest that vicious matters have been 'placed' or disposed of, there is here a sense of being weighed down. The categorizations are witty and precise, but the voice is flat and rasping, not buoyant with those righteous energies with which Pope and Fielding can outmatch the most viciously animated turpitudes. I suggest that this astringency is Swift's rather than Gulliver's, so far as we bother to disentangle them. This is not (once again) to say that Gulliver and Swift are identical, but that the feeling seems to come from behind the Gulliver who is speaking. Within a page of the last passage, in the same conversation or series of conversations, Gulliver gives this, not astringent but high-spirited, account of human war (which has already been discussed from another point of view):[44]

> I could not forbear shaking my Head and smiling a little at his Ignorance. And, being no Stranger to the Art of War, I gave him a Description of Cannons, Culverins, Muskets, Carabines, Pistols, Bullets, Powder, Swords, Bayonets, Sieges, Retreats, Attacks, Undermines, Countermines, Bombardments, Sea-fights; Ships sunk with a Thousand Men; twenty Thousand killed on each Side; dying Groans, Limbs flying in the Air: Smoak, Noise, Confusion, trampling to Death under Horses Feet: Flight, Pursuit, Victory; Fields strewed with Carcases left for Food to Dogs, and Wolves, and Birds of Prey; Plundering, Stripping, Ravishing, Burning and Destroying. And, to set forth the Valour of my own dear Countrymen, I assured him, that I had seen them blow up a Hundred Enemies at once in a Siege, and as many in a Ship; and beheld the dead Bodies drop down in Pieces from the Clouds, to the great Diversion of all the Spectators (IV.V).[45]

The note of animated pleasure is at odds with the preceding astringency, and with the notion (see especially the *later* stress on this, IV.vii)[46] that he was in these conversations already disenchanted with humanity: but there is a very similar, complacently delighted, account of war given to the King of Brobdingnag before Gulliver's disenchantment (II.vii).[47] The method of the *Travels*, putatively written after the disenchantment, is often to have Gulliver present himself partly as he was at the relevant moment in the past, and not merely as he might now see himself, so that in both chapters (II.vii and IV.v) twin-notes of affection and dislike might be felt to mingle or alternate. Unless we are prepared to regard Gulliver as a very sophisticated ironist or rhetorician (let alone a highly-developed Jamesian consciousness)—and some readers are—we must feel that the alternations are modulations of Swift's ironic voice. Even if we deny Gulliver's pleasure in the list about war, we cannot deny the list's comic exuberance, and its difference from the dry epigrams of a moment before. However we describe Gulliver's attitude at this time, the shift cannot be attributed to any significant variation in his feelings, just as the inordinate and chaotic cataloguing cannot be accounted for as a subtly motivated departure from Gulliver's earlier announcement in IV.v that he is only reporting 'the Substance' (and an ordered summary at that) of these conversations.[48] The modulations in the *actual* atmosphere as we read emphasize again the abstractness of any separation of Swift from his speaker (even where that speaker, unlike the *Tale*'s, has a name, wife, family and other tokens of identity). Swift's most expansive satiric energies kindle not at those sharp and witty summations which would have delighted Fielding or Pope, but at the humour of Gulliver's anarchic submission to an evil whose chaotic vitality has not been subdued to epigrammatic definition. At the mental level at which we, as readers, respond to such transitions, we are face to face with Swift's inner fluctuations, without intermediaries. Big men, little men, Gulliver and the rational horses, become so many circus animals, deserting. The encounter is, of course, unofficial: we do not admit it to ourselves, as distinct from experiencing it, and no suggestion arises of Swift's conscious design. When Swift participates harshly in Gulliver's tart epigrams there is no formal difficulty in imagining that the two converge, almost *officially*. But when the tartness unpredictably gives way to Gulliver's unruly exuberance (whether Gulliver is felt *at that instant* to hate war or to relish it is not a problem which occurs to us in the reading, as distinct from knowing Swift hates it, and sensing the exuberance), Swift's participation is unofficial and closer, a variant form of that mirror-relationship I have already suggested between an unruly and right minded Swift who wrote the *Tale*, and the *Tale*'s unruly but mad and wicked 'author'.

These identities establish themselves in that very charged penumbra where the satirist's personality overwhelms his own fictions, in a huge self-consciousness. It is no coincidence, from this point of view, that Swift's *Tale* is both a pre-enactment and an advance parody of Sterne; nor that the self-irony, at once self-mocking and self-displaying, of Sterne, or Byron, or Norman Mailer (whose *Advertisements for Myself*, for example, use every trick that the *Tale* satirically *ab*used, digressions, self-interruptions and solipsisms, solipsistic reminders of digression or solipsism, etc.) sometimes develops from Swift or shares formal elements with his work. The major formal difference is that Swift's 'authors' (the hack, the proposer, Gulliver) are predominantly satirized figures, officially Swift's complete antithesis most of the time, whereas the speakers or narrators of the later writers are either identical with their creators (as in many of Mailer's *Advertisements*), or projections and facets, hardly massively dissociated. The satiric plots and formulae which guarantee this dissociation in Swift may be thought of as immense protective assertions of the Super-Ego, part of the same process which sees to it that potentially 'gratuitous' effects of any length are in fact more or less subdued within frameworks of moral allegory. Because Swift's person is not *openly* permitted to take the slightest part in the affair, his self-mockery (for example) is denied all the luxuries of coy self-analysis available to the later writers. (Where he does, however, speak through voices which are direct self-projections, as in *Cadenus and Vanessa* or the *Verses on the Death*, a tendency to such luxuries becomes evident.) The fact that Swift's presence remains felt despite the formal self-dissociation creates between the reader and Swift an either/or relation whose very indefiniteness entails more, not less, intimacy. In that whirlpool of indefiniteness, where any tendency to categorize is arrested, individual characters become fluid and indefinite, as in Sterne, despite the unSternelike (but rather nominal and cardboard) firmness of 'characters' like the modest proposer, or like Gulliver in his more self-consistent interludes. There is a relation between this and Swift's readiness in some moods to think of the human mind as prone to bottomless spirals of self-complication. An implication that hovers over both is that human behaviour is too unpredictable to be usefully classified in rounded conceptions of 'personality', as 'in (or out of) character'. Despite its strong moral point of reference, Swift's self-implicating sense of our anarchic tortuosity is close in conception to some of those visions of complexity which in our time are often embodied in the extraordinarily recurrent image of a spiral (and its relations, vortex, whirlpool, winding stair, endless ladder, vicious circle), with all its suggestions of perpetual movement and interpenetrating flux. We think of the Yeats of 'Blood and the Moon', who charged the image with a direct and passionate self-commitment, and with splendours and miseries which Swift would shrink from as too grandiloquent,

> I declare this tower is my symbol; I declare
> This winding, gyring, spiring treadmill of a stair is my
> ancestral stair;
> That Goldsmith and the Dean, Berkeley and Burke have
> travelled there.
>
> Swift beating on his breast in sibylline frenzy blind
> Because the heart in his blood-sodden breast had dragged him down
> into mankind,

but whose inclusion of Swift shows part of Yeats's strangely inward insight into Swift; of 'those endless stairs from the buried gaming rooms of the unconscious to the tower of the brain' in Mailer; of the dialectical psychologies of Sartre or R. D. Laing.[49]

A reflection of this on a more or less conscious, or 'rhetorical', plane are those familiar fluidities of style: the irony seldom docile to any simple (upside-down or other) scheme; 'masks' and allegories seldom operating in an unruffled point-by-point correspondence with their straight non-fictional message, or with sustained consistency to their own fictional selves; stylistic procedures at odds with one another, or deliberately out of focus with the main feeling of the narrative; contradictory implications on matters of substance. The effect is to preclude the comforts of definiteness, while blocking off retreats into woolly evasion, so that both the pleasures of knowing where one stands, and those of a vagueness which might tell us that we need not know, are denied.

Pope's writing, by contrast, depends on a decorous clarity of relationship (with the reader and subject) without the active and radical ambiguity we find in Swift. Pope's speakers (outside the *Dunciad*) are usually not enemies, from whom he must signpost his dissociation, but rhetorically simplified projections of himself (as urbane Horatian commentator, righteously angry satirist, proud priest of the muses). The somewhat depersonalized postures are traditional and 'public', secure within their rhetorical traditions (and so not subject to unpredictable immediacies), and they permit certain grandeurs of self-expression precisely because the more intimate self recedes from view. Urbane or passionate hauteurs

('Scriblers or Peers, alike are *Mob* to me', 'I must be proud to see/Men not afraid of God, afraid of me')[50] can then occur without opening the poet to easy charges of crude vanity. The 'masks' of Pope may thus be thought of as melting the poet's personality in a conventional or public role, but also as a release for certain acts of authorial presence. The finalities of the couplet form serve Pope in a similar way. They formally sanction a degree of definiteness which might otherwise seem open to charges of arrogance or glibness. The clearly patterned artifice hardly engulfs Pope. He moves within it with so much vitality and such an assurance of colloquial rhythm, that a powerfully dominating presence is always felt. But it remains a simplified presence, and Swift is in many ways paradoxically closer to his parodied enemies than is Pope to his own rhetorical selves.

But if couplets help Pope to formalize his presence, and to free it from certain inhibiting vulnerabilities, the effect is largely personal to Pope, and not primarily a cultural property of the form. Couplets do not, in Johnson, guarantee to suppress vulnerability, nor create triumphs of self-confidence; and their prose-counterparts do not in Swift (as they do in Fielding) attenuate the close intimacy of the satirist's presence. The balanced orderliness of couplet-rhetoric need not, even in Pope, reflect a serenity of outlook, nor a civilization which is confident, stable and in harmony with itself. The *Dunciad*, like the *Tale* and *Gulliver*, envisages cherished ideals not only under threat, but actually collapsing. The absurd moral universes which are locked away in the neat satiric patternings of both Swift and Pope often show 'order' parodying itself in its nasty uncreative antithesis. Each vicious 'anti-system' seems the ironic expression not of an Augustan order, but of a 'rage for order' gone sour. Pope's later style (at least) suggests no easy dependence on stabilities visibly and publicly achieved, but (like Swift's) highly personal encroachments on chaos.

Pope's way with chaos, however, is to keep his distance. He is temperamentally one of those for whom categorization and wit offer satisfactions which as such reduce chaos, or keep it at bay: not only aesthetic satisfactions as, once labelled by 'ruling passions', 'the prospect clears', but the comforting moral solidity of a decisive summation, however damaging or pessimistic. A style had to be forged for this, since the hostile realities to be mastered were pressing and vivid enough to expose the smallest verbal evasion or complacency. Pope's rhetoric suggests not denial but *containment* of powerful and subtle forces, and thrives on an excited decisiveness. If his lapses lead to complacency and patness, his strengths are those of a thrilling and masterful vision, in which delicate perceptions and massive urgencies of feeling marvellously cohere. Swift's rhetoric is no less masterful, but its whole nature is to suggest forces which cannot be contained, thus tending away from categorization. This is often evident at moments of clinching finality, and nowhere more clearly than in the phrase about the 'Fool among Knaves'. The clear and uncompromising lines of the completed epigram imply, as we saw, that 'knaves and fools divide the world'. But the surprise of this implication, its violation of the general run of the preceding argument, and our impulse to discount something (we do not know what, nor how much) because the words are formally spoken by the mad 'author' cause a blur of uncertainty to play over the cheeky patness of the phraseology. Categorization yields to unresolved doubts. The clinching phrase, subverting its own finality, becomes disorderly and inconclusive. If it is also a self-assertion, buoyant with the satirist's masterful grasp over his material, it is not, in Pope's manner, part of a steady rhetoric of definition, but seems a dazzling momentary victory wrested from chaos. Of course, the playing for sudden dazzling victories, and to some extent the chaos itself, are also a rhetoric, though not (like Pope's) self-announced and openly visible as such.[51] It is important to Pope's manner that he should seem to stand clear-sightedly on top of his material; and essential to Swift's to appear, as the phrase from *Lord Jim* puts it, in the destructive element immersed.

This is evident not merely in the mechanics of verbal style, narrowly conceived. Whole allegorical sequences, whose straightforward message has Swift's full endorsement, dissolve in a self-undercutting inconsistency, or explode in violence. The most unsettling thing about the Academy of Lagado in *Gulliver's Travels*, III.v-vi, and especially its School of Political Projectors, is not the allegorical *substance*, but the Swiftian manoeuvres which force changes of focus in the midst of an apparent moral certainty. The projectors are associated not only with predictably silly and repugnant programmes, but, by an astonishing redirection in III.vi, also with 'good' schemes ('of teaching Ministers to consult the publick Good', etc.). These 'good' programmes in turn dissolve into a 'cruel' Ubu-like absurdity, as in the crazily beneficent proposal to eliminate political dissension by sawing off the occiputs of 'each Couple' of opponents, and interchanging them 'in such a Manner that the Brain may be equally divided' between both men in a new balanced mixture of 'two half Brains'. After this beneficent 'cruelty', the redirections continue, by way of further 'good' proposals reminiscent of the *Project for the Advancement of Religion*, intermixed with some silly nastiness, until we arrive at crude totalitarian horrors.[52]

Or consider this initially straightforward allegory from section IV of the *Tale*:

> whoever went to take him by the Hand in the way of Salutation, *Peter* with much Grace, like a well educated Spaniel, would present them with his *Foot*...

This is one of several Swiftian jokes about the papal ceremony, and the passage so far is adequately accounted for in Wotton's gloss, which Swift prints in a note: *'Neither does his arrogant way of requiring men to kiss his Slipper, escape Reflexion'*. The passage then continues:[53]

> and if they refused his Civility, then he would raise it as high as their Chops, and give them a damn'd Kick on the Mouth, which hath ever since been call'd a *Salute*.

This development is outside the scope of Wotton's comment, outside the clean outlines of the allegory. It is not, as with the school of projectors, a redirection of the allegory, but an overspilling. One may argue it into the allegorical scheme by saying (accurately enough) that it represents the authoritarian brutality of the Roman Church. But the real force of the passage is to explode the emphasis away from the domain of allegorical correspondence as such.

The sudden violence is only one of several means of subversion, capping other subversions inherent in the context. Swift's appropriation, here and throughout the *Tale*, of Wotton's hostile exegesis, is not merely a means of explaining the allegory. Various piquancies of attack and of mocking self-exhibition, which lie outside the mere purposes of allegorical translation, are at work: the bravura of exploiting an enemy's attack for the serious illumination of one's own work; the tendency of this trick, while explaining the text, to mock it as requiring such solemn annotation, and from such a source; all the conventional seasoning of mock-scholarship, and so on. These effects combine with the fact that the allegory, like everything else, is spoken by the crazy 'author', and that it is an allegory which parodies allegories. The straightforward import of the story of the three brothers is thus not only undercut, but fragmented by a host of competing energies. Swift's real commitment to the direct import or core (the potted history of the Church) and to the primary satiric implications (the 'Abuses in Religion') becomes complicated by huge and distracting pressures: of self-mockery, of self-concealment, of tortuous and exuberant self-display. To say that this self-mockery simply subverts the allegory, or satirizes allegories in general, would be too crude, not only because part of the allegory somehow survives straight, but also because that diffusive spikiness injected by Swift is an attacking thing, *adding* to the satire's total fund of aggression and reinforcing the allegory's attack by that fact. But there is certainly, in practice, an exposure of the limits of the allegory to express all that Swift wants, to a degree which far exceeds the superficial and routine self-deflations of 'self-conscious narrative'.

The centre cannot hold. These unharnessed centrifugal energies of the form, its huge disruptive egotism, mirror the satirist's conscious vision of man's self-absorbed mental restlessness endlessly spiralling away from the rule of sense and virtue. The satirist is reflected in that mirror, 'satirized' beyond all his rhetorical reaches, yet *aptly* implicated, since his attack, so deeply rooted (as we saw) in a *psychological* diagnosis, extends to all mankind. The violence which Swift deplores is mirrored by the violence with which he charges his own style, just as, in the *Modest Proposal* and elsewhere, the murderous projects he satirizes in others are paralleled by aggressive velleities of his own, like the half-ironic desire to include in the cannibal project those Irish girls who wear foreign fineries.[54] The authoritarianism and the extremism which he exposes in others correspond to powerful authoritarian and extremist elements in himself, while his professed admiration for compromise, moderation and the common forms is balanced by moods or by contexts of suspicion or dislike for these very things, or things for which he uses uncannily similar language.[55] He is temperamentally given to subverting his own positives, as the treatment of Martin in the *Tale* tends to show.[56] He is quick to see in himself, as in all men, those anarchic proclivities of the inner man which may emerge in a hypertrophied and institutionalized form in sectarians, free thinkers and similar factious or individualistic groups. The controls which he requires that the law should place upon dissenters, free thinkers and proponents of 'innovations in government' closely resemble the controls which he expects himself and others to impose upon their own spontaneously subversive impulses and thoughts.[57] The King of Brobdingnag's comment upon 'the several Sects among us in Religion and Politicks', that there was 'no Reason, why those who entertain Opinions prejudicial to the Publick, should be obliged to change, or should not be obliged to conceal them' (*G.T.*, II.vi)[58] closely parallels Swift's own views in 'Some Thoughts on Free-Thinking':[59]

> I cannot imagine what is meant by the mighty zeal in some people, for asserting the freedom of thinking: Because, if such thinkers keep their thoughts within their own breasts, they can be of no

> consequence, further than to themselves. If they publish them to the world, they ought to be answerable for the effects their thoughts produce upon others.

The passage occurs in work in which (as we shall see) Swift is deliberately blurring the distinction between 'free thinking' in the technical or religious sense, and the looser etymological sense of 'unrestricted flow of thought', arguing that the sanity of every man depends on his ability to control his own internal 'free thinking'. And it is not surprising therefore that the passage is very similar not only to the King of Brobdingnag's views about the control of public free thinkers, but also to Swift's own statements about the limits of his answerability for his inner subversive doubts, provided he took care to conceal these doubts, tried to subdue them, and prevented their visible influence on his conduct of life ('Thoughts on Religion').[60]

These introspective statements, I suggested earlier, are very close to Johnson's mode of thinking, and the whole Swiftian vision of the psychologically rooted restlessness of human nature, including that of the satirist himself, is one which Johnson shared very deeply (it may be that Johnson's dislike of Swift was indeed partly motivated by an unconscious sense of likeness). Johnson was to take that vision a step away from moral censure, but largely by means of compassion and a rueful self-tolerance rather than by any radical reappraisal of moral standards. It is only much later that one hears of a 'human condition', psychologically determined, but without God and without attribution of sin.[61] Nevertheless, the vicious spirals, and those related energies (of sudden violence, or of deliquescence) which overspill their official (didactic or discursive) purposes, have the further point in common with black humour and the cult of the 'gratuitous' that their world is no longer secure in its values. When straightforward categorizable vice has dissolved into the unpredictabilities of the *Tale*'s freewheeling madness (the vice/madness equation is commonplace, but the *Tale* is surely something special), the most cherished finalities no longer seem to solve anything. A conclusiveness where, 'Nature well known, no prodigies remain,/Comets are regular, and Wharton plain', yields to conclusions in which 'nothing is concluded'.[62] Swift and Johnson clung, of course, with an urgency often authoritarian and sometimes close to despair, to their faith in a traditional morality, to their Anglican piety and Augustan ideals of order. They had no consciously formulated sense that traditional values cannot any longer apply. This partly explains the tendency of Swift's 'gratuitous' effects to dovetail into a moral argument, especially if they are protracted; and it doubtless has something to do with Swift's and Johnson's stylistic attachment to the perspicuous finalities of couplet-rhetoric, Swift's in some of his prose, Johnson's in prose and verse. But Johnson's laboured, eloquent sadness in this mode, and Swift's imprisoning harshness, also tell their story. So, I believe, does the corresponding tendency of Swift's prose to kindle to a ferocious vitality in proportion as (in much of the *Tale*, and in Gulliver's list about war) its subject grows anarchic. The radical difference from Pope lies here, for all Swift's conscious closeness to Pope's outlook, and for all the likelihood that he would have given Breton and the other modern theorists a most comfortless home in his *Tale*. The matter transcends official themes, and outward feelings, as it transcends mere couplets. Cultural disorder for cultural disorder, the Academy of Lagado's relatively lighthearted or low-pitched inconsequence (not to mention the *Tale*'s hectic craziness) seems more disturbing than the *Dunciad*'s Fourth Book, Miltonic Darkness and all. This is perhaps part of what Leavis meant about Pope being more 'positive' than Swift, and if so it leads me to an exactly opposite valuation of the two men. For if Pope's positives, even in defeat (when the massive heroic ruin of the *Dunciad* proclaims the world that has been lost), are vividly adequate to the crisis as Pope so brilliantly re-creates it, they do not measure up to the evoked quality of deepest malaise with which Swift *relives* that crisis. Swift's writing exists at a level where no act of containment, however complete and resourceful, can in the end be validated, its subject being, not Augustan culture, but the nature of man. And the matter of Swift's vitality in anarchic contexts is not wholly accounted for by Leavis's notion (in what is, despite its hostility, the most acute general discussion of Swift ever written) that Swift is most creatively alive in 'rejection and negation'.[63] The slow harsh epigrams negate and reject just as much, and when it comes to the Yahoos having 'all the life',[64] we may wonder whether (as in the *Tale*) Swift is not most profoundly in his element not merely as a scourge of anarchy, but as its *mimic*; participating inwardly, as well as protesting at those limitless escalations of folly and vice, those feverish spirals of self-complication. As the satire finally devolves from the third on to the first person, from world to gentle reader and back to the satirist, we could do worse than entertain the thought that Swift, in that place where all the ladders (and the spirals) start, was and sensed that he was, in all rebellious recalcitrance, himself Yahoo.

CHAPTER III

'TIS ONLY INFINITE BELOW

Swift, with Reflections on Yeats, Wallace Stevens and R. D. Laing

HAMLET A man may fish with the worm that hath eat of a king, and eat of the fish that hath fed of that worm.
KING What dost thou mean by this?
HAMLET Nothing, but to show you how a king may go a progress through the guts of a beggar.

(*Hamlet*, IV.iii)

All flesh is grasse, is not onely metaphorically, but literally true, for all those creatures we behold, are but the hearbs of the field, digested into flesh in them, or more remotely carnified in our selves. Nay further, we are what we all abhorre, *Anthropophagi* and Cannibals, devourers not onely of men, but of our selves; and that not in an allegory, but a positive truth; for all this masse of flesh which wee behold, came in at our mouths: this frame wee looke upon, hath beene upon our trenchers; In briefe, we have devoured our selves.

(Sir Thomas Browne, *Religio Medici*, I.xxxvii)

He is devoured
  by his devouring fear of
  being devoured by
  her devouring desire
for *him* to devour *her*.

(R. D. Laing, *Knots*)

Wallace Stevens has a poem entitled 'Frogs Eat Butterflies. Snakes Eat Frogs. Hogs Eat Snakes. Men Eat Hogs'.[1] The poem, like many of

Stevens's, is about poetry and its relation to the great processes of life and death. The cycle of rapacity which the title describes is an ineluctable fact of nature. From this, squarely recognizing death, the poet starts. With an odd aptness this poem does not elaborate on its title, but moves on from it. It tells not of frogs, snakes and hogs, but of rivers, which are *like* the hogs, 'nosing like swine,/Tugging at banks, until they seemed/Bland belly-sounds in somnolent troughs'. These belly-sounds are familiar in Stevens: they are the ugly invigorating call of reality, booming us free of 'poetic' sentiment, and releasing *true* poems. In other poems, they may come from frogs, oxen, lions or an archetypal dead shepherd booming 'tremendous chords from hell'.[2] Here they belong to rivers that are like hogs, hogs being (in the title's chain of rapacity) the last pre-human stage: they eat the rest, man eats them.

The rivers flow past the man 'who erected this cabin, planted/This field, and tended it awhile', not conscious of poetry, of 'the quirks of imagery', a man perhaps of the true poverty, of the 'essential' or the rocklike 'barrenness',[3] in 'his indolent, arid days'. Yet he and the rivers merge, as the hog merges with the man who eats him, and a heavy reciprocity of relationship complicates the cycle. Man not only eats hogs, but 'the swine-like rivers' and 'the hours' of heavy thundery summer feed on him, and on themselves:

> the hours of his indolent, arid days,
> Grotesque with this nosing in banks,
> This somnolence and rattapallax,
>
> Seemed to suckle themselves on his arid being,
> As the swine-like rivers suckled themselves
> While they went seaward to the sea-mouths.

The sea and its liberations are also a devouring, as the final word suggests. The ambiguities, of barrenness and creation, of heavy entrapment and vital release, are characteristic of Stevens's vision. A section of the *Man with the Blue Guitar* surveys first an uncreative aspect of the life-cycle, and then retorts:[4]

> The sea returns upon the men,
>
> The fields entrap the children, brick
> Is a weed and all the flies are caught,
>
> Wingless and withered, but living alive.
> The discord merely magnifies.
>
> Deeper within the belly's dark
> Of time, time grows upon the rock.

These liberations and rebirths are not only rooted, very often, in a bleak and heavy dryness, in black and muddy rivers of the mind,[5] but also in ambiguous images of self-suckling, of a creative Narcissism or cannibalism ('These days of disinheritance, we feast/On human heads .../... men eating reflections of themselves' says a poem wittily entitled 'Cuisine Bourgeoise'.)[6] Such things are partly a good circularity,[7]

> the merely going round,
> Until merely going round is a final good,
> The way wine comes at a table in a wood,

creative finalities 'For a moment final',[8] the table restored to its original element in the wood, plus the pleasure of wine. We are not allowed to forget that these experiences are charged with death, and that the supreme fiction depends on death and change: 'Death is the mother of beauty', 'Poetry is a Destructive Force'.[9] It is momentous associations of this kind which underlie the seeming irrelevance, the cheeky buoyancy of the title of a poem itself deliberately heavy and unbuoyant: 'Frogs Eat Butterflies. Snakes Eat Frogs. Hogs Eat Snakes. Men Eat Hogs.'

Swift also has a poem about poetry, *On Poetry: A Rapsody* (1733), in which various images of self-nourishing, reciprocal feeding, and a chain of rapacity occur. Chickens take a month to fatten, but are quickly eaten; similarly, poems long toiled over 'Are swallow'd o'er a Dish of Tea' and go 'where the *Chickens* went before' (ll. 61ff.).[10] Again, if you have published a poem anonymously and the town is running it down, keep the secret, 'Sit still, and swallow down your Spittle' (ll. 117ff.).[11] (The experience was autobiographical for Swift. On 10 November 1710 he wrote to Stella: 'I dined to-day at lady Lucy's, where they ran down my [*Description of a City*] *Shower*; and said *Sid Hamet* was the silliest poem they ever read, and told Prior so, whom they thought to be the author of it').[12] Most famously, there is a picture of universal devouring in the animal kingdom:[13]

> *Hobbes* clearly proves that ev'ry Creature
> Lives in a State of War by Nature.
> The Greater for the Smallest watch,
> But meddle seldom with their Match.
> A Whale of moderate Size will draw
> A Shole of Herrings down his Maw.
> A Fox with Geese his Belly crams;
> A Wolf destroys a thousand Lambs (ll. 319-26).

Poets, and fleas, are like this too, differing only in three special emphases or implications. They reverse the order of nature, so that it is the smallest who bite the greatest; they do this in an unending chain; and the chain is cannibalistic:

> The Vermin only teaze and pinch
> Their Foes superior by an Inch.
> So, Nat'ralists observe, a Flea
> Hath smaller Fleas that on him prey,
> And these have smaller Fleas to bite 'em,
> And so proceed *ad infinitum* (ll. 335-40).

There is no need to insist that Swift's emphases, unlike Stevens's, are satirical. He is dealing with bad critics and bad poets. The self-feeding, and the cannibal activity, are unproductive, barren, but not with the paradoxical 'aridity', the true 'poverty' of Stevens's poet, which 'becomes his heart's strong core'.[14] Characteristic Swiftian effects quickly develop. *Unnaturalness* is massively emphasized, not only the simple reversal of 'due Subordination' (l. 314), but perversions of natural feeding patterns which compound, and cut across, the cannibal chain. Thus, the poetasters have left their native Grub Street, are now not only tolerated outside (and above) their proper station, but actually fed by the Court:[15]

> Degenerate from their ancient Brood,
> Since first the Court allow'd them Food (ll. 365-6).

The whole fantasy is elaborated with a sour loftiness of which Swift was a unique and perfect master.

My special emphasis, however, is on the *infinity* of the flea-biting chain. This infinity is not one which completes itself in a circle, like the constant renewals of the life-cycle. It is a teeming but negative endlessness, applicable especially to poetry, which (unlike other things in nature) has an upper but no lower limits:[16]

> From bad to worse, and worse they fall,
> But, who can reach the Worst of all?
> For, tho' in Nature Depth and Height
> Are equally held infinite,
> In Poetry the Height we know;
> 'Tis only infinite below (ll. 387-92).

The ever-receding limits of badness ('who can reach the Worst of all?') recall an important satiric pattern in *Gulliver's Travels*. But against this denial of a closing circle, where end and beginning, top and bottom, meet, runs another configuration. In the damaging sense, there *is* a circle, and top and bottom *do* meet in the '*low Sublime*' (ll. 370, 469ff.):[17]

> With Heads to Points the Gulph they enter,
> Linkt perpendicular to the Centre:
> And as their Heels elated rise,
> Their Heads attempt the nether Skies (ll. 401-4).[18]

Such polarizations and circularities are an old preoccupation of Swift's, going back at least as far as the *Tale of a Tub* and the *Mechanical Operation of the Spirit*:[19]

> whereas the mind of Man, when he gives the Spur and Bridle to his Thoughts, doth never stop, but naturally sallies out into both extreams of High and Low, of Good and Evil; His first Flight of Fancy, commonly transports Him to Idea's of what is most Perfect, finished, and exalted; till having soared out of his own Reach and Sight, not well perceiving how near the Frontiers of Height and Depth, border upon each other; With the same Course and Wing, he falls down plum into the lowest Bottom of Things; like one who travels the *East* into the *West*; or like a strait Line drawn by its own Length into a Circle (*Tale*, VIII).

The unending series, and the closed circle, can, by a happy chance, coexist mathematically, and Swift is quick to seize on the joke (though its use in satire was not new: Marvell used it in the *Rehearsal Transpros'd*).[20] What really interests Swift is not the mathematical viability of this joke, but the opportunity it gives the satirist for having it both ways. Endless chains, closed circles, crossing poles and the like would be thrust into unsettling proximities even if scientific explanations had not been available for some of them.

Of course Swift is at the same time laughing at scientific propositions about the ultimate circularity of the straight line, or whatever; and at the paradox-mongering which 'makes us fond of furnishing every bright Idea with its Reverse':[21]

> Whether a Tincture of Malice in our Natures, makes us fond of furnishing every bright Idea with its Reverse; Or, whether Reason reflecting upon the Sum of Things, can, like the Sun, serve only to enlighten one half of the Globe, leaving the other half, by Necessity, under Shade and Darkness: Or, whether Fancy, flying up to the imagination of what is Highest and Best, becomes over-shot, and

spent, and weary, and suddenly falls like a dead Bird of Paradise, to the Ground. Or, whether ... I have not entirely missed the true Reason....

The *Tale* is concerned with the human mind, not merely bad poets, and the example helps us to see the Grub Street hacks of the poem, like their ancestor in the *Tale*, resolving themselves into instances of a radical perversity of man, endlessly refining or 'modernizing' itself into fresh heights or depths of folly. The Bird of Paradise was popularly supposed to lack feet, and to be doomed to fly in the air until death. Bacon has a mocking remark about this bird, which Swift may be recalling.[22] But in Coleridge's *Eolian Harp* there was to be a lovely celebration, where 'Footless and wild' and 'hovering on untam'd wing', neither pausing nor perching, the bird of Paradise becomes an emblem of high imaginative enchantments, associated with 'Melodies round honey-dropping flowers'—sweetness and light! As so often, Swift's mockeries of mad moderns prefigure the imaginative explorations of later men, as though the modernism had finally come into its own, outfacing Swift. We may well also feel a kind of tragic beauty erupting lawlessly from Swift's own jeer about the bird, Swift himself becoming a modern *malgré lui*, unruly in his restless intensities.

R. D. Laing's haunting meditation, *The Bird of Paradise*, is a journey into the self, and an exploration of the radical madness of the human condition, of the kind (it might be said) which Swift's *Tale* both mocks, and *is*—the resemblance is intensified by sudden eruptions of violence, by street-glimpses of suffering horror not unlike that of Swift's flayed woman, by a preoccupation with medical dissection and with images of bodily dismemberment. There the bird is a symbol of transfiguring insight ('I have seen the Bird of Paradise ... and I shall never be the same again'),[23] and the author seeks precisely to grasp 'how near the Frontiers of Height and Depth, border upon each other', and to do so by what Swift repudiates as a soaring 'out of his own Reach and Sight'. It is an ancient kind of quest, and Laing's epigraph comes from the apocryphal gospel according to Thomas:[24]

> Jesus said ... :
> When you make the two one, and
> when you make the inner as the outer
> and the outer as the inner and the above
> as the below ...
> then shall you enter the Kingdom.

The antiquity of this example would not make the issue seem any less 'modern' for Swift. 'Modernity' was for him a symptom of restlessness fundamental to man's nature, and thus primitive or atavistic. Swift shied, partly in self-defence, from all traffic in transcendentals, and is quick to repudiate 'dark Authors', of all periods, as mad moderns.

Laing's example is that of a psychiatrist exploring, and asserting, the alienated condition of man in our time, and he does so with a degree of compassion and of self-implication a good deal removed from the externalized stance of the scientific observer. But he offers to the student of Swift a particularly poignant demonstration, at a level of medical understanding, of that interplay between configurations of imprisoning circularity, of limitless (*ad infinitum*) escalation, and of starkly polarized opposites, which Swift explored through wit.[25] The madness of *The Divided Self* is a 'self-enclosure', in which 'The place of safety of the self becomes a prison. Its would-be haven becomes a hell' without 'even ... the safety of the solitary cell', because inside this prison the 'inner self is persecuted' by an 'uncontrollable' fragmentation.[26] The fragments are an endless atomization, or (to rephrase) the prison consists precisely of a limitlessly multiplied process of self-entrapment, the closed circle becoming 'vicious',[27] or turning into a paradoxically 'open' figure: the spiral, vortex, whirlpool.[28]

The spiral is that of the 'bitter furies of complexity' of Yeats's 'Byzantium', an irreducibly complex and unceasing flux of activity or consciousness:[29]

> Those images that yet
> Fresh images beget,
> That dolphin-torn, that gong-tormented sea.

The example of Yeats helps to demonstrate the further paradox, of irreducible spirals of complexity submitted to the simplification of starkly polarized oppositions: 'Between extremities/Man runs his course'.[30] The interlocking spirals of Yeats's gyre-mythology presuppose a ceaseless traffic between absolute (but interpenetrating and mutually completing) opposites, the infinite scale of relativities between the extremes becoming, somehow, of secondary importance, '*mere* complexities'.[31] R. D. Laing, writing on the pathology of an individual's failure to achieve 'genuine mutuality' with others, talks of an oscillation, *ad infinitum*, between opposed absolutes:[32]

> the polarity is between complete isolation or complete merging of identity rather than between separateness and relatedness. The individual oscillates perpetually, between the two extremes, each equally

unfeasible. He comes to live rather like those mechanical toys which have a positive tropism that impels them towards a stimulus until they reach a specific point, whereupon a built-in negative tropism takes over again, this oscillation being repeated *ad infinitum*.

But the Yeatsian gyres, or similar conceptions of infinite spiralling between two opposed absolutes, are only one form of the paradox which brings into mutual relation the idea of a limitlessly self-complicating activity on the one hand, and the simplifications of a polarized vision on the other. Another variant of this paradoxical pattern is the 'dialectic spiral', familiar in certain philosophical and political systems, and in the dialectical psychology of Laing (and of Sartre).[33] The dialectic spiral describes an unceasing 'process of conflict and reconciliation which goes on within reality itself, and within human thought about reality'. But the unresting complexities of this process are at the same time simplified and concentrated 'into an obvious protagonist and antagonist', and its infinite relativity is regularly transformed, by means of the so-called dialectical 'leap', into provisional but absolute syntheses, or 'totalizations', of the conflicting opposites.[34]

This configuration, like that of the interlocking gyres, attempts to fuse complexity and flux with an element of radically inclusive (indeed sometimes of *violent*) simplification. It certainly rejects the cult of 'intermediate positions', or the Jamesian novelist's delicate and unpolarized recording of 'fine consciences' (just as it tends to reject the relativities and compromises of a 'liberal' outlook in politics). When Conrad praised the 'nice discrimination of shades of conduct' of James's 'fine consciences', he was careful to speak also of an irreducible complexity. The 'fine conscience' is 'a thing of infinite complication and suggestion'. But he felt also that 'None of these escapes the art of Mr Henry James'. The 'art of the novelist' imposed upon this material a kind of mastery, an intricate and rounded inclusiveness which, though provisional and limited ('not final'), was yet 'eminently satisfying' in suggesting a kind of rich completeness: 'He has mastered the country, his domain, not wild indeed, but full of romantic glimpses, of deep shadows and sunny places.' There, the 'fine consciences', with their 'abiding sense of the intangible, ever-present, right', fulfil themselves in an 'ultimate triumph' of character which is described by Conrad as 'energetic, not violent'.[35] This may be contrasted with Mailer's feeling that the novel has nothing to do with such satisfying arrangements, that 'characters' are falsifications and that persons or 'beings' in novels must be rendered, with an essential and radical incompleteness, as very fluid and open: 'A character is someone you can grasp as a whole ... but a being is someone whose nature keeps shifting'. Mailer goes on to say that the novelist's 'craft' is itself a consoling evasion of the spiralling abysses, of 'the terror of confronting a reality which might open into more and more anxiety and so present a deeper and deeper view of the abyss. Craft protects one from those endless expanding realities of deterioration and responsibility.'[36]

The protagonist of his 'Prologue to a Long Novel' in *Advertisements for Myself* 'had a love affair ... with the form of the spiral': 'in truth the form of his thought was also spiral: he would have to make that all but circular voyage through experience before he would come back to contemplate the spiral again.'[37] This circularity is very different from the intricate discriminations and rounded resolutions of the 'historian of fine consciences'.[38] Nor, as in Conrad's account of James, is 'violence' deprecated. The 'bitter furies of complexity' can only, in Yeats's words, be *broken* by some form of simplifying or overwhelming violence (it is apposite that Mailer admires 'The Second Coming' as 'the best short poem of the twentieth century'),[39] and Mailer's protagonist has a 'lover's sense of the moment of crisis': his predicament, which is both flux and impasse, can only be 'breached' by a murderous act.[40] Or, as Lawrence put it in *Fantasia of the Unconscious*: 'There is no way out of a vicious circle ... except breaking the circle.'[41]

Such short-circuits of violence find their stylistic reflection in certain 'gratuitous' shocks in what we have become accustomed to call the literature of 'cruelty'. I argued earlier[42] that certain sudden violences in Swift's prose style, notably at moments of rambling tortuosity or in other mimicries of protracted or limitless folly, may be taken as an intuitive (though doubtless not in those terms conscious or avowed) rendering of this.

Violent interruption is not the same as polarized vision, but it has here a similar purpose, of breaking the spinning formlessness of 'all complexities of mire or blood'. In Swift, and in Yeats and Mailer, there is a powerful tendency, at their most vivid moments or in their most crucial writings, to think in terms of strongly paired opposites. The whole range of Yeats's doctrines of the mask and antiself, Mailer's dichotomizing of Hip and Square (and his related interest in the concept of the 'White Negro') or Cannibals and Christians,[43] have a real relation with Swift's pairing of Ancients and Moderns, Fools and Knaves, big men and little men, Houyhnhnms and Yahoos.

Politically, such polarizing outlooks tend to be 'radical' (whether of the left or of the right) rather than 'liberal',[44] fostering a Hobbesian domination of unruly human nature, or an opposite project of 'perpetual revolution'.[45] Swift knew the old truths about the closeness of anarchy to tyranny, of the extreme left to the extreme right, and he professed himself a 'moderate'. But we should not be misled by that. His professed 'moderation' and his conservative attachment to the 'common forms', and to established accommodations and 'middle ways', were accompanied by an often strongly manifested element of dislike for these selfsame things. Swift saw man's condition as being by its psychological nature inclined to 'perpetual revolution' (an eternal 'modernism'), and he did not exempt himself from this. His moderation is itself an extreme position, committed to the *status quo* and slow piecemeal improvement as a desperate protection from the disruptive forces that are, in himself as in all of us, ready to erupt at the least failure of vigilance.

His political outlook is thus profoundly pessimistic. Where the Marxists regard the 'dialectic spiral' as tending upwards, towards 'higher reformulation' at each dialectical 'leap' or synthesis,[46] Swift saw the spiral as most characteristically tending downwards. Indeed, as he said, ' 'Tis only infinite below'. This is so because of that restless perversity of our psychological constitution, of which the 'moderns', Grub Street hacks and flea-like poetasters, are a particularly disreputable manifestation. That perversity, as we know especially from the *Tale*'s 'author', involves an unchecked submission to instantaneous impulse, and an undisguised cherishing of mere undisciplined experience. It is interesting to compare this with the Mailerian hipster's dedication to 'the perpetual climax of the present', liberated from 'the Super-Ego of society'. Mailer writes in 'The White Negro' of 'the instinctive dialectic through which the hipster perceives his experience, that dialectic of the instantaneous differentials of existence in which one is forever moving forward into more or retreating into less'.[47] Swift was considering essentially the same thing, but he would not have accepted that the 'instantaneous differentials' contained in themselves any hope of forward (or upward) movement. The very readiness to consider that in such conditions the spiral could go up as well as down would for Swift be a guarantee that it can only go down.

Mailer is not, on this point, complacent. More often than not the figure of the mental spiral entails an intensely unhopeful contemplation of the human lot, despite the readiness to believe in and to celebrate the possibility of 'moving forward' (and despite some well-known moods of programmatic jauntiness). There is a haunting bleakness (and not only a witty gesture of positiveness) about Rojack's feeling, after the murder of his wife in *An American Dream*, that an internal 'magician who solved all riddles was on his way, ascending those endless stairs from the buried gaming rooms of the unconscious to the tower of the brain'.[48] There are terrors in this condition, even though the moral sanctions of the Super-Ego are rejected; and the spiral holds active threats of a bottomless drop. We may also compare Laing's account of the tragic paradoxes of self-destruction in the schizophrenic state:[49] moral blame is not in question, and healthy alternatives are presupposed, but the medical madness has a grimly vivid force as an emblem of a human self-entrapment much more extensive than medical classifications recognize.

Closest to Swift, however, and directly imbued with his spirit, are those Beckettian heroes, whose minds and lives are trapped in those very prisons of the self which Swift mocked, and suffered, as symptoms of the radical madness of the race. 'I must have got embroiled in a kind of inverted spiral', says the Unnamable, 'the coils of which, instead of widening ... grew narrower ... and finally ... would come to an end for lack of room.' When this dead-end is reached, 'having screwed myself to a standstill', the only way is the return journey, widening out (but not, as in Yeats's gyres, to an opposite pole, and back again), this time forever, 'ad infinitum, with no possibility of ever stopping'.[50]

The Unnamable's broodings go on to explore alternative patterns. For the moment, however, his configuration is like Swift's, but even bleaker. Both posit that the spiral has a limit in one direction, and none in the other:[51]

> For, tho' in Nature Depth and Height
> Are equally held infinite,
> In Poetry the Height we know;
> 'Tis only infinite below (ll. 389-92).

But for Swift the limit is a fixed and positive height, while for Beckett's hero it is just a dead end. Of course, that Swiftian 'positive' is flattened and back-handed, since, unlike its opposite, the goodness has its limits, and since, by a queer kind of irony I have already noted, it is made to appear *unnatural*: for in *nature*, height or depth *are* infinite. The passage should be taken seriously. That its main business is to jeer at 'bad poets' does not reduce it to a mere specialized joke, for 'bad poets' are (as in the *Tale*) human nature in its unregulated state and also (as in both the *Tale* and Pope's *Dunciad*) a desperate symptom of cultural sickness. Still, Swift can laugh at them in the name of established standards, and his treatment of them or of the hack in the *Tale* is, despite some self-implication, at least sufficiently externalized to prevent compassionate sympathy. Beckett's Unnamable, like the *Tale*'s 'author', is quizzically conscious of himself as a writer, and of his predicament as a mad one. 'How, in such conditions, can I write, to consider only the manual aspect of that bitter folly?' he asks.[52] The Unnamable's *physical* difficulties are more absolute than those of Swift's occasionally bed-ridden and hungry garreteer, since his very shape and physical identity are in question. But the mental anguish of his consciousness is very stark. 'And yet I am afraid, afraid of what my words will do to me, to my refuge, yet again': 'Labyrinthine torment that can't be grasped, or limited, or felt, or suffered, no, not even suffered, I suffer all wrong too, even that I do all wrong too'.[53] The Unnamable would resemble Camus's Sisyphus, sufferer of ever-renewed, 'absurd' and meaningless torment, if it were not for the ultimately affirmative and heroic joy of Camus's absurdist hero. Swift would not have denied meaning to the suffering, but would have hung on to a belief in its 'decorum', as well as its justice. For this reason, it might almost be said, he held back from attributing serious suffering to his hacks. That would not only have dignified them unduly, but perhaps removed their difference from himself.[54]

These torments Swift, like Beckett or Camus, regarded as given, as well as self-inflicted. But the quality of self-infliction was, for him, a peculiarly culpable thing, and he shows what Beckett and certainly Camus do not: the special exasperations of guilt, and of a rigid commitment to values which are perpetually under subversion from that condition of restlessness which is given. The bottomless chain of self-complicating perversity in *Gulliver* is seen in relation to very uncompromising and very plain standards of Nature and Reason. The plainness gives an added hopelessness to the sense of the folly of sin, but also an inevitability, since only the most irrepressible energies could be supposed strong enough to break such strong and simple rules. Hence the peculiarly personal testiness which enters into Swift's uses of the satiric commonplace of the world's unmendability: the 'I told you so' spikiness with which he renders Gulliver's annoyance that the world is still uncured six months after the publication of his book, or the Modest Proposer's belief that a cannibal-project will seem more acceptable than the sensible 'other Expedients' which he (and Swift) had once been 'visionary' enough to advocate.[55] The rhetorical posture of a noble, protesting madness is allowed to curdle into a pathological absurdity, in which the distinction between the vicious and the virtuous folly becomes horribly and insultingly blurred, and in which rhetorical madness (of both kinds, vicious and virtuous) becomes medical—perhaps incurable.

The configurations of limitlessness and incurability in *On Poetry: A*

Rapsody are, of course, in a lighter vein. The cannibalism *ad infinitum* of the poetic fleas should not be approximated too closely to the outrageous nastiness of the *Modest Proposal.* That Swift was capable, in moods ranging from an unsettling playfulness to the most chilling sarcastic astringency, of himself expressing certain destructive velleities not unlike that of the *Proposal*, we have already seen.[56] My concern here is with his own paradoxical involvement in the bottomlessness of the fleas' cannibal activity, and with the simultaneous very rigid sense that the bottomlessness (as well as the habit of eating people) is wrong. The playfulness does not remove a powerful element both of self-involvement and of distaste.

Another highly stylized, and perhaps more externalized, variant of the *ad infinitum* configuration occurs earlier in the poem, when Swift advises critics who want to quote Longinus, but do not know Greek, to buy Welsted's translation,[57]

> Translated from *Boileau*'s Translation,
> And quote *Quotation* on *Quotation* (ll. 261-2).

The quip takes its place among the whole network of jokes about circularities or infinities of consumption in the poem, and calls to mind the *Tale*'s joke about nesting boxes: 'But not to Digress farther in the midst of a Digression, as I have known some Authors inclose Digressions in one another, like a Nest of Boxes . . .' (*Tale*, v).[58] The example shows the set of boxes not, as in the poem, externalized into a fairly specific (and actually finite) perversion of plagiarism, but instead internalized into wanderings of mental self-elaboration. Moreover, the 'author' not only says he will no longer do what he has just done, but is soon actually to give us a formally labelled 'Digression in Praise of Digressions'. These playful notions of circularity or of infinite regression are, of course, a highly patterned, self-completing joke, and have some effect of taming or enclosing infinity itself. In both poem and *Tale*, however, they co-exist with another kind of open-endedness. Both works contain the old mock-learned joke that what we are reading is a scholarly edition of itself, with a scholarly apparatus or other indications that draw attention to the fact that there are gaps in the MS., and in particular that it is unfinished at the end. Thus the poem ends with asterisks and *Caetera desiderantur*,[59] and the *Tale* with the 'author' planning to resume his pen, after a pause for feeling the world's pulse and his own.[60]

If the poem and *Tale* become, in these ways, the thing which they mock, that is partly the mere nature of the parody, although many critics have felt (with the *Tale* at least) that Swift's self-implication runs deeper than that. The infinities evoked by these open endings are part closed-system, and part gaping void. The *Tale*'s 'author', in particular, is considering a modern experiment to *'write upon Nothing'*, letting 'the Pen still move on' beyond the exhaustion of his subject and the exhaustion of his book.[61] Compare his fellow-dunce, Cibber, 'Sinking from thought to thought, a vast profound!', whose mental abyss is of Miltonic dimensions:[62]

> Plung'd for his sense, but found no bottom there,
> Yet wrote and flounder'd on, in mere despair.

Swift's 'author' has not made the 'mere despair' conscious to himself, and it would be unlike Swift to claim Miltonic splendours and miseries for his creatures, or for himself (though a 'despair' of the modern 'vast profound' he did, in another and very anguished sense, share with Pope). But the aptness of Milton's Chaos and Milton's Hell to our subject is real, for his Satan saw Hell as both mental prison and bottomless drop:[63]

> Which way I flie is Hell; my self am Hell;
> And in the lowest deep a lower deep
> Still threatning to devour me op'ns wide.

This kind of 'vast vacuitie' (II.932) is the reward, and the domain, of guilty folly: it is infinite space, yet totally imprisoning, and, in one important sense, *situated in the mind* (the spiralling mental hell of Dostoyevsky's *Notes from Underground* is a still more completely psychologized version).[64]

The freedoms of these spaces of the mind, and their entrapments, are Swift's subject, in anguish and in wit. In his parody of Anthony Collins, *Mr. C——ns's Discourse of Free-Thinking, Put into plain English, . . . for the Use of the Poor*, Swift shows his foolish Freethinker asserting the right of all men to 'think freely', even those who are incapable of 'thinking freely':[65]

> whoever cannot *think freely*, may let it alone if he pleases, by virtue of his Right to *think freely*; that is to say, if such a Man *freely thinks* that he cannot *think freely*, of which every Man is a sufficient Judge, why then he need not *think freely*, unless he *thinks* fit.

The parody is gross. But the notion it conveys of spiralling vacuities which are both unlimited and self-imprisoning is vividly and characteristically Swiftian, even if it distorts what Collins really said. Swift's Free Thinker was answering the objection that most men are not qualified to think at all, 'and if every Man thought it his Duty to *think freely*, and trouble his Neighbour with his Thoughts (which is an essential Part of *Free-thinking*,) it would make wild work in the World'.

Troubling one's neighbour with one's thoughts, that 'essential Part of *Free-thinking*', takes up the point made a little earlier, that 'free-thinking', like all forms of schism or anarchy, quickly turns tyrannical: 'It is the indispensable Duty of a *Free Thinker*, to endeavour *forcing* all the World to think as he does, and by that means make them *Free Thinkers* too.'[66] Swift's belief that dissenting attitudes in religion or politics should be tolerated so long as they are not expressed or displayed in public is well known. But since dissent and doubt are radical to man, his point extends beyond the political forms of dissent to that potential private subversiveness which is in himself also. Hence his insistence on a peculiarly reductive moral discipline, and on massive self-restraint and self-suppression, rather than on any hopeless project of eradicating the vicious impulses themselves. In one of his 'Thoughts on Religion' he said 'I am not answerable to God for the doubts that arise in my own breast' provided he conceals them from others, tries to subdue them, and prevents their 'influence on the conduct of my life'.[67] His extension, in *Mr. C——ns's Discourse*, of the more technical and restricted sense of 'free-thinking' to the most literally anarchic implications of the term, is no mere debating-point, but rooted in a profound sense of real relation. The 'wild work in the World' which he foresees from any spread of free-thinking must be understood in the light of a short undated piece, 'Some Thoughts on Free-thinking', in which he approvingly quotes a remark made to him by an Irish prelate, 'that if the wisest man would at any time utter his thoughts, in the crude indigested manner, as they come into his head, he would be looked upon as raving mad'. This made it clear how essential it was to keep our thoughts, 'as they are the seeds of words and actions', under 'strictest regulation': 'So that I cannot imagine what is meant by the mighty zeal in some people, for asserting the freedom of thinking...'[68]

That way madness lies. And when in 1738 Swift wrote, with a tart jokeyness, of his 'Age, Giddyness, Deafness, loss of Memory, Rage and Rancour against Persons and Proceedings', he chose to convey this self-mocking portrait of senile decay in an image of endless spiralling regression from his former healthy self: 'I have been many months the Shadow of the Shadow of the Shadow, of &c &c &c of Dr. Sw—.'[69] We should not take this too solemnly (and certainly not as evidence of actual insanity!) But this infinite chain of self-attenuation may reasonably be put side by side with the equally playful and equally tart image of the cannibal chain of fleas and poets in *On Poetry: A Rapsody*. Grub Street poets and sectarian free thinkers are but images of the unregenerate self, and their mad cravings and hungers, including that of the man in the Digression on Madness who is engaged in a cycle of eating his own excrement,[70] can, at a certain level, be translated and internalized into 'that hunger of imagination which preys incessantly upon life' which was Johnson's more compassionate formulation of man's radical restlessness.[71]

Modern psychology has taught us to think of the internalized self-reference of cannibal fantasies, and of related fantasies of eating and devouring.[72] We need not suppose that Swift or Johnson would be conscious of this in any cold technical sense. Nor was Wallace Stevens being cold or technical (although he may have been more conscious of the modern psychologist's or anthropologist's symbolism) when he wrote, not merely about the life-cycle, but about the imagination's rootedness in, as well as analogy with, that cycle: 'Frogs Eat Butterflies. Snakes Eat Frogs. Hogs Eat Snakes. Men Eat Hogs'. Where, he asked in another poem,[73]

> shall we find more than derisive words?
> When shall lush chorals spiral through our fire
> And daunt that old assassin, heart's desire?

'That old assassin' is Johnson's 'hunger of imagination', turned into affirmation. It is perhaps not too fanciful to say that he is also the Swiftian flea, not mocked but celebrated in 'more than derisive words'. In yet another poem, Stevens spoke of 'the never-resting mind', but saw (unlike Swift, or Johnson) 'in this bitterness, delight'—the source of poems, 'flawed words and stubborn sounds': 'The imperfect is our paradise'.[74]

In the Introduction to *Paradoxia Epidemica*, Rosalie L. Colie summarizes the paradoxes contained 'in the emblematic figure of the circle'. She notes that it is a 'figure traditionally regarded as at once limited and limitless. The circle-figure is also the figure for zero; the snake with his tail in his mouth may eat around to his head.'[75] The self-devouring of the snake is an annihilation, but it is at the same time an ancient symbol of eternity and renewal,[76]

> Because in your vast mouth you hold your Tayle,
> As coupling Ages past with times to come.

Cyclic theories of history, as contemplated by Plato or by Swift, are frequently focused on 'that part of the cycle which leads to decay',[77] on thoughts of a present and continuing degeneration. But many archetypal myths of cyclic destruction and regeneration have their principal emphasis on what Eliade has called the 'eternal return'.[78] On a smaller scale, the cycle of the seasons, or the alternations of day and night, are of course similarly open to a positive or negative symbolism.

The circle is endless, an infinite process of living, creative aspiration, fulfilment of God's purposes; or an equally infinite cycle of monotony, and suffering, and unfulfilled aspiration. It is also a comforting assurance of limits, 'supreme proof of limitation',[79] the most enclosed of forms, enfolding the whole Universe, or the smallest of little worlds made cunningly, a drop of dew, the soul, which[80]

> Does, in its pure and circling thoughts, express
> The greater Heaven in an Heaven less.

It is everything, utter plenitude, the 'greater Heaven'; and nothing, zero.[81] It is totally self-sufficient, yet totally vulnerable: 'Nothing more endlesse, nothing sooner broke.'[82] It is free because totally inclusive and perfect, 'the Circle of Perfection', and also completely penned in, imprisoning, 'vicious': 'Prenez un cercle, caressez-le, il deviendra vicieux!'[83]

So too with spirals. Vladimir Nabokov, recalling how he grew up steeped in the spiralities of Hegelian dialectic, says amusingly: 'In the spiral form, the circle, uncoiled, unwound, has ceased to be vicious; it has been set free.'[84] Spirals can 'become vicious circles again';[85] and their infinities, as we have seen, can in any case readily appear as imprisoning closed systems because they extend endlessly through all possibilities, excluding nothing and showing no way out. The openness of the form can also release a wild gaiety, as when Stevens wants 'lush chorals [to] spiral through our fire'[86] in Orphic celebration, or when his Doctor of Geneva, who knew only the burgherly lake of his home city, first sees the sea, and experiences a whirling, bracing, 'unburgherly apocalypse',[87]

> his simmering mind
> Spinning and hissing with oracular
> Notations of the wild, the ruinous waste.

But the burgherly Doctor is simultaneously troubled by all this excitement; and the openness of the spiral may, as we saw, reveal the bleaker and more negative energies of teeming abundance, of fleas devouring fleas and Grub Street on the march. I shall argue in a later section that the same is true, *a fortiori*, of less ordered and still more 'open' configurations, like the satiric lists or catalogues to which Swift was so notoriously addicted.

The spiral and its closest analogues (nests of boxes, regularly graduated sequences or chains, infinite progressions or regressions, and various forms of circularity) have about them not only the unruliness of perpetual movement but also a self-enclosing regularity of form. If this contributes a buoyancy of play, it also imposes the restraints of stylization and certain embodiments (or at least simulacra) of order. A heightened interest in such simulacra of order, in highly stylized closed systems, is surprisingly common among authors who have a strong sense of the bottomless untameability of the human condition. Infinite regression in particular mocks the sense of order in an especially teasing way, for it is a pattern which defies the solaces of pattern by having no end. In Borges's story, 'The Library of Babel',[88] the universe is conceived as a terrifying orderly building, with 'interminable' vistas arranged in an 'invariable' regularity, a 'spiral staircase, which plunges down into the abyss and rises up to the heights', 'a mirror, which faithfully duplicates appearances' and gives an impression (true or false?) of infinity. The 'polished surfaces' and the rigorous symmetry of the whole system (shelves, books, etc., disposed in unvarying order) 'feign and promise infinity',[89] but in another sense contain all possibilities, and are at the same time exhaustive and finite: the library's contents are permutationally complete, containing all combinations of words, letters, punctuation, in all possible languages, with books differing from other books by a single comma, and with books about books about books, commentaries upon commentaries, and catalogues of books and books about catalogues. How is the library infinite, yet permutationally complete? The narrator finds a solution in the notion of an endless exhaustion and recurrence of the permutation, a disorder become order by repetition:

> It is not illogical, I say, to think that the world is infinite. Those who judge it to be limited, postulate that in remote places the corridors and stairs and hexagons could inconceivably cease—a manifest absurdity. Those who imagined it to be limitless forget that the possible number of books is limited. I dare insinuate the following solution to this ancient problem: *The Library is limitless and periodic.*[90] If an eternal voyager were to traverse it in any direction, he would find, after many centuries, that the same volumes are repeated in the same disorder (which, repeated, would constitute an order: Order itself). My solitude rejoices in this elegant hope.

'The Library of Babel' is full of Swiftian themes. It is written by an 'unknown author' and has a *Tub*-like mock-annotator. It has flashes of violence, death, madness, emanating from the frustration of restless human quests (for 'the catalogue of catalogues', the 'cyclical book [which] is God', 'the basic mysteries of humanity'), from religious controversy, from wild fanaticisms and asceticisms. Sectarian enthusiasts destroy millions of books with an 'ascetic, hygienic fury'. Mad pedantries of 'system' open up gaping voids of 'unspeakable melancholy'. Men hidden in privies perform Laputian exercises in letter-shuffling, in the hope of 'composing, by means of an improbable stroke of luck, the canonical books', thus feebly mimicking 'the divine disorder'. Cryptographic and other inquiries take place into the meaning of books and the 'allegorical justification' of nonsense titles. Codes and compendia are restlessly sought, including a particular mysterious Book 'which is the cipher and perfect compendium of *all the rest*'. (Compare the Laputian projector who hoped 'to give the World a compleat Body of all Arts and Sciences'.)[91] Borges's story is in some ways a 'perfect compendium', or concentrated version, of Swift's vision of the world as a literary Babel, of that *Tale of a Tub* which in turn is a 'perfect compendium' of 'modern' absurdities, including the recourse to 'large *Indexes*, and little *Compendiums*' to make up for the lamentable fact 'that our *Modern* Wits are not to reckon upon the Infinity of Matter, for a constant Supply' (*Tale*, VII).[92]

Like Borges, and like Swift, Beckett too is exercised by concepts of the unending series, and of the self as 'infinite and void'.[93] Like Borges (more than like Swift) he has at the same time a notoriously obsessive interest in circularity and permutation. Beckett's lists and inventories, of actions or of objects, frequently tend to permutational exhaustiveness. Their clockwork activity exhibits a more or less playful abundance paradoxically fraught with austere, rationalist sterility. The compulsive finalities give barren satisfactions, a kind of bleak shelter which is yet perpetually 'assailed by proliferation and menaced by mystery'.[94] In Beckett, as in Borges, there is often a combination of grimly unmanageable chaos and of rigorous arrangement, an order frozen to anti-order, a sense of system both infinite and totally imprisoning in its stylish and elaborate symmetries, with occasional moments of violence which do not so much disrupt these symmetries as add to their already powerful feeling of menace.

Such interplays of ordered circularity and its various opposites (the open-ended spiral of infinite regress, the threatened or actual violence which breaks or disturbs the circuit) are a radical element in Swift's analysis of the madness of the world. They are not confined to Swift.

Paradoxes of liberty and imprisonment, of self-indulgence and self-entrapment, of exclusion and confinement, of the open and the closed, are pervasive in the history of madness and of conceptions of madness, as Michel Foucault has vividly shown. In the old Ships of Fools, the madman is excluded from the town and let out in the free element of water, of rivers flowing to the open sea; but he is also imprisoned 'in the interior of the exterior':[95]

> A highly symbolic position, which will doubtless remain his until our own day, if we are willing to admit that what was formerly a visible fortress of order has now become the castle of our conscience... Confined on the ship, from which there is no escape, the madman is delivered to the river with its thousand arms, the sea with its thousand roads, to that great uncertainty external to everything. He is a prisoner in the midst of what is the freest, the openest of routes: bound fast at the infinite crossroads.

Eighteenth-century discussions examined by Foucault are frequently informed by more or less internalized versions of this paradox: the madman imprisoned by the liberty of hallucination; the sane quotidian pressures of life, the rhythm of the seasons and the discipline of work, conversely constraining madness, 'freeing man from his freedom'; the concept of cure as a restoration of liberty by means of these constraints upon the other and fatal liberty.[96] Links were even made between the political liberty of England, and the prevalence of melancholia and madness there; and the link which Swift made between an unregulated liberty of conscience and the sort of 'free thinking' that leads to madness is suggested also by medical writers.[97]

A similar interplay of conceptions of 'openness' and 'enclosure' may be found, in one form or another, in much modern psychiatric or meta-psychiatric literature.[98] I confine my examples to Laing only because of his particular relevance to an understanding of Swift. In his Foreword to *Reason and Violence*, Sartre congratulated Laing and Cooper on their constant effort to realize an 'existential' approach to mental illness, and registered his agreement with them that mental illness is the free organism's chosen solution to an intolerable situation ('l'issue que le libre organisme, dans son unité totale, invente pour pouvoir vivre une situation invivable').[99] Laing himself, in *The Politics of Experience*, has incorporated Sartre's formulation into his own thinking: '*without exception* the experience and behaviour that gets labelled schizophrenic is *a special strategy that a person invents in order to live in an unlivable situation*.'[100] *The Politics of Experience* also puts forward the view that madness may be a form of release and authentication, a liberating journey away from the falsehood of social living into the truths of the inner being: 'Madness need not be all breakdown. It may also be break-through. It is potentially liberation and renewal as well as enslavement and existential death.'[101]

If 'madness' is a freedom from the imprisoning falsehood of modern life, modern life may itself, by a paradox familiar equally to Swift and to Laing, be described as mad, an Academy of Modern Bedlam. This madness of the so-called sane exhibits the same paradoxical configurations of 'open' and 'closed', in reverse directions. The social attitudes of the officially sane, like the biting of Swift's fleas, exhibit the imprisoning freedoms of the infinite series, freedoms which, like those of the free-thinking Mr Collins (whose recipe for freedom of thought, as paraphrased by Swift, involves making the whole world and his neighbours think the same free thoughts)[102] lead straight to a crude repressiveness: 'Each person is thinking of what he thinks the other thinks. The other, in turn, thinks of what yet another thinks. Each person does not mind a coloured lodger, but each person's neighbour does. Each person, however, is a neighbour of his neighbour.'[103] What distinguishes Swift's attitude from Laing's is that we cannot imagine him consciously accepting the notion of 'breakdown' as 'break-through'. Swift feared *both* freedoms, the freedom of the social lie, and the freedom of the inner truth as realized in a submission of the self to its spontaneous impulses. 'Free-thinking' is Mr Collins, the Dissenting sects, the whole of 'modern' hypocrisy, but also the 'raving madness' of our spontaneous mental processes, the 'crude indigested' thoughts of all of us.[104]

This impasse gives a peculiar poignancy and a peculiar complexity to the patterns of 'openness' and 'enclosure' which we find in Swift. It helps to account for the fact, which is discussed in the next two chapters, that his configurations of enclosure are not only very imprisoning, but also more infrequent, more radically incomplete, more often breached by a violence of tone or incident, than those of other comparable writers (including Borges and Beckett). He is also much less given to games of exhaustive permutation, and much more given to the chaotic open-ended catalogue (of vices, follies, malefactors, etc.).

His images of conflict and disruption are rough, explosive, unresolved. The contrast with Pope, in this matter, is particularly great. For Pope, whether early (as in *Windsor-Forest*) or late (as in the *Essay on Man*), 'strife' tends to be a natural ritual with a vitalizing function or happy ending within the scheme of things, 'The lights and shades, whose well accorded strife/Gives all the strength and colour of our life', 'All Discord,

Harmony, not understood'.[105] For Swift, strife is a bottomless, unceasing affair, and truly disruptive, like the sectarian violence in the *Tale*. Pope's devotion to the Chain of Being, whatever the degree of his literal belief in it, is a positive expression of a sense of order, so that his imaginative play or intellectual flirtation with the idea has a vivid and genuinely upward thrust. Swift's version of the Chain is the infinite descent downwards of the cannibal fleas.[106] Martin Price has written aptly of the spiralling release evoked by the *Essay on Man*, once Pope has imagined the contraction of our minds 'from soaring presumption to humble minuteness': 'The contraction to a point is like the inward-turning spiral of a vortex; once man reaches the center, his mind can open out again into selfless love.'[107] This is like Stevens's 'lush chorals' spiralling, or Yeats's gyres in a positive phase. In Swift's spirals, there is only the '*low Sublime*',[108] a rising to airy heights or a sinking to bottomless depths, meeting in some region of empty space, coming to the same thing.

The nature of the 'open' and 'closed' configurations of circle, spiral, chain and the rest in the writings of Swift and Pope parallels or reflects certain important differences in their stylistic manner, and most notably, as we saw earlier, in their respective uses of couplet-rhetoric.[109] Couplet-rhetoric may be described as a 'closed' stylistic form. It exists in both Swift and Pope, and may sometimes, in both authors, describe situations of mental imprisonment. But it has a tendency, in Pope but not usually in Swift, to delimit the scope of these situations. The formal configuration of enclosure, as the line, couplet or epigram complete themselves, encapsulates the subject in a way which might readily imply the existence of a freer world outside. Neatly balanced finalities induce a feeling that standards are sufficiently secure to make decisive summations possible, that the world has a certain tidiness and symmetry, and that the author has the wit and moral grasp to reduce complexity to its appropriate pattern. This feeling of release through enclosure does not occur in Swift, as we have seen. Moreover, Swift's 'open' forms, his tendency to avoid couplet-rhetoric both in prose-syntax and metrical arrangement, as well as his suggestions of limitless spiralling or his chaotic catalogues, become paradoxically more confining or imprisoning than the 'closed' forms of Pope or of Fielding.

Swift's 'rage for order' was as great as Pope's, and the 'order' he sought was in many respects the same. If the patterned finalities of the couplet-style, or the symmetries of circle, spiral or graduated chain, are expressions of that 'order', Swift's uses of them (to the extent that he does use them without deliberately or ostentatiously violating their symmetries) imply an aspiration betrayed or thwarted, an order turned into a hideous parody of itself. If Swift did not delight in the orderly ideals of Augustan culture, it is not because he rejected the ideals but because he felt hopeless of their fulfilment. Pope and Fielding did not, and their use of couplet-rhetoric is not only more frequent but more natural. Their delight in summation as such, in the satisfactions of definition and limitation, suggest an ability to imagine the order as existing or at least attainable. This is felt even in contexts where the uses of the couplet-style suggest a tense over-confidence or even outright anguish, rather than unruffled ease; and it certainly survives in a work as grim as the *Dunciad*, which describes order under threat of anarchic destruction (I believe, however, that it does not survive in the latest and most anguished writings of Fielding).[110]

If the 'closed' forms of Pope and Fielding can be liberating, the 'open' forms of Swift have the opposite paradoxical effect. They deny the release that comes from the defining or containment of unruly forces, just as they lack the sense of release which may be felt in the more expansive 'open' forms of other writers (in Stevens's or Nabokov's spirals, or, as we shall see, in the rhetorical catalogues of Rabelais or Whitman). Unruly forces are not only not *contained*, but are simultaneously indulged and made *unwelcome*, by Swift's style, even as it mimics them: for the mimicry suggests that they are freewheeling, unpredictable, inordinate, yet not vitalizing or enriching in their abundance. When the moral or psychological nature of man is in question, as it almost always is in Swift, unpredictable and inordinate forces easily acquire a quality of damaging absoluteness. Where unruliness is mental, as I have argued in relation to both Swift and Johnson, it may seem independent of the external checks provided by reason, moral codes, or circumstance, and therefore theoretically limitless. Hence partly that suggestion of the *bottomlessness* of human perversity which emanates from *Gulliver's Travels*. Efforts to escape such an absolute predicament seem excluded by an irreducible obstacle, and any attempt at containment is likewise blocked. Anarchy (whether political or psychological) was for Swift a worse totalitarianism, a more absolute prison than most forms of arbitrarily imposed order. It also seemed the more immediate threat, and more actual and vivid too than those *good* forms of order and tradition on which his positive values were based.

It is for such reasons that Swift seems, in both verse and prose, to be most characteristically in his element, and his imagination most powerfully engaged, in stylistic configurations which reflect not a limited and definable human wickedness, but one so restless and irrepressible that it overspills all boundaries, and makes nonsense of any idea of containment by explanation. In this sense even his 'open' forms are more imprisoning than the *closed* forms of Augustan couplet-rhetoric usually are: they suggest a chaos more radical and more pervasive, a kind of vicious infinity, which blocks off all serious hopes of general improvement. In the same way, his circles and his spirals are usually vicious, not benign.

CHAPTER IV

CIRCLES, CATALOGUES AND CONVERSATIONS

Swift, with Reflections on Fielding, Flaubert, Ionesco

Hélas ! les vérités élémentaires et sages qu'ils échangeaient, enchaînées les unes aux autres, étaient devenues folles, le langage s'était désarticulé, les personnages s'étaient décomposés; la parole, absurde, s'était vidée de son contenu et tout s'achevait par une querelle dont il était impossible de connaître les motifs...

Pour moi, il s'était agi d'une sorte d'effondrement du réel. Les mots étaient devenus des écorces sonores, dénuées de sens; les personnages aussi, bien entendu, s'étaient vidés de leur psychologie et le monde m'apparaissait dans une lumière insolite, peut-être dans sa véritable lumière, au-delà des interprétations et d'une causalité arbitraire...

Le texte de *La Cantatrice chauve*..., composé d'expressions toutes faites, des clichés les plus éculés, me révélait, par cela même, les automatismes du langage, du comportement des gens, le 'parler pour ne rien dire', le parler parce qu'il n'y a rien à dire de personnel, l'absence de vie intérieure, la mécanique du quotidien, l'homme baignant dans son milieu social, ne s'en distinguant plus.

(Eugène Ionesco, *Notes et Contre-Notes*, Part III)

In *The Breaking of the Circle*, Marjorie Nicolson documents the decline, in the seventeenth century, of that concept of a harmonious universe which is embodied in the image of the 'Circle of Perfection', and in attendant notions of the correspondence between macrocosm, geocosm and microcosm.[1] The old order, conceived in terms of circles, and of their concentric disposition in a harmonious universe, gave way to a more fragmented vision, in science as in other domains:[2]

> Gone was Nature's nest of concentric boxes, evidence of permanence and stability, gone even more the supreme proof of limitation—the limits of the universe. The great circles were broken, the universe dispersed into a nebulous infinity that had no shape or pattern.

A suggestive passage in her Introduction notes how, in a later age and 'under the influence of the evolutionary theory and belief in progress', the image of the circle turned into that of a spiral, and how in Yeats it 'has suffered still another change. "Things fall apart. The Centre cannot hold" ... His is no closed circle but a spiral in which the movement is both upward and downward.'[3]

Miss Nicolson is right to see that Swift occupies a crucial place in the transition. The changes of outlook in the seventeenth century were in large part due to 'the discoveries of science', but it was the literary consciousness of Swift that most powerfully registered the demise of the old order:[4]

> Whatever the effect of science ... perhaps the literary death-blow to the microcosm was given by that son of the Enlightenment, Jonathan Swift. *A Tale of a Tub* is the greatest parody of its time, in which Olympian laughter was turned against the whole seventeenth century: its styles, its manners, its religion, its learning, its science, its enthusiasms.

She goes on to instance specifically the 'parody of the macrocosm and microcosm' embodied in the Clothes' Philosophy of section II.[5] And Swift's parody has an obsessively ship-shape quality which is appropriate to his sense of the frozen, stubborn pedantry of all such 'systems', great circles, nesting or concentric boxes, and the rest. If he sometimes mimicked their bogus neatnesses, he was also vigorously alive to opposite implications, of limitless process and bottomless folly, of infinite and imprisoning circularity. But above all, his interest in circles and spirals focused less on their properties of geometric regularity or shapeliness, than on the proneness of such false systems to be shattered by unruly fact. Even a close mimicry of system-making like the Clothes' Philosophy is sometimes disturbed by eruptions of satiric intensity which break the smooth surface of the mock-argument, if only by a quickened harshness of tone or a sudden sarcastic pay-off (as in the famous sequence which begins 'Is not Religion a *Cloak*', continues with a series of similar, relatively predictable parallels, and then develops into an unexpectedly elaborate and highly-charged anti-climax: 'and Conscience a *Pair of Breeches*, which, tho' a Cover for Lewdness as well as Nastiness, is easily slipt down for the Service of both').[6] Sometimes, Swift enacts or displays a pattern of neat circularity which is breached or disfigured by some violent or grotesque action, as in this account of a belching ritual of Aeolist priests in section VIII:[7]

> At ... times were to be seen several Hundreds link'd together in a circular Chain, with every Man a Pair of Bellows applied to his Neighbour's Breech, by which they blew up each other to the Shape and Size of a *Tun* ... When, by these and the like Performances, they were grown sufficiently replete, they would immediately depart, and disembogue for the Publick Good, a plentiful Share of their Acquirements into their Disciples Chaps.

Similarly, with nesting configurations:[8]

> It were much to be wisht, and I do here humbly propose for an Experiment, that every Prince in *Christendom* will take seven of the *deepest Scholars* in his Dominions, and shut them up close for *seven* Years, in *seven* Chambers, with a Command to write *seven* ample Commentaries on this comprehensive Discourse. I shall venture to affirm, that whatever Difference may be found in their several Conjectures, they will be all, without the least Distortion, manifestly deduceable from the Text. Mean time, it is my earnest Request, that so useful an Undertaking may be entered upon (if their Majesties please) with all convenient speed; because I have a strong Inclination, before I leave the World, to taste a Blessing, which we *mysterious* Writers can seldom reach, till we have got into our Graves. Whether it is, that *Fame* being a Fruit grafted on the Body, can hardly grow, and much less ripen, till the *Stock* is in the Earth: Or, whether she be a Bird of Prey, and is lured among the rest, to pursue after the Scent of a *Carcass*: Or, whether she conceives, her Trumpet sounds best and farthest, when she stands on a *Tomb*, by the Advantage of a rising Ground, and the Echo of a hollow Vault (*Tale*, x).

A precisely calculated nesting arrangement begins with overtones of imprisonment as taut and as stylishly designed as in a tale by Borges, then opens into a ragged fragmentation as the scholars produce differing conjectures all deducible from the text, and finally leads into imagery of violence and loudness, birds of prey pursuing carcasses, the vast and hollow sound of the Trumpet of Fame.

The paradoxical relationship between the symmetries of an infinite spiral, and a fragmentation and disorder in which 'Things fall apart;

the centre cannot hold',[9] Swift seems to have understood as well as Yeats. Characteristically, however, he showed a great deal less interest than Yeats in the geometric and systematic factor in this relationship. He makes no formal attempt to fit the 'bitter furies of complexity'[10] into sharply defined pairs of interlocking gyres, and for Yeats's larger system, as developed in *A Vision*, he would have expressed the same contempt as for all other 'dark Authors' pilloried in the *Tale of a Tub*. The 'bitter furies' themselves were more vivid to him than any system, however open-ended and however unresting in its processes, as were the violences which suddenly 'break' these furies (and all experience for that matter), redirecting them with a peremptory antithetical force. We have already seen that he sometimes plays satirically with closed systems, little worlds made cunningly, nesting boxes, and infinite chains, parodying all 'system', and also exposing the limitlessness of folly, enclosing digression within digression within digression, jeering at translators translating from translations, becoming himself the shadow of the shadow of the shadow of himself.[11] Yet even when the stylized symmetry of these things remains unbreached by the kind of violent eruption in tone or in description which occurs in the account of the circle of Aeolist priests, or that of the seven scholars locked for seven years in seven chambers, there is very little sense of refuge to be derived from the stylized ordering itself, which tends to imply closed prisons rather than happy havens.

More important, however, is the fact that these stylized regularities are in themselves relatively rare in Swift. The digressive ramblings of the *Tale*'s 'author', for example, exhibit no symmetrical plan, only mental chaos.[12] And a statistical examination of Swift's style has shown that his own not very frequent stylistic or syntactical tendencies towards 'nesting' arrangements, as when he inserts one list within another, are notable for 'irregularity'.[13] More generally, we may add, Swift is much more given to the list, the disorderly satiric catalogue, than he is to the patterned escalations of the infinite series, for lists are a truer token of chaos, unordered as well as infinite.

Lists need not, of course, in all cases suggest a painful sense of unending openness. They may, instead, convey a comforting and inclusive abundance. W. B. Carnochan says of epic lists, and of the celebrations of abundance in Whitman:[14]

> In ... the epic or ... the romantic sublime, the expanding catalog implies that all experience can be assimilated in the heroic world. It is important to Homer, or ... to Walt Whitman, that nothing be felt

> as inevitably, and by its nature, left out; nothing ... is too mean for inclusion.

In a post-Romantic poet like Whitman, writing outside any of the settled or ordered world-views which belong to older traditional cultures, it is left to the individual to create his own cosmos out of chaos, to create himself as ordering principle and microcosm.[15] 'I am large, I contain multitudes', explains Whitman in the famous phrase in which he accepts contradiction and self-contradiction as part of life's rich multiplicity, instead of seeking to resolve them into a conventional order: 'Do I contradict myself?/Very well then I contradict myself,/(I am large...).'[16] And by the same token, as Leo Spitzer pointed out, Whitman's abundant 'chaotic' lists of things, places, people, and experiences tend paradoxically away from chaos: 'The chaotic enumeration [in 'Out of the Cradle Endlessly Rocking'] ... is intended to show the collaboration of the whole world ... toward that unique event—the birth of a poet out of a child who has grasped the meaning of the world.'[17] This collaboration or unity is a secular one: 'no reference is made in Whitman's poem to the world harmony of the Christian Beyond in the manner of Milton.'[18] It differs also from the feats of ordering found in a modern religious poet like Claudel, who accepts and absorbs multiplicity into the 'higher order' of his Catholic faith instead of meeting 'the confusion of our world by imposing thereupon a rigid orderliness of his own making'.[19] But this higher order, itself traditional, the property of an ancient and widely shared faith, has in Claudel to be reasserted *by means* which are untraditional, by a 'modern' imagery of disorderliness, by 'new devices', a new vision 'comparable with that of the modernist architect who designed the Catholic cathedral in Barcelona'[20] (and perhaps as individualist in some respects as Whitman's?). Spitzer speaks of Claudel as in some important ways an imitator of Whitman,[21] and he notes with specific reference to Claudel one particular property of 'chaotic enumeration' in the modern post-Whitmanian poet, which differs from the exuberant cataloguing of older writers like Rabelais and Quevedo, namely a tendency to subvert or to cut across *categories*:[22]

> While the exuberant enumerations, the lists, the 'catalogues' to be found with Rabelais or Quevedo still respected the distinctions between the different realms of Nature, the post-Whitmanian writer can enumerate things and thoughts detached from their frames, in order to evoke the plenitude of the world.

'Thus Claudel will list', adds Spitzer, the following variegated things, all as signs of the inclusive plenitude: his house, the station, the town-hall, the man in a straw hat, space, the keeping of accounts (his own, or those of a shoe-shop or of mankind). On the crossing of categories, which has a particular bearing on Swift, I shall have more to say later.

The lists of both Claudel and Whitman show two ways in which a poet's personal vision may turn the chaotic catalogue into an image of coherence and order. In both, as in the catalogues of ancient epic and in similar traditional exploitations of the rhetorical list, are conveyed a sense of rich completeness, of 'the plenitude of the world', and the suggestion, in Carnochan's phrase, that 'nothing ... is too mean for inclusion'.[23] Carnochan goes on to compare this with Swift's satiric lists, which also convey the notion that they may be extended to include everyone: the suggestion of enclosure, it might be added, tends in satire, and especially in Swift, to become that of a vast incriminating net rather than of a bountiful home. Carnochan argues that the implication of total inclusiveness, though useful to the satirist, is emotional rather than logical, and that the reader can, 'at the moment of self-defense', comfort himself with the 'more rational view' that the attack is not indiscriminately applicable to all. He considers that this potential comfort is available in books I-III of *Gulliver*, but not easily in book IV.[24]

In all books of *Gulliver*, however, as well as elsewhere in Swift, the satiric catalogues have in common a quality of teeming vitality, an exuberant profusion of ugliness and disorder. The moods which underlie this may range from the playful to the very bitter, but the sense of sheer anarchic energy is often strong. Ralph Cohen has shown in some lists in Swift's poems an emphasis on fragmentation and dismemberment.[25] Writing of the 'Description of a City Shower', he notes in particular 'a harmony of garbage'.[26] The phrase is suggestive. For Cohen, it seems to reflect Swift's apprehension of chaos as somehow rooted in a final order, but also as mimicking a society which, though it 'may be capable of resembling natural beauty',[27] is shaped into a squalid anti-order. The phrase also conveys the organizational bravura of the poem, and the pleasures of setting down so much intractable life into a disciplined if loose-seeming form.

Although I am in agreement with a good deal of Cohen's argument (so far as I can understand it), I shall later be playing down this orderly element in Swiftian lists, perhaps more than Cohen's reservations allow. But his discussion of 'additive repetition of details', of 'figures of extension'[28] and of related forms of enumeration in Augustan poets confirms the observations of Spitzer, Carnochan and others, that abundant enumeration need not always imply chaos or anarchy. He goes on to give an enlightening account of the 'prospect view', in Pope and other Augustan poets, where enumeration and multiplicity arrange themselves into real order, with landscapes becoming signs of God's blessedness, and physical space sometimes turning into an 'infinite space' which is 'beyond man's comprehension' yet in a way comfortingly enclosed because the 'world is a whole, though only partially known'.[29] In one form or another, lists have long existed in various literary genres as recognized rhetorical devices whose function it was to reinforce the sense of order rather than subvert it. The epic catalogues 'of ships, and captains, and kings reigning'[30] express an abundance not of chaos but of cohesiveness. They are pageants of heroic collaboration. Other enumerations (the conventional lists of trees, or whatever, in Ovid, Chaucer, Spenser, for example, which Curtius describes as 'bravura interludes')[31] suggest a decorous abundance that is part of the natural order, or the order of art, a ritual sense of abundance and variety held in due gradation or place, and sometimes specifically arranged in what Swift's *On Poetry: A Rapsody*, mocking its desecration in modern Grub Street, and typically standing the ideal on its head, called 'due Subordination' (l. 314).[32] Even when the details are not arranged into 'prospects', or listed hierarchically, they are enjoyed as rehearsals of known, familiar things,[33] rituals satisfying a sense of expectation not only in their matter, but in their style. Rosemond Tuve has argued that one should not infer from the frequency among Renaissance poets of rhetorical forms of *copia*, or variegated repetition, and of related devices like the *congeries* or *'heaping figure'* (which Puttenham describes as 'multitude of words & speaches, not all of one but of diuers matters and sence'), that these poets took a particular delight in 'plentiful imagery' or in copiousness for their own sake, since the forms had rhetorical *functions* (e.g. to 'be exact and forceful').[34] This is probably less true of catalogues proper, where the abundance tends to be of things rather than of words, and where the greater emphasis is on accumulation of detail rather than verbal variegation. But catalogues too have rhetorical *functions* which are partly independent of abundance as such, and which have to do, for example, with the need to discriminate exactly between types, to give an impression of exhaustiveness, to generate ironies of one kind or another. And catalogues (of warriors, or trees, for example), though perhaps less frequently discussed by rhetoricians than other devices of amplification and variegation, are like them conventionally established features of style, which tend to reassure or to please by virtue of their conventionality itself, and of the sense which they give that recognized or agreed or well-loved forms of discourse are being upheld.

I argued earlier, in a different connection, that in some of Swift's contemporaries, and most notably in Pope, certain stabilities, which may be described as *style-induced*, proceed from particular stylistic contexts which create their own expectations of pattern partly from the conventionality as such of specific devices.[35] This will, however, tend to occur only when the tone of a passage or work manifests the author's loyalty to, or delight in, the stylistic configuration and the sense of order which is ideally implied by it. The fulfilment of rhetorical or stylistic expectation normally turns, in Pope, into a ceremony of rich satisfaction, however scabrous the context. In Swift, on the other hand, even when he fulfils the predicted pattern of a figure or formula, satisfaction is denied or expectation defeated. His rhetoric may in many ways be conscious, conventional and controlled, but its whole force is to violate rhetorical expectation even when that expectation has been fulfilled in an outward or formal sense. His figures of enclosure, as we have just seen, denote not the security of a sheltered home or garden prospect, but a dry imprisonment. His uses of a patterned couplet-style are not only rare, in comparison with Pope's or Fielding's, but also notably tart and uncompromising. The buoyancies of epigrammatic definition, the triumphant finalities, in Pope or Fielding suggest the kind of enclosure which, by conveying reassurance rather than confinement, releases a fresh lucidity of understanding and a freer field of action. For Pope, as definition becomes exact, 'the prospect clears'.[36] In front of Fielding's home base of solid understanding and secure values stretches what some critics call (perhaps more truly than they mean) an 'open road'—a road which, though stretching wide and spacious on to clear and distant horizons, yet finally and surely brings the hero home again.

Swift's configurations of openness (his satirical catalogues, as well as his chains of infinite escalation or regress) are by contrast as imprisoning as his uses of the closed forms of couplet rhetoric. Fielding's catalogues tend towards a comforting limitation, which prevents abundance from turning into an imprisoning infinity, and which, like his and Pope's closed or couplet-forms, evoke a positive rather than negative combination of enclosure and release. Like Swift, Fielding was interested in the cant-phrases of 'polite conversation', and he many times gave little catalogues of the vocabulary of snobbery, haughty pique, outraged virtue, and other 'polite' absurdities. In the 'dissertation concerning high people and low people' in *Joseph Andrews*, II.xiii, Fielding notes how

the people of fashion [and] ... the people of no fashion ... seem

> scarce to regard each other as of the same species. This, the terms 'strange persons, people one does not know, the creature, wretches, beasts, brutes,' and many other apellations evidently demonstrate; which Mrs. Slipslop, having often heard her mistress use, thought she had also a right to use in her turn...

Fielding's list is a 'catalogue' in so far as it records various discrete linguistic formulas which are all in use in society at large. But the near-synonymity of these formulas turns the list into a satirical version of the *copia* of 'varying', an exercise in the accumulation of alternative phrasings of the kind of which Erasmus's *De Copia* is the classic handbook.[37] Some of the free inventiveness of playing with words comes through, despite the fact that the usages are all actual rather than 'invented'. And if the *copia* is an anti-copia, because it records disreputable usages which the satirist would have us *never* use whereas the examples of the rhetorician Erasmus are offered for direct imitation, Fielding is satirizing not the *copia*, but social snobbery. In its aspect of *copia*, in the collecting and displaying and classifying, there is a buoyant delight. And even in its aspect of social satire, delight exists in the firmness of the moral 'placing', the sense of completeness, the confident refusal to multiply details beyond a certain point. The easy finality of 'and many other apellations evidently demonstrate' closes the discussion because we and the author share a knowing and superior sense of the world's foolish ways, and an ability to generalize about it without exhausting the examples. The effect is very different from such a typical Swiftian formula as 'and the like', which, as we shall see, opens up discreditable vistas of unlimited viciousness not easily subsumed in a confident generality, yet too numerous and wearisome and depressing to specify beyond the first dozen or more instances.

It could be argued that Fielding's generalizing is the less likely to seem imprisoningly inclusive because it arises out of individual situations involving particular named persons, whereas Swift's takes place in a genre of satire whose reach is, in the nature of the kind, more universal. Even *Gulliver's Travels*, where the fiction is more or less precisely localized, and where the protagonists are named and given various personal qualities, the real emphasis is away from the novelistic realization of individual persons or episodes for its own sake. But on the other hand many of Fielding's satiric passages are set-pieces which stand out from, or even digress from, the normal movement of the fiction, and which more or less overtly ask to be taken as generalizing comments on society at large. The passage I quoted, for example, has its point of departure in the specific, purportedly surprising fact that the low Mrs Slipslop behaves uppishly to Fanny. The 'dissertation concerning high people and low people' is ostensibly introduced to 'explain' the particular phenomenon. But it is also labelled a 'dissertation', and leads Fielding to assemble a list of typical usages in generalized abstraction, outside actual conversations. In other places, even when purporting to record an actual conversation, Fielding in fact enacts a dialogue which reads, primarily, not as a particular record so much as an anthology of ritual formulas:

> Miss Grave-airs said, 'Some folks might sometimes give their tongues a liberty, to some people that were their betters, which did not become them: for her part, she was not used to converse with servants.' Slipslop returned, 'Some people kept no servants to converse with' etc., etc.

Like the 'dissertation', this 'smart dialogue between some people and some folks' (*Joseph Andrews*, II.v), stands partly as a set-piece, its formal identity as a 'smart dialogue' firmly indicated, its resemblance to the moral disquisition of a periodical essay unmistakable, its 'typicality' clearly insisted on locally, just as, in a larger sense, Fielding insists that his whole novel describes 'not an individual, but a species'.[38]

But although both lists have this powerful generalizing emphasis, they are in effect liberating, rather than confining. They are rounded and assured, carefully organized round a very precise attitude towards uppish affectations. By making clear exactly what they are attacking, they also leave a good deal of freedom outside the sharp outlines of the definition. Because the notation is so firm, we incline to trust the author's moral grasp, and to feel that his standards are secure enough not to extend blame untidily, beyond its proper limits. This is doubtless helped by the fact that the passages arise out of particular situations in a novel. But it is probably the fact of their 'typicality', rather than their notionally 'individual' contexts, which prevents the satiric set-pieces from closing in on humanity at large. This is so for two reasons. Because Fielding mocks specifiable types (low-born persons with uppish airs, the servant who pretends to gentility, etc.), the satire leaves out other types by definition. And because the 'typicality' of the satirized usages is taken for granted by Fielding, so that his enumeration can be frankly selective, giving enough examples to suggest the kind of thing, and no more, there need be no effort at limitless extension, and no place for Swift's imprisoning exhaustiveness.

Swift's generalizations, on the other hand, seem often to be less about specific types than about humanity as a whole. When he produces his long catalogues of human types, as in Gulliver's final invective in IV.xii, 'a Lawyer, a Pick-pocket, a Colonel, a Fool, a Lord, a Gamester, a Politician, a Whoremunger, a Physician, an Evidence, a Suborner, an Attorney, a Traytor, or the like',[39] the list of types does not limit the satire, but threatens to extend to everybody. The generalizing is a matter not of summation, as in Fielding, but of the multiplication of an endless series of particulars, tending away from a classifying of types and towards a universal exposure of all. And where there is a limitation of types in both authors (e.g. to the 'polite' world and its low imitators), Fielding's little anthologized lists of 'polite' usages are in sharp contrast to Swift's *Complete Collection of Genteel and Ingenious Conversation*, which is very extensive.[40] It has none of Fielding's knowing air of giving a few choice examples and leaving the rest unsaid. At the same time, though labelled a 'Complete Collection', it could be added to indefinitely.[41] Swift spent years putting the materials together,[42] and the whole configuration suggests fulfilment only in a nominal sense: its real point is limitless absurdity. Although the 'polite' clichés are made to unfold themselves in what looks more or less like a conversation, the conversation frequently lacks sense or sequence and exists for no other purpose than to record the clichés. Needless to say, the dialogue is not related to any significant situation, as it would be in a novel, and such circumstantial setting as it has serves only to get or to keep the speakers talking.[43] It is all inventory, and no drama. There are named speakers, with 'type' names, like Lord Sparkish, Sir John Linger, Lady Answerall, and others, but the individual statements might in many cases have been given interchangeably to any of them, and are unrelated to character.[44]

One result of this is that where Fielding's foolish speakers have a kind of clockwork reality, a predictable pedantry in the social forms, Swift's become oddly detached from context, unreal, moving in vacuous space. The reduction of fashionable manners to 'pedantry' is a commonplace of Augustan satire, found in Swift as well as in Fielding: 'There is', Swift tells us in 'On Good-Manners and Good-Breeding', 'a pedantry in manners, as in all arts and sciences; and sometimes in trades'.[45] The formula reduces any satiric victim to social meanness, and enables the satirist to indulge a gentlemanly hauteur at his expense. But where Fielding does this by suggesting that his victims are predictable automata, operating within stiff and awkward forms which are wholly within the grasp of his own superior understanding to classify or account for,[46] Swift shows them enacting their absurdities in a kind of hideous void, outside the domain of rational explanation. Continuing his discussion of the 'pedantry in manners', he says of professional court-functionaries, 'from the gentleman-usher (at least) inclusive, downward to the gentleman-porter':[47]

> being wholly illiterate, and conversing chiefly with each other, they reduce the whole system of breeding within the forms and circles of their several offices: and as they are below the notice of ministers, they live and die in court under all revolutions, with great obsequiousness to those who are in any degree of favour or credit: and with rudeness or insolence to every body else.

This vacuous enclosed existence within 'forms and circles' is exactly what happens in the disembodied world of the *Complete Collection*. There is a tendency towards that void created by Ionesco's exploitation of the verbal platitudes of our own time, a void which is at the same time an imprisoning anti-order, and about which Richard Coe has said: 'the utter pointlessness of a language which has degenerated into formulae whose acceptance, by those who utter them, is symbolic of an inner abdication, of submission to an order "which is defined exclusively by its own slogans"'.[48] Ionesco tells us that his first play, *La Cantatrice Chauve* (*The Bald Prima-Donna*) was inspired by the conversational clichés of a French-English conversational handbook.[49] The play turned into an exposure of the 'idées reçues' and the conformism of the 'petite bourgeoisie universelle', a demonstration of ready-made language, of speech with nothing to say, of the absence of all inner life, the automatism of the everyday in the hollow undifferentiating social milieu in which the 'petit bourgeois' lives.[50] The focus is on a different social class from that satirized by Swift, but some of the feeling is the same. Ionesco, however, openly and radically moves beyond satire.[51] His phrase-book illogicalities carry a fundamental sense of discontinuity and emptiness beyond the mere registering of linguistic or social absurdities. He speaks of the collapse of the real ('une sorte d'effondrement du réel'), words becoming stripped of their meanings, characters emptied of their psychology.[52] This effect can to some extent be detected in Swift too, although Swift's primary orientation, unlike Ionesco's, *is* satirical, and although his tendency to go beyond satire, here as elsewhere, is unofficial. Swift, for example, confines himself to a notation of actual spoken clichés: 'there is not one single Sentence in the whole Collection,' says Simon Wagstaff (Swift's 'author') in the Introduction, 'for which I cannot bring most authentick Vouchers ... from Courts, Chocolate-houses, Theatres ... from Persons of both Sexes'.[53] By contrast, Ionesco allows his platitudes to transform themselves, to become denatured and unruly ('se dénaturèrent ... se déréglèrent').[54] Instead of listing the seven days of the week, the hero Mr Smith asserts that there are three days in the week, Tuesday, Thursday, and Tuesday.[55] Mrs Smith states it as a law that when the door-bell rings, there is nobody at the door wanting to get in. Mr Smith says ribbons are a useless but absolutely necessary precaution for colds. Mr Martin declares that social progress is better with sugar.[56] Cliché is no longer merely mimicked, but becomes distorted into a disturbing linguistic surrealism, which goes hand in hand with other tokens of radical disorientation, such as the choice of *Bald Prima-Donna* for the play's title, partly because no prima-donna, bald or otherwise, appears in the play.[57]

No such discontinuity is allowed to overwhelm the outward form of Swift's discourse. The official appearance of a formal satiric dialogue, mocking the clichés of social types whose names are labels which indicate their typicality, stands out very clearly when we contrast Swift with Ionesco rather than with Fielding. In both Swift and Ionesco characterization is broken down into disconnected absurdity and the clichés arrive in a pure state. But Ionesco's refusal to define character contrasts with Swift's opposite inclination to reduce it crudely to rudimentary type. I suggested that the meaningless banalities of Swift's speakers could, in many cases, emanate interchangeably from any one of them or any typical member of 'polite' society. But in fact they are uttered by Lord Sparkish, Sir John Linger, Lady Answerall, and the rest, whereas Ionesco's are uttered by a Mr and Mrs Martin and a Mr and Mrs Smith. Swift's fluidities and discontinuities are played off against a formal appearance of clear definition and of categorizability, even though part of his effect is to melt the categories into the wild hotch-potch that he conceives social intercourse to be. Ionesco explicitly insists on the interchangeability, saying that Smith could be replaced by Martin, and vice-versa, without anyone noticing.[58] The play actually ends by beginning again with the Martins replacing the Smiths in the opening scene,[59] while even the characters themselves are unsure of their own or each others' identities: thus Mr and Mrs Martin converse with all the clichés of strangers who think they may have met before, discovering that by coincidence they travelled by the same train, live in the same house and must be husband and wife[60] (though doubt is cast on that too, and on their names; while an earlier conversation between the Smiths discusses a family in which everyone, father, mother, children, uncles, are called Bobby Watson).[61]

Ionesco's discontinuities are rigorously disciplined and stylized. The plays in which they occur have a hard finish, a peculiar shapely conclusiveness not unlike that of a 'well-made play' turned inside out. He spoke of *La Cantatrice* as an 'anti-play',[62] and if there can be such a thing as a 'well-made anti-play', that is what it is and what many of his other plays are. In their firmness of formal outline, in the elegant precision of their nonsense, and in their outward appearance of severe logic and clear pattern, they resemble some of Swift's 'closed' configurations, the mad systems and giddy circularities, the nesting boxes and spiralling chains. Within such frameworks, as we have seen, both authors are given to introducing glimpses of disruptive illogicality or violence or grotesquerie, so that disturbance is never far from the hard polished surface.

But such surfaces are, as I argued earlier, fairly rare in Swift, and his most natural idiom is one in which the explosive loose end, the raggedly unfinished, flourish in a state of formal freedom, so that a work like the *Tale* can digress anywhere it likes, pretend to gaps in the manuscript, and end, if not actually unfinished, at least with the declared readiness of the 'author' to resume his pen. And among the major post-Swiftian cataloguers of 'idées reçues' the one who perhaps resembles Swift most closely is not Ionesco but Flaubert. In some ways Swift's so-called 'complete' record of polite conversation is closer to the incomplete labours of Bouvard and Pécuchet, and to Flaubert's own failure to complete the novel to which they belong, as well as the *Dictionnaire des idées reçues* which is related to it. Swift and Simon Wagstaff, Flaubert and Bouvard and Pécuchet all took years compiling their records, seeking an impossible exhaustiveness, exposing on the way the manifold vacuities of modern language, modern thought, modern scientific experiment.[63]

René Girard has said that in *Bouvard et Pécuchet*, 'L'individualisme petit-bourgeois s'achève par l'apothéose bouffonne de l'Identique et de l'Interchangeable.'[64] The terms resemble those of Ionesco. But Girard's fine account of that Flaubertian void which emanates from the 'fausses énumérations' and the 'fausses antithèses' exposed in his novels, the nonsensical openness of the lists and the anti-order of the symmetrical paired arrangements ('aristocrates et bourgeois, dévots et athées, réactionnaires et républicains...')[65] has a striking relevance to Swift. Even more directly applicable to Swift is Hugh Kenner's argument in that very Swift-minded book, *The Stoic Comedians*, that *Bouvard et Pécuchet* shows us the 'hack writer' as 'supreme realist', and that Flaubert's novel seeks its reality precisely through a kind of transcendent parody of the bad novel in which 'the book itself aspires *directly* to the idiot accuracy of second-rate fiction'.[66] The hack 'author' of the *Tale* is likewise a meticulous recorder of experience, and the *Tale*'s formidable power depends on its being, in a curious way, the best of all the bad books that it mocks. An important difference is that it is *novelistic* fiction which Flaubert, unlike Swift, is both writing and burlesquing. Bouvard and Pécuchet acquire solidity as characters, with differences from one another in their appearance, their reactions and their motives, which arouse our interest and affection quasi-independently of the absurdities which they reveal or catalogue for us. In Swift's *Tale*, 'modern' absurdities are rendered in a pure state, as anonymous, universal, and more or less free of context. And the kind of sympathy which we come to feel for Flaubert's satirized characters, because we get to know them as people (with amiable weaknesses, endearing habits, etc.), is impossible in the tart ambience of absolute rejection which we find in Swift's attitude towards the hack 'author' of the *Tale*.

It is true, however, that in the case of Simon Wagstaff, the supposed compiler of the *Complete Collection*, we do not feel this sense of absolute rejection, partly because he tends to be somewhat more directly Swift's spokesman. His Introduction is often ironic, and since Swift mimics certain 'projector' follies through him, he cannot be taken as simply equivalent to Swift. But he is not a totally upside-down 'mask', like the *Tale*'s 'author', and his methods of collecting his material are those of Swift himself.[67] Moreover, in the dialogues themselves he is totally effaced from the scene. We are therefore unlikely to have strong feelings either of rejection or of sympathy for him, and our whole attention is focused instead on the inanities of the polite dialogues which he has transcribed. In *Bouvard et Pécuchet*, by contrast, we are invited to contemplate not only the absurdities recorded by the two compilers, but also their experience in recording them, their stubborn commitment and their moments of impulsiveness, their timidities and their obsessive persistence, their relations with each other and with others. The difference from Swift remains essentially the same as that revealed in the comparison with the *Tale*. As in the *Tale*, Swift invites us in the *Complete Collection* to contemplate absurdities in their pure state, with this difference, that the absurdities are lodged not in a single, inclusive, anonymous personality, but in vacuous forms of speech uttered nakedly and with a wild freedom from any live or meaningful context.

It would be wrong, however, to conclude that this difference really brings Flaubert closer to Fielding than to Swift. It is true that, in both Fielding and Flaubert, the novelistic imagination, with its wider tolerance, its greater interest in individual persons, its tendency even in satirical contexts to record a good deal of unsatirical detail for its own sake, prevents satirical hostility from becoming absolute in the manner of Swift. But Fielding differs as much from Flaubert as from Swift in his feeling that the follies he satirizes are a phenomenon limited to certain types, unlikely to overwhelm the whole fabric of life, and in any case held in control by the satirist's knowing wisdom. The easy selectiveness of his enumerations is in sharp contrast not only with Swift's various ways of hinting at *inexhaustible numbers*, but also with the sheer mass of Flaubert's attempt to record these inexhaustible numbers item by item, and his visible failure to exhaust or to complete this record. The large bulk of *Bouvard et Pécuchet* is to Fielding's short anthologies of usage in the novels (e.g. the 'dissertation concerning high people and low people' and the 'smart dialogue between some people and some folks')[68] what the *Dictionnaire des idées reçues* is to the short satirical 'Modern Glossary' in *Covent-Garden Journal*, no. 4.[69] In both cases, moreover, Flaubert is not only massive where Fielding is brief, but also unfinished where Fielding is, for his own selective purposes, complete and conclusive. Swift does not bother to achieve Flaubertian mass. His own two longest efforts at recording folly or vice in exhaustive detail and in a more or less tabulated form, namely the *Complete Collection* and the *Directions to Servants*, are much shorter than *Bouvard et Pécuchet*. But what he lacks in mass, he makes up in rhetorical or stylistic suggestion, in lists which, though relatively short by Flaubertian standards, are meant to seem long, and to hint at endless extension beyond themselves. The lists are unfinished not merely because, as for Flaubert, there wasn't time, but because he could not see the limits, and wished to make that point too. In this sense, Swift goes even further than Flaubert in registering the radical unruliness of things. His catalogues are ragged and disorderly, as well as incomplete. Each item appears to emerge randomly, pell-mell, instead of being, like Flaubert's, meticulously arranged by topic, or in alphabetical order, with a consequential tendency towards the ultimate inclusiveness of an encyclopedia. The hint, inherent in Flaubert, that such an inclusiveness might just about be possible, however difficult to achieve or sterile in its final consummation, is one which Swift always withholds.

CHAPTER V

CATALOGUES, CORPSES AND CANNIBALS

Swift and Mailer, with Reflections on Whitman, Conrad and Others

> Of every hue and caste am I, of every rank and religion,
> A farmer, mechanic, artist, gentleman, sailor, quaker,
> Prisoner, fancy-man, rowdy, lawyer, physician, priest.
> (Walt Whitman, *Song of Myself*, No. 16)

> Our society is a plural one in many senses. Any one person is likely to be a participant in a number of groups, which may have not only different membership, but quite different forms of unification.
>
> Each group requires more or less radical internal transformation of the persons who comprise it. Consider the metamorphoses that the one man may go through in one day as he moves from one mode of sociality to another—family man, speck of crowd dust, functionary in the organization, friend. These are not simply different roles: each is a whole past and present and future, offering differing options and constraints, different degrees of change or inertia, different kinds of closeness and distance, different sets of rights and obligations, different pledges and promises.
>
> I know of no theory of the individual that fully recognizes this. There is every temptation to start with a notion of some supposed basic personality, but halo effects are not reducible to one internal system. The tired family man at the office and the tired business man at home attest to the fact that people carry over, not just one set of internal objects, but *various internalized social modes of being* from one context to another, often grossly contradictory.
> (R. D. Laing, *The Politics of Experience*, ch. IV)

This journey is experienced as going further 'in', as going back through one's personal life, in and back and through and beyond into

> the experience of all mankind, of the primal man, of Adam and perhaps even further into the being of animals, vegetables and minerals.
>
> (*Politics of Experience*, ch. v)

Swift's lists have been shown statistically to be more numerous, and also individually longer, and less patterned, than those of Addison and several other eighteenth-century writers, some of whom (Johnson, Gibbon) by contrast use more often than Swift does those short shapely lists (doublets, triplets) which tend towards balances of parallelism or antithesis.[1] Even when using doublet-devices, Swift avoids and sometimes mocks such balances, as he avoids and sometimes disrupts 'regularity, both in rhetoric and in grammar'.[2] This reflects, as the statistician says, 'his general suspicion of predictability'.[3] It is also, we may add, an active onslaught on the complacency which too readily assumes that all hangs neatly together.

The long list is an anarchic configuration, because it does not contain within itself any intrinsic need to end, or any stylistic promise that an end is forthcoming:

> I am not in the least provoked at the Sight of a Lawyer, a Pick-pocket, a Colonel, a Fool, a Lord, a Gamester, a Politician, a Whoremunger, a Physician, an Evidence, a Suborner, an Attorney, a Traytor, or the like (*Gulliver's Travels*, IV.xii).[4]

This list ends only because any discourse must, not because it exhausts itself. One of the implications of 'or the like' (a type of phrase which occurs frequently in Swift's satiric lists) is that the list could perpetuate itself, given time, patience, a freedom from those extrinsic and practical factors which limit speech or any other human activity.

But 'or the like' has a second tonality, the flattening effect of a sarcasm. Moreover, if in one sense it opens the possibility of innumerable further examples, in another sense it simply stops the list. Lists stopped by such etceteras, flattened by sarcasms of equivalence and by the colloquial drops of an angry rhetoric (these effects occur here in potent combination, but they may occur singly), are characteristic of Swift. Lists nearly always generate in his writings some combination of exuberance and astringency. In the present list, headlong abundance is made to coexist with weary predictability, and Gulliver's nagging bombination is the drearily sobering underside of that touch of aggressively playful buoyancy with which Swift is felt to be getting something off his chest. And where, as in Gulliver's earlier war-list,[5] Gulliver and Swift share a degree (though opposite kinds) of exuberance, the fundamental nastiness of the situation combines with the sarcasms, the colloquial drops, and the bland notation of shocking ironic twists and countertwists ('to set forth the Valour of my own dear Countrymen, I assured him,...', 'to the great Diversion of all the Spectators', etc.)[6] to exercise a downward pull. The combination of exuberance and astringency permits some hideous energies to come to life, without letting the exuberance itself turn into a Rabelaisian joy in abundance. Lists are the obvious place for such combinations to occur, since they trade by definition in abundance, though often a negative abundance, checked by inappropriate blandness or a savage moderation ('every Day *dying*, and *rotting*, by *Cold* and *Famine*, and *Filth*, and *Vermin*, as fast as can be reasonably expected').[7] But the combinations are not confined to lists, and are, as the *Modest Proposal* and parts of *Gulliver* show, a natural consequence of the trick of giving extreme or monstrous thoughts to moderate speakers. The imprisoning energies of an open style, energies of a viciously pullulating abundance, become doubly imprisoning because the only outlet they might have offered, an expansive delight in their sheer vitality and excess, becomes blocked.

A comparison with Rabelais is instructive, since (though neither author holds the copyright) it is partly from him that Swift acquired the habit of the long outrageous list. Rabelais's lists declare that sheer delight in abundance which Swift's astringency constantly checks, even when he is mimicking the energies of viciousness with an angry abandon. The abundance is of words as well as of things.[8] Hence not only the enormous itemizations of every kind of object, but also torrents of synonymous redundancy ('le blanc luy signifioit joye, plaisir, delices et resjouissance')[9] and of self-contradictory nonsense ('un gros, gras, grand, gris, joly, petit, moisy livret, plus, mais non mieulx sentent que roses').[10] Instead of stinging afterthoughts which freeze the feeling and arrest the list's momentum ('*dying*, and *rotting*, ... as fast as can be reasonably expected'), those of Rabelais's lists which issue in a final surprise or anticlimax do so with the expansive gaiety of a happy joke ('plus, mais non mieulx sentent que roses').[11] Even Rabelais's abusive lists contain a massive feeling of release. When Gulliver, in IV.x, lists all the disreputable types not to be found in Houyhnhnm society, beginning with physicians, lawyers and informers, and proceeding, by way of 'Murderers, Robbers, Virtuoso's' and 'strolling Whores, ... Poxes ...

ranting, lewd, expensive Wives', to 'Lords, Fidlers, Judges [and] Dancing-masters', he specifies at great length, concludes with an astringent finality, and leaves it at that. When Rabelais tells us who will not be admitted to *his* Utopian society, the abbey of Thélème, namely variously deformed, ugly, insane and unhealthy men and women, he then redirects, or opens up, the entire mood by saying who *will* be admitted: 'les belles, bien formées et bien naturées, et les beaulx, bien formez et bien naturez'.[12] But even where such formal redirection is absent, there is often in Rabelais's abusive lists a *built-in* feeling of liberation. In the characteristic one in I.xxv, for example, the abuse flowers with such sheer supererogation and at times with so much near-synonymity, that what one mainly senses is not the additional variation or nuance brought by each new word, but the pleasure as such of adding word to word. Swift on the other hand does not allow his precisions to get lost in torrents of undifferentiating fun;[13] nor does he often, in his major satiric writings, playfully let them dissolve in nonsense-antitheses (like Rabelais's description of the book which is both large and small). Instead of huge synonymities, he provides incongruous equivalence, instead of preposterous contraries, an unexpected but pointed clash of categories: 'Murderers, Robbers, Virtuoso's', 'a Lawyer, a Pick-pocket, a Colonel, a Fool'. The world's teeming variety of human types thus emerges, step by step and shock by shock, as a reductive amalgam of knaves and fools. Where Rabelais is too happily outrageous to encourage such radical, simplifying and imprisoning redefinitions, Swift frequently forces them upon us.[14] Where Rabelais will even (quite deliberately) discard precision to permit a free expansiveness, Swift's precisions extract their full value of shocked attention, and hold abundance back.[15]

Rabelais's lists, with their deliberate semantic irresponsibility, their free piling-on of synonyms and antonyms, exist partly in a dimension of pure verbal play. The delighted exploitation of rich resources of language has the effect of proclaiming an aesthetic *order*, which transcends and triumphs over the mere unruly abundance of fact. In this it resembles the (otherwise dissimilar) operation of Pope's couplet-rhetoric, which also asserts reassuringly that the order of art has the measure of life's teeming and apparently limitless disorder. Something akin to that comforting and liberating sense of enclosure which we find in Pope exists paradoxically in the copious infinities of Rabelais, whereas Swift's infinities, as I argued in earlier chapters, evoke a very different counter-image of enclosure, that of the prison rather than the rich haven.[16]

Swift was, of course, like Rabelais, notoriously given to verbal play.

But his main impulses in that direction found their outlet in the verbal games which he played with his friends (in convivial punning sessions and the like),[17] and not in the serious business of his major writings. His playing was, in an important sense, largely confined to games, and in serious contexts (especially in the great satires) quickly becomes charged with pointed and acrid significance. This seems to be true even in the invented or fictional languages, where outlandish words have a grating, unsettling harshness even when they do not (unlike 'Laputa', or 'Yahoo') carry suggestions of a more openly semantic kind.

Swift none the less looks back to Rabelais. The formal device of the satiric catalogue he learned partly from him. Both share a degree of playfulness, and a certain unruly abundance. That Rabelais's exuberance evokes a happy release, while Swift's animated tribute to mankind's vicious energies has an imprisoning force, should not be allowed to obscure the important likenesses between the two authors, likenesses to which Pope (at the beginning of the *Dunciad*)[18] and many other critics have referred. And if, as we have seen, the vitalities of abundance are themselves prevented, in Swift, from flowering into joy, they are nevertheless there to be prevented. Their world may in some ways be a dry one, but the soul of Rabelais, as Coleridge said, does inhabit it.[19] Whilst Swift's lists look back to Rabelais, where the keynote is comic exuberance, they nevertheless also look forward, with their quality of biting obsessiveness, to certain anguished intensities in post-Romantic authors, notably in the literature of protest, and of violent or extreme situations, in our own time. Allen Ginsberg's 'Howl', and other poems which similarly redirect Whitmanian exuberance of celebration to a high pitch of urgent anxiety, come to mind (in some ways, Beat poems of protest are to Whitman as Swift is to Rabelais). Or this passage by Eldridge Cleaver, very much like Gulliver's war-lists[20] in its angry desperation, and its achievement of a strange generalized vividness through the piling on of painfully particularized typicalities:[21]

> One thought of blood and guns and knives, whips, ropes and chains and trees, screams, night riders, fear, nightsticks, police dogs and firehoses, fire, wounds and bombs, old women in pain and young women defiled, lies, jeers, little boys frozen in their first heat and young men *de*studded and old men burnt out, little girls psychically vitiated and physically massacred.

Or such passages as this 'most appetizing menu', which catalogues the guests at a party in a story in Norman Mailer's *Advertisements for*

Myself, and which recalls particularly Gulliver's incongruous lists of human types:[22]

a queer
a cop
a crook

a Negro
a war hero
a movie star

an athlete
a dope addict
a socialite

a fisherman
an analyst
a call girl

a whore
a businessman
a mother
a father

a child
a sibling
a television entertainer
a politician

a writer
a painter
a jazzman
a rapist

a Timeless wonder (originally a man but altered
to a facsimile of woman)....

In Mailer's list, however, we neither have Swift's firm implication of moral culpability, nor Swift's sense of the essential categorizability of human types. Mailer made his narrator say of Marion Faye, the protagonist for whom the party was convened, that he prided himself for being 'one of the few to have climbed beyond the killing precipice of manners, morals, the sense of sin and the fear of germs'.[23] In a sense, Faye's position is that of the exceptional hero, 'one of the few', and he pays the Romantic Agonist's price (exhaustion, dulling of 'the finer knives of his brain').[24] But he is powerfully endorsed by all the overheated loyalties of Mailer's imagination. And even if his high freedom from manners, morals and the rest is not that of ordinary people, there is also in Mailer's list a more ordinary or low-pitched sense in which incongruous juxtapositions are not, as in Swift, primarily and sarcastically concerned with making a moral critique. For Mailer, the discontinuities are largely outside the domain of simple moral judgments; for Swift, they urgently demand moral judgments, and the simpler the better.

This is true not only in the domain of moral imperatives, but also in that of categories of definition. Thus Mailer's discontinuities radically confound any suggestion that character is definable in terms of accepted psychological or professional types. They are thus not mere equivalences sharply demarcated from one another, but fluid interpenetrating identities, several of the listed 'persons' being one and the same, and several also being facets of more than one individual. We are warned beforehand that the list is 'a peculiar list, for it included everyone, and yet there were more items on the list than people present, and titles applicable to more than one, as if some of the guests contained several categories within themselves'.[25] Categories have become meaningless or irrelevant. The 'expectations' which are violated are of course real, and perhaps widespread, but only, one supposes, as vague invalid residues of an older, spent culture. And for Mailer it is therefore only the 'expectations' which are violated, because the categories no longer exist in their old form. In Swift, on the other hand, the categories themselves, not just the expectations, do still very much exist, however often transgressed, with the implication that when they are violated, something unnatural is taking place.

Gulliver's juxtapositions ('a Pick-pocket, a Colonel ... a Politician, a Whoremunger ...') are damaging equivalences. A clear moral standard we are all expected to share asserts that colonels should not be though they sometimes *are* like pickpockets, and that politicians should not be though they sometimes are like whoremongers. These equivalences are damaging, but they remain mainly equivalences, not identities. There is no powerful suggestion that the pickpockets and the colonels are the same persons, only that (in a bad modern world) the types approximate to one another. If mixed identities are not excluded (colonels *could* be pickpockets), the stronger implication is that the various types are categorizable and more or less separate, though less different from one another than they should be. This relatively clear categorizability or 'typicality' differentiates them from the people in Mailer, just as in another sense it differentiates the speakers of Swift's *Complete Collection of Genteel and Ingenious Conversation* from the amorphous or fragmented cliché-mouthing automata of Ionesco's dramatic dialogues.

A good recent discussion of Swift's poems by A. B. England places a rather different emphasis on some lines in *On Poetry: A Rapsody*, where Swift mocks the practice in satiric poems of substituting 'initials for the full name of the person satirized':[26]

> On A's and B's your Malice vent,
> While Readers wonder whom you meant.
> A publick, or a private *Robber*;
> A *Statesman*, or a South-Sea *Jobber*.
> A *Prelate* who no God believes;
> A [Parliament], or Den of Thieves.
> A Pick-purse at the Bar, or Bench;
> A Duchess, or a Suburb-Wench (ll. 159-66).[27]

Mr England compares this passage with a passage from *Hudibras* on which it may have been modelled, and comments:

> Swift exploits the antithetical structures suggested by the couplet form, not to bring sharp separates ironically together and to mock those who don't see the falsity, but to throw apparent unlikes into conjunctions that are valid and real. In doing so he conveys a sense of actuality as something amorphous and indistinct, not to be resolved into simple partitions.

This emphasis may seem apt enough. But a comparison with Mailer's passage, where there is a much more radical coalescence of categories, suggests that it needs to be qualified in some important ways. Swift's categories are 'amorphous and indistinct' only if certain aspects of moral behaviour are viewed in isolation. The indistinctness would largely disappear if names were named, or if (as I think we are entitled to suppose) we saw the members of each pair at their actual daily business (in Parliament, or Den of Thieves), or in their actual physical appearance (as Duchess, or Suburb-Wench). The irony is essentially the one made familiar by the *Beggar's Opera*, that the 'manners in high and low life' are so alike 'that it is difficult to determine whether (in the fashionable vices) the fine gentlemen imitate the gentlemen of the road, or the gentlemen of the road the fine gentlemen'.[28] Standards of behaviour have become deplorably blurred, but not the categories themselves. If, as Fielding's version of the same irony puts it, 'the splendid palaces of the great are often no other than Newgate with the mask on',[29] there is no suggestion that 'the splendid palaces' are not identifiable as such, or that the 'mask' which differentiates them from Newgate is insignificant. On the contrary, a salient irony of both Gay and Fielding is the fact that this 'mask' ensures that one category will prosper and the other be punished, although both categories practise the same vices. More important, Fielding was not at all times sure that this discrepancy should necessarily be removed;[30] and both he and Gay would certainly hold, with Swift, that different behaviour was, ideally, expected of each category, those in high places being especially expected to practise high virtues. Hence the particularly pointed incongruity when boundaries are crossed:[31]

> The truth is, as a very corrupt state of morals is here represented, the scene seems very properly to have been laid in Newgate; nor do I see any reason for introducing any allegory at all; unless we will agree that there are without those walls, some other bodies of men of worse morals than those within; and who have, consequently, a right to change places with its present inhabitants.

Fielding is answering critics who found 'personal applications' in *Jonathan Wild*, where no names of high persons were explicitly given. The situation which Swift described in *On Poetry: A Rapsody* is here actually enacted in essence, since Fielding's omission of names leads to free-wheeling decipherments by the critics, who take the novel's low characters as an allegory about actual persons in high places. Fielding is, of course, being at least partly disingenuous in pretending that no 'personal application' was intended. But his phrase about the 'right to change places' does not imply indistinguishability. On the contrary: the irony depends on distinctions, and highlights a violated sense of fitness. The blur is really a mock-blur. And if, as Swift argued in the poem, such a blur or mock-blur comes from the satirist's refusal to name names, it serves for Swift as for Gay and Fielding to emphasize a satiric situation whose contours and divisions are in one sense very precise. I have argued at some length that there are certain deliberate and radical intermergings and indistinguishabilities in Swift's satire. In this he is unlike Fielding and probably unlike Gay. But the special point of the lines in *On Poetry: A Rapsody* is that Swift was actually in favour of naming names, of satirizing, at this particular level, with the greatest possible *distinctness*: once again, the most unsettling fluidities of Swift's style occur in a context of fixed standards and fixed targets.

In this pattern, as in so much of Swift's writing, opposite extremes maintain a polarized coexistence instead of entering into compromise combinations on middle ground. In the maintenance of sharp outlines, in the insistence on naming names and on similar satiric precisions, Swift went much further than Fielding and, for that matter, than most other eighteenth-century writers. He also, and often simultaneously, went further than most in an opposite process of universalizing his satire through the calculated and aggressive blurring of boundary-lines. The satiric catalogue, with its ordered juxtaposition of incongruous pairs and its simultaneous air of chaotic and inexhaustible numerousness, is a particularly effective vehicle for Swiftian satire. Although neither the catalogue nor the trick of juxtaposition was new or unique to Swift, his ability to combine the two in a very highly charged way is his own. It may even be that he used the combination as such more frequently than other writers. Fielding's satiric lists tend, I believe, to enumerate in coherent groups, as in these examples from *Covent-Garden Journal*, no. 3: 'Rakes, Beaux, Sharpers, and fine Ladies', 'Lawyers, Physicians, Surgeons, and Apothecaries', 'Officers of State, and wou'd-be Officers of State, (honest Men only excepted,) with all their Attendants, and Dependents, their Placemen, and wou'd-be Placemen, Pimps, Spies, Parasites, Informers, and Agents'.[32] (It is also characteristic of Fielding, unlike Swift, to remind us, in the thick of the passage, of the actual existence of 'honest Men'). Swift also has such more congruous groupings, of course.[33] But the less orderly examples I have been considering have his own strongly individual flavour. And if the several types of person listed within each group are in themselves more precise and more self-contained than those in Mailer's passage, Swift's imagination is powerfully exercised by notions of disorder, of merging identities, of categories under pressure from human impulse and activity. In this he approximates to Mailer, and perhaps to some other modern authors whom he would have castigated as mad 'moderns', in a way that Fielding does not.

I am using 'modern' mainly in Swift's sense, which evokes among other things the dissolution of orderly standards and categories, rather than in a merely chronological sense. The distinction between the two is not hard and fast. But just as not all eighteenth-century authors are like Swift, so not all twentieth-century authors are like Mailer. And, in particular, Mailer's list must be distinguished from various other catalogues in twentieth-century authors in which persons acquire multiple identities, for example the famous passage in Joyce's *Portrait of the Artist* where[34]

> Stephen began to enumerate glibly his father's attributes.
> — A medical student, an oarsman, a tenor, an
> amateur actor, a shouting politician, a small landlord,
> a small investor, a drinker, a good fellow, a
> storyteller, somebody's secretary, something in a
> distillery, a taxgatherer, a bankrupt and at
> present a praiser of his own past.

Despite the fact that all these identities belong to one man, we hardly get the sense of an intimately-rendered blurring of identity. Indeed, the passage has a clear externality of portraiture which would not be out of place in a comic novel of the tradition of, say, Fielding or Smollett. An inclusive pen-portrait is being rounded out, whose various components (past and present, simultaneous and successive) go to make up Mr Dedalus, with all his changeability, into a 'typical' figure of considerable coherence and solidity. (The almost classical nature of the portrait is reinforced by the echo of Horace's *laudator temporis acti*, *Ars Poetica*, l. 173, at the end of the passage.) No doubt Joyce felt able to be so comically pat only by hiding behind Stephen's 'glib enumeration'. But his effect could hardly be more unlike the fluid intermergings and discontinuities of Mailer's list, where categories combine with one another not in a coherent or typical mixture, nor in a straightforward temporal progress, but in the unstable melting-pot of a confused present; and where we remain unsure of which categories do or do not enter into combination, and in whom.

Mailer's passage differs similarly from this self-portrait by Wyndham Lewis:[35]

> I am a novelist, painter, sculptor, philosopher,
> draughtsman, critic, politician, journalist, essayist,
> pamphleteer, all rolled into one, like one of those
> portmanteau-men of the Italian Renaissance.
> I am a portmanteau-man (like 'portmanteau-word').
> I have been a soldier, a yachtsman, a baby, a *massier*,
> a hospital patient, a traveller, a total abstainer,
> a lecturer, an alcoholic, an editor, and a lot more.

Wyndham Lewis's passage is a jaunty prefiguration of those potted biographies of the Versatile-and-Much-Experienced-Author that one finds on the covers of certain paperbacks, but with a sense of humour thrown in. As with Joyce, there is a sense of the rounded, though perhaps mock-untidy, portrait of a single person, and none of the Mailerian feeling of blurred boundaries. There is in addition a coy joke about Renaissance versatility, cut down to modern sub-heroic size ('portmanteau-man'), a joke and an ideal which, as it happens, also receive passing mention elsewhere in Mailer's story.[36] It would be an over-simplification to say that such an ideal is necessarily outside the range of imaginative aspiration of a modern writer, unless ironically transposed, as in Wyndham Lewis, to a lower key. Yeats's Major Robert Gregory gets full heroic measure. But even he (or especially he) has to be imagined in terms of an older time, as 'Our Sidney and our perfect man'.[37] Kermode has shown that Yeats borrowed for his elegy the stanza of a late Renaissance poem, Cowley's 'On the Death of Mr. William Hervey'.[38] It is sometimes forgotten that Gregory's description,[39]

> Soldier, scholar, horseman, he,
> As 'twere all life's epitome,

is also, consciously or otherwise, a heroic restatement or inversion of a satirical portrait by another seventeenth-century poet, Dryden, who described the giddy changeable nobleman Zimri ('Chymist, Fidler, States-Man, and Buffoon') as[40]

> A man so various, that he seem'd to be
> Not one, but all Mankinds Epitome.

Yeats might be said to be putting back on its feet an ideal that Dryden stood on its head, perpetrating a sort of mock-heroic in reverse. If Wyndham Lewis's 'portmanteau-man' in some sense revalidates the Renaissance ideal by laughing it into a smaller, more viable size, Yeats boldly reasserts it in the teeth of one of the Renaissance's own mocking or ironic versions. In both cases, however, the modern author needs to make us aware that the ideal is a Renaissance one, and that its restatements in our time must be viewed against that background, seen as something special, and protected, perhaps, by irony.

The examples by Joyce, Wyndham Lewis, Yeats (and Dryden) all presuppose that a person's multiple roles cohere to produce a definable personality, even though that personality has sometimes to be defined in terms of inconsistency, self-contradiction, imbalance, fickle unsteadiness. The versatile Renaissance Man is in some ways an idealized form, peculiarly high and harmonious, free of all imbalance, and charged instead with aristocratic ease and authority. But all differ equally from the shifting and multiple identities of the figures in Mailer's list, and especially of a modern consciousness like that of Mailer's speaker, or the Tiresias of Eliot's *Waste Land*:[41]

> Tiresias, although a mere spectator and not indeed a 'character', is yet the most important personage in the poem, uniting all the rest. Just as the one-eyed merchant, seller of currants, melts into the Phoenician Sailor, and the latter is not wholly distinct from Ferdinand Prince of Naples, so all the women are one woman, and the two sexes meet in Tiresias. What Tiresias *sees*, in fact, is the substance of the poem.

Like 'Tiresias', the principal 'I' of Eliot's poem (a fact which Eliot's term 'mere spectator' slightly obscures), Mailer's speaker merges into the figures in his list, as we shall see. (Swift's derided 'author' in the *Tale of a Tub* is also many persons: 'author', annotator, bookseller, etc., a shifting embodiment of many modern absurdities). And if the older, more stable conception of rich or varied personality finds its ideal form in the Renaissance Man, the more fluid and discontinuous conception is idealized in the romantic and post-romantic figure of the 'camelion Poet'.[42] Thus Mailer's speaker notes that he 'will probably travel from the consciousness of one being to the emotions of another—a house, a tree, a dog, a cop, a cannibal...'[43] (For a parallel to Tiresias's 'two sexes', see the last item in Mailer's list as quoted on p. 105.)

If there is some mock-heroic residue in Eliot's narrator, and a powerful mock-heroic quality in the poem as a whole, there is very little in Mailer—Mailer does not invert a Renaissance ideal: such an ideal simply does not enter into play in his story, except as a passing verbal flourish. This perhaps links him with Swift, where one would least expect it. Swift was fond of indicating our shortcomings in relation to high ideals, and often wrote in parody of high-flown forms. But he had a modern's scepticism of heroic possibilities, and his list of colonels, pickpockets and fools is a fragmented 'modern' miscellany *tout court*, though issuing from the stern values of a classical moralist. It is not offered as the squalid underside of the Renaissance Courtier (or of any other similarly magnificent concept), only as a set of examples of low-pitched failures of virtue. Swift gives few positive examples of the Renaissance ideal of the nobleman of high moral and civic principle who is also a man of judgment and taste. Perhaps Lord Munodi in *Gulliver's Travels*, III.iv, is the nearest example, and he is a shadowy figure compared with, say, Pope's Burlington. This is what we should expect. For Swift, the Renaissance Man had dwindled to mere *virtuoso*, in the lowered Augustan sense of that word, and Swift's satire seldom sketches the lineaments of the older, respected type, even for ironic contrast. Dryden's portrait of Zimri is full of derision, but there is behind it an essential and active loyalty to the old ideal. It is mock-heroic in a sense which Swift shied from; and it is a rich irony that Dryden, a more straightforward traditionalist than Swift, should have been pilloried as a leading mad 'modern' in the *Tale*.[44]

What Swift's rhetorical catalogues have most in common with Mailer's against virtually all the other examples so far, is a quality of strident wit, a peculiar amalgam of high spirits and anguished intensity. Swift evolved stylistic procedures for keeping the two ingredients of this amalgam at least nominally separate. Thus in Gulliver's war-list, discussed earlier, Swift feels all the anxiety while an unregenerate mankind, and up to a point Gulliver himself, show all the high spirits, as 'the dead Bodies drop down in Pieces from the Clouds, to the great Diversion of all the Spectators' (IV.v).[45] But we have seen that in another, more unofficial sense, a kind of wild exuberance on Swift's own part is inevitably manifested, even though it is formally ascribed to a wicked world. In Mailer, and also perhaps in some of the long catalogues in Allen Ginsberg's poems, a quality of celebration enters into some of the most acutely pained intensities more directly and less guardedly than Swift would have allowed himself: compare the anti-war passages in *Gulliver's Travels* with Ginsberg's 'Howl', or the many ambiguous passages in Mailer in which protest against violence coexists openly with violent fantasy and an 'instinctive taste for violence'.[46]

As with the energies of violence and of abundance, so with those of incongruity, which are so often related to violence and abundance. Mailer's narrator is able to express a near-ecstatic and at the same time witty wonder at the disharmonies of the long list of party guests, the first section of which I quoted on p. 105 above: 'I wonder if in the history of our republic there has been a party equal in montage: a movie star and a rat, a rapist and a war hero, a psycho-analyst and a call girl'.[47] Gulliver, and I believe Swift, can be just as entranced, but Swift will sometimes adopt a formal position ironically opposite to Gulliver's, or at other times make Gulliver express Swift's own conscious distaste, while Mailer's relationship with his narrators is less defensive. In Ginsberg's 'Howl', the speaker is directly and openly the poet himself, and it is perhaps even more difficult than in Mailer to separate celebration from pain, and either of these from wit, as in the evocation (in the course of a long Whitmanian anaphora) of those 'who copulated ecstatic and insatiate with a bottle of beer a sweetheart a package of cigarettes a candle...'[48] The detailed content of such a passage is doubtless something Swift would not openly allow into print, although he may be felt to come close to it in the anal or onanistic parts of the *Tale* or the *Mechanical Operation*; but there is a pained and witty exuberance about it which is not unSwiftian. By contrast, Pope does in a major work deal with a similar content of erotic fantasy, when, in the Cave of Spleen, 'Maids turn'd Bottels, call aloud for Corks',[49] but without the touch of pain, the helpless yet excited sense of disorder, the feeling of close authorial participation (compassionate or derisive, friendly or hostile), that exist in Ginsberg as so often in Swift. For one thing, Pope's passage has an overall quality not of incongruity, but of harmony. Its material is, of course, aberrant, but this fact tends if anything to emphasize the order which the poet has imposed upon it. The section devoted to the Cave of Spleen is a well-enclosed, sharply defined set-piece, in which a whole set of mental antics are categorized with inventive virtuosity and self-delighting exactitude. The examples succeed one another in line-units or in couplets, the vivid suppleness of Pope's verse modulating without strain into triumphant couplet-finalities. The whole is a highly ordered and stylized vision of disorder, well-wrought urn rather than melting-pot, a series of brilliant show-cases rather than a teeming market-place.[50] Even though its point is to display absurdities of fantasy, each absurdity tends to have a coherence or logic of its own:

> Here living *Teapots* stand, one Arm held out,
> One bent; the Handle this, and that the Spout (IV.49-50).

Once grant the fantastic assumption, the rest follows exactly, and Pope lovingly registers each consequential gesture or attitude. Similarly with 'Maids turn'd Bottels': if the fantasy takes this particular form, it follows that erotic yearnings will be for a cork. The satisfactions of the logic predominate over any readily imaginable reality, let alone a reality typical enough to take its place in an allegorical account of Spleen, as though the category of cork-craving maidens who thought they were bottles were to be taken for granted as an everyday thing,[51] and the poet only needed to remind us where the fantasy originated. Part of the wit depends on the implied claim of typicality, contrasted with the fact that what we are given is a fiction whose wild logicality hardly seems *possible* in the real world, let alone typical, with Pope dominating the whole nonsense (his own fiction, and the girls' yearnings, both fantastic) with a cheeky detachment.

Ginsberg's passage, on the other hand, has neither the detachment, nor the neat logic. He is expressing a suffering involvement with the persons he describes, without any assurance that their doings are merely mental fancies which we are invited to patronize, and without any of the self-completing congruence of Pope's cork-and-bottle image. Where Pope's maids do not actually mate with their corks, Ginsberg's persons are presumed to perform their strange couplings in fact as well as fantasy (and if fantasy at all, the fantasy of actual sexual longings, rather than that of stylized allegories of longings), so that what is conveyed is the ragged authenticity of sexual loneliness, or deviation, or individualism—or normality! 'A bottle of beer a sweetheart...': the unexpected merging of the normal and the unorthodox, and the taking for granted of their coexistence, are close to Swift, but not to Pope.

The same is true of Mailer's juxtapositions: 'a queer, a cop, a crook', 'a dog, a cop, a cannibal'.[52] As with Swift, the taking for granted is edged with a strident, witty sense of discord, although Mailer's wit, like Ginsberg's, suggests the dissolution or melting down (as in a 'heat-forge')[53] of categories, rather than, like Swift's, their *violation*. Hence an element of constatation, rather than, as in Swift, of a mock-constatation really implying the classical satirist's moral outrage. But Mailer's constatation, though lacking in outrage, is hardly cool. Indeed, it is fraught with drama, and even melodrama, enough to make the outraged satirist seem cool in comparison. Just before the tabulated list of party guests, Mailer's narrator tells us not only that its categories are not neatly distributed among the people present, but also that it was found on a dead body, after a party. The fact contributes a quizzical note of violence, different from Swift in its melodramatic immediacy, but also suggesting a queer resemblance. For in both writers, the anguished discontinuities of the catalogues issue from men in extreme situations: the body of a suicide or murder victim, a crazed Gulliver, a modest proposer of cannibal schemes. This is one of the things which makes it appropriate that Swift should sometimes be thought of in relation to a modern literature of violent and extreme situations, and significant (though hardly, as a value judgment, persuasive) that Jack Kerouac should have chosen to praise William Burroughs as 'the greatest satirical writer since Jonathan Swift'.[54]

Mailer's strange and haunting piece, with its imagery of spirals and of impasses breached by violence,[55] is one which (as I have already suggested) Swift would have understood. The religious aberrants of Swift's *Tale* are given not only to sexual excess but to aggressive violence,[56] and he would also have understood the peculiar combination of violence and a sense of the sacred, the use of a 'melodramatic mode' of imagination 'to renew contact with the sacred', which runs through Mailer's story and many of his other writings;[57] just as he might have sensed that behind the rhetorical devices of catalogue and anaphora there is often a sacral element of celebration or denunciation, of liturgical repetition or chant[58] (Allen Ginsberg habitually opens recitations of his poems with a spell of mantric incantation). As an anti-rhetorician and scourge of 'enthusiasm', he would also have repudiated these things, instead of allowing his pained exuberance to turn into that high-pitched Mailerian jauntiness which can celebrate fear and self-importance, splendours and miseries, held in a single view. Swift's response to Mailer's compulsively spiralling forms of experience, inextricable and 'vibrating with sensuality and anguish',[59] would be to impose a rigorous absolute upon them, after first trying to exorcize as much of them as he could into the mimicries of *A Tale of a Tub*. If both writers see themselves as in the destructive element immersed, Swift keeps his head above water, precariously, lightening his load by parodic rejection, and clinging to solidities of discipline and faith, while Mailer's way is to come out the other side (or, as Marion Faye himself put it in *The Deer Park*, to 'push to the end ... and come out—he did not know where, but there was experience beyond experience').[60]

Mailer frequently toys with the idea of violence as containing sacred, or at least deeply cleansing, properties, noting in 'The White Negro' the hipster's ability 'to envisage acts of violence as the catharsis which prepares growth',[61] and exploring in fiction and in essays the possibility of self-renewal and of religious experience through extreme or violent action. The same is true of the 'vibrations' of 'sensuality'. He speaks of the awakening of the senses through sexual experience as an avenue to God, and is interested in Reichian notions of the relationship of orgasm and God.[62] If his references to hipster or 'White Negro' attitudes on such matters, or his reference to Reich, are not always clear of irony, he is always ready to assert the sacramental quality of violence and of orgasm, and their power to renew and purify. In *The Prisoner of Sex* he speaks of both suicide and coitus as 'religious acts'[63] and says that the 'projects' (the term, by a happy accident, has Swiftian associations, though not the usual Swiftian sense) 'of the months and the years can be overturned, or put in disorder, or accelerated by sudden new sexual experience, by a fierce fuck which lights a fire, or a splendor of velvet in the night'.[64] And in the story with which I am principally concerned, the 'Prologue to a Long Novel', there is this excited speculation on Time, not 'passive' or 'onanistic' Time ungalvanized by murder and love, 'but Time as growth, Time as the excitations and chilling stimulations of murder, Time as the tropical envelopments of love ... the hard of a hoodlum or the bitch on her back looking for the lover whose rhythm will move her to the future'.[65] The image of orgasm as marking decisive and violent 'leaps' in the process of history, both private and cosmic, inner and outer, is recurrent in Mailer.[66] It is partly derived from the Yeats of 'Leda and the Swan' and 'The Second Coming' (it has already been noted that Mailer regards the latter as 'the best short poem of the twentieth century').[67] Like Yeats, Mailer finds the notion of such 'leaps' seductive as well as frightening. The contrast with Swift's treatment in the Digression on Madness of the sexually determined innovations and revolutions in Empire, Philosophy and Religion is in one sense very great. But the distinctions between Swift and the later writers are not in every way clear cut. All three, for example, have a vivid sense of the close interinvolvement of excrement and sex:[68]

> ...Love has pitched his mansion in
> The place of excrement.

The stark grandeurs of Yeats's rhetoric are not in Mailer. In being more intimately specific, less grandly aloof from the details, Mailer is rather closer to Swift. He is even sometimes satirical in a manner basically similar to Swift's. The novel *Why Are We in Vietnam?* links military conquest with a pungent mixture of frustrated sexuality and anal fixation not essentially different from Swift's exposure in the Digression on Madness of the forces which cause 'a Great Prince to raise mighty Armies, and dream of nothing but Sieges, Battles, and Victories'.[69]

Mailer is not always satirical however. If he lacks the stark magniloquence of Yeats's Crazy Jane, defiantly proclaiming the proximity of excrement to love, he is not only much readier than Yeats ever was to celebrate the facts of this proximity in particular and graphic detail,[70] but no less inclined to be rhetorical about it in his own way. Feverish vibrancies of style are to be found in all Mailer's presentations of the anal or excremental factor as an integral part of the sacredness of sexual experience: witness the black-humorous ecstatics of the episode with the German girl in the second chapter of *An American Dream*,[71] or the language with which he praises Henry Miller as one of the discoverers of the divinity of the sexual act, who saw that it was 'the mirror of how we approach God through our imperfections, *Hot*, full of the shittiest lust'.[72]

This is one of the 'mysteries', in a holy or 'dark' sense of that term, to which Mailer, like many of Swift's derided moderns, is peculiarly drawn. In the same passage, Mailer says Henry Miller revealed to us 'that there were mysteries in trying to explain the extraordinary fascination of an act we can abuse, debase, inundate, and drool upon...'[73] And consider this sentence: 'the fruitfulness of his imagination led him into certain notions, which ... were not without their mysteries and their meanings, nor wanted followers to countenance and improve them.' This last sentence has a real Mailerian cadence, and something of Mailer's way with the large heady abstraction ('mysteries', 'meanings'). In this case, however, it is not Mailer praising Miller, but Swift mocking Brother Jack (I merely modernized the appearance, by decapitalizing the initial letters of nouns).[74] The entranced contemplation of Mysteries and Meanings is an activity which Swift's 'author' shares with Mailer and his narrators, and like them he readily proceeds from mystery to cosmic relationship and universal analogy, i.e. to what Swift dismissed in general as system-mongering, and in particular as 'that highly celebrated Talent among the *Modern* Wits, of deducing Similitudes, Allusions, and Applications, very Surprizing, Agreeable, and Apposite, from the *Pudenda* of either Sex, together with *their proper Uses*' (*Tale*, VII).[75]

Both Mailer and Miller offer good examples of this 'celebrated Talent', and they give them straight. Thus Miller, quoted approvingly by Mailer, 'deducing' cosmic relationship from female pudenda: 'perhaps a cunt, smelly though it may be, is one of the prime symbols for the connection between all things'.[76] In one sense, this is precisely the kind of arcane analogizing which Swift satirized in mad moderns. But some of his own 'Similitudes, Allusions, and Applications, very Surprizing', deduced 'from the *Pudenda* of either Sex', need also to be accepted as valid. The assertion of a close connection between erotic (including anal) processes, and the activities of conquest, philosophy and religion only damages Swift's victims if Swift is telling us that the connection is real, and not merely a parody of analogizing. Such connections are a staple of anti-Puritan satire,[77] but Swift is generalizing not only about Puritans or religious 'enthusiasts' at large, but also about other important human types.[78] It is wrong simply to credit him with proto-Freudian insights, and some of the critics who have written against Norman Brown's view of a proto-Freudian Swift have pointed out that the Digression on Madness and the *Mechanical Operation of the Spirit* expose a more or less conscious hypocrisy or self-deception rather than repressed unconscious drives.[79] But hypocrisy will hardly cover such a case as that of Louis XIV, for example, unless we are to suppose that the king's conquests are simply motivated by a desire to conceal the fact of his anal fistula. Swift's pseudo-scientific description of how the connection works is of course all parody or spoof:[80]

> the *Vapour* or *Spirit*, which animated the Hero's Brain, being in perpetual Circulation, seized upon that Region of the Human Body, so renown'd for furnishing the *Zibeta Occidentalis*, and gathering there into a Tumor, left the rest of the World for that Time in Peace. Of such mighty Consequence it is, where those Exhalations fix; and of so little, from whence they proceed. The same Spirits which in their superior Progress would conquer a Kingdom, descending upon the *Anus*, conclude in a *Fistula* (*Tale*, IX).

But if this medical hocus-pocus, with its mechanics or psycho-mechanics of vapours and exhalations, is to be rejected as pseudo-science, the *fact* of the connection has, somehow, to stand. And since Freud's way of making such a connection medically intelligible was not available to Swift or to his readers, we are left with an undeclared implication that the 'mysteries' of analogy are indeed to some extent at work.

In this passage, one of the chief targets of Swift's mockery is the Paracelsan version of the 'connection between all things', namely that 'Microcosmical conceit' which, as summarized by Sir Thomas Browne, 'divideth the body of man' in accordance with 'the Cardinal points of the World': 'therefore working upon humane ordure, and by long preparation rendring it odoriferous, he terms it *Zibeta Occidentalis*, Western *Civet*; making the face the East, but the posteriours the *America* or Western part of his Microcosm.'[81] It is painful to imagine the use which Swift would have made of this geographical localizing had Norman Mailer and Allen Ginsberg, and their excremental cosmologizing, been available for parody in the *Tale*. Compare the excremental pantheism of Ginsberg's 'Magic Psalm':[82]

> Asshole of the Universe into which I disappear . . .
> Desire that created me . . .
> that makes my flesh shake orgasm of Thy Name . . .
> cover my belly with hands of moss, fill up my ears with your
>   lightning, blind me with prophetic rainbows
> That I taste the shit of Being at last, that I touch Thy
>   genitals in the palmtree,
> that the vast Ray of Futurity enter my mouth . . .

with this scatological statement or mock-statement, which comes earlier than the previous example in the Digression on Madness:[83]

> the *upper Region* of Man, is furnished like the *middle Region* of the Air; The Materials are formed from Causes of the widest

> Difference, yet produce at last the same Substance and Effect. Mists arise from the Earth, Steams from Dunghills, Exhalations from the Sea, and Smoak from Fire; yet all Clouds are the same in Composition, as well as Consequences: and the Fumes issuing from a Jakes, will furnish as comely and useful a Vapor, as Incense from an Altar. Thus far, I suppose, will easily be granted me; and then it will follow, that as the Face of Nature never produces Rain, but when it is overcast and disturbed, so Human Understanding, seated in the Brain, must be troubled and overspread by Vapours, ascending from the lower Faculties, to water the Invention, and render it fruitful.

Like the other passage from the Digression, this not only derides analogizing (mysteries, systems, self-indulgent metaphor-making), but also condemns certain facts of human nature which the analogizing brings to light in this case: facts about the sources of 'enthusiasm', of deluded and self-centred idealisms, of the power-hunger which drives men to empire by conquest, or to 'innovation' in philosophy and religion. The passage comes early in the Digression, and thus follows almost immediately upon the satire of the Aeolists in the previous Section, sharing with it an imagery of vapours and other gaseous activity.[84] Although the Aeolist satire is ostensibly linked with Brother Jack and the Puritans, that fact is only revealed at the end, almost as an afterthought, and even then in terms which positively suggest a wider application.[85] The Aeolist satire as a whole, apart from the brief mention of Jack, generates wider applications *a fortiori*. And in the Digression on Madness which follows, things widen even further, first by the introduction of the three types of innovator (conquerors, and propagators of new philosophies and new religions), and then by the universalizing force of the passages about fools and knaves, and about the Academy of Modern Bedlam. So the analogizing passage I quoted is teasingly poised between a relatively localized satire of specific human types and a universal exposure of the madness-and-badness of the whole race. The whole passage see-saws characteristically between opposite implications, both true. Mysteries of analogy are mocked as obscurantist hocus-pocus, yet positively exploited to reveal factual truths. The truths refer to deplorable particulars, yet turn into generalizations about the human animal. Satire with a strongly antimetaphysical flavour tends towards metaphysical statement.

Because Swift's contempt for 'system', for Clothes' Philosophies, Aeolist universes and their like, as well as for the emotional ecstatics (of religious fervour, learned pedantry, or whatever) which go into their making, remains so strong, any universalizing pattern he proposes will seem metaphysically incomplete. Generalizations which tend to 'system' are mocked or undercut, yet there is a tendency for satirical exposures to become globally inclusive. Attacks on the Puritans, for example, tend to expose the whole unregenerate nature of man, because Puritan turpitudes are embodiments of universal human impulse, unchecked. But this universalizing implication is itself metaphysically incomplete or untidy. This is partly because the immediate and *overt* targets are the Puritans or other peccant groups, not (or not always) mankind as a whole, and the larger implication, though aggressively vivid, remains undefined, an unsettling loose end generated by energies of style rather than crystallized into clear inclusive statement. The entranced invocation of universal fusion in Ginsberg's 'Magic Psalm' outdoes the analogies which Swift mocks. Part of Swift's mockery is directed at religious ecstatics of a kind to which Ginsberg's psalm, somewhat extremely, belongs. Ginsberg might be said to have actualized, or made literally true, a satire which Swift had presumably intended as, in the first place, metaphorical. The Puritan enthusiasts and other religious individualists whom Swift was exposing did not normally worship in literally excremental terms, and Swift's use of excremental imagery was not in this respect mainly a description or mimicry, however exaggerated, but a degrading insult, which the Puritans would have taken as such. Swift knew that they would deny the accusation, and that they would normally agree with him that such accusations, where true, would be profoundly damaging.[86] Although we should beware of oversimplifications which would translate Swift's satirical insults into Freudian insights, the fact that latter day 'enthusiasts' like Ginsberg and Mailer have openly incorporated excremental and anal-erotic experience into their religious vision and their religious celebrations does in some ways bear on the universality of his satiric reach. If they can recognize and celebrate as human fact the connections between excremental and religious experience which Swift and his Puritan victims would see only as insulting metaphor, it becomes possible to say that behind Swift's use of the metaphor lurks an unacknowledged truth which is more than metaphorical.

What is certain is that in this, as in other spheres, 'moderns' of a later day have taken to themselves, often without any consciousness of Swift, some of the most outrageous details of Swiftian mockery. Mock-blasphemies to the effect that 'the Fumes issuing from a Jakes, will furnish as comely and useful a Vapor, as Incense from an Altar' have in Swift a quality of heady daring, of witty experiment with the outrageous, which transcend satire and tend towards a certain kind of Mailerian utterance:[87]

> To say that the oceans of the world are but one tear of God's compassion is a metaphor so excruciatingly empty that the flatulence of a celibate must have been its first wind. But to believe that God like man can suffer occasionally from diarrhoea is an infectious thought that stimulates all but the churchly and the vicious.

The *Tale* would have categorized such exuberant blasphemy as 'the very *bottom* of all the *Sublime*' (Preface), an example of what the Aeolist or Wind chapter pillories as that lamentable tendency whereby[88]

> the mind of Man, when he gives the Spur and Bridle to his Thoughts, doth never stop, but naturally sallies out into both extreams of High and Low, of Good and Evil.

But we have seen that this satire of the 'extreams of High and Low' modulates into the genuinely ambiguous sublimities of the Bird of Paradise,[89] with a suggestion of quick Swiftian forays into the heights he mocks. And it is possible to feel, as Wotton and other contemporary readers of the *Tale* did, that mock-blasphemies about the fumes of jakes and altars have also about them a primary blasphemous tang.[90]

The fact that Swift satirized what Ginsberg or Mailer propound does not produce the clear-cut distinctions between them that we might expect. Instead, teasing similarities and approximations jostle with the stark oppositions. Mailer's jibe about 'the flatulence of a celibate' sketches out a familiar Swiftian connection between inadequate religions, sexual frustration, and wind, although Swift could probably have endorsed the sentiment whose 'flatulence' is scorned by Mailer, and repudiated (despite a vigorous flirtation with such 'infectious thoughts') the excremental theism which Mailer sets up in its stead. Swift too mocked the Romish rule of priestly celibacy (*Tale*, IV), although he himself remained celibate, and jeered at the Roman clergy for taking whores in the place of wives.[91] As for 'the churchly and the vicious', Swift would doubtless not have equated the one with the other as totally as Mailer's passage appears to do, but his writings abound in exposures of the arrogance, cruelty, hypocrisy, venality and careerism not only of Romish priests and Dissenting ministers, but of men of his own church, men of aldermanly discretion who grow fat on the common forms, while persons of real distinction and integrity suffer neglect, or disgrace, or worse.[92]

As a member of an institutional church, and a strong believer in institutions, and as one who would have felt bound to reject Mailer's 'infectious thought', Swift must finally be counted among 'the churchly'. The category, for Mailer, would include not only Papist and Puritan, but also anyone whom Swift would accept as orthodox. Where Swift attacked the Dissenting sects for their departure from sanctioned institution and their assertion of religious individualism, Mailer would reject that form of individualism as itself institutional. The religious experience invoked by Mailer or by Ginsberg is a matter of personal epiphany, free of sectarian codification, an extremer manifestation of 'the *Spirit* ... proceeding entirely from within'[93] than anything envisaged in the *Mechanical Operation of the Spirit* or in the *Tale*. In so far as Mailer or Ginsberg envisage a genuine collectivity of religious experience, that collectivity is non-sectarian, fluid, uncodified, that of the mass-rally or the love-in, of indeterminate membership and free-flowing half-secularized 'soul'. Swift understood the psycho-mechanics of such gatherings, and his *Discourse Concerning the Mechanical Operation of the Spirit* gives as good an account as anything in the later writers of the play of erotic incantation and the stimulus of rhythmic movement, and even of the role of drugs and the resemblance to Eastern cults ('the *Jauguis* [i.e. Yogis], or enlightened Saints of *India*' are specifically mentioned).[94] Even so, Swift's *Mechanical Operation* is more concerned with sectarian groups, however fragmented or divisive or individualist, than with wholly free-lance 'operators', so that not only Swift himself but even those whom he attacks belong to organized religious associations. It is a paradox and an irony that, in a truly 'modern' context in which personal values have more force than those of the group, it is the highly private modes of 'vision' in Ginsberg or in Mailer which reach out to inclusive notions of universal harmony, whilst Swift, a rigid and conservative institutionalist of an older time, is shy of any suggestion that things hang together in a cosmic, or any other, arrangement.

The 'perpetual Game at *Leap-Frog* between ... *Flesh* ... and ... *Spirit*'[95] (Swift's phrase, in a passage which Wotton found blasphemous, because it 'affects ... not the Private Interpretations of this or that Particular Sect' but St Paul himself on carnality,[96] although Swift was being satirical from an essentially Pauline point of view) is, then, one which both Ginsberg and Mailer choose frankly to play. Both find a sense of connection with the universe, and a vision of the universal connection between all things, through a form of sexual-excremental epiphany. A difference between them, however, is that Ginsberg's 'Magic Psalm' has a Whitmanian openness, a quality of free, exuberant indulgence of the whole experience, including the powerful homosexual aspect of the anal imagery, without inhibitions of guilt, or at least with a strong desire to annihilate guilt. Mailer, by contrast, rejects homosexuality and, more important, desiderates guilt. Both points are made, for example, in a passage in *Armies of the Night* in which, after scoffing at advocacies of a super-hygienic, guilt-free homosexuality with its 'medicated Vaseline', he asserts that he wanted his sex not only heterosexual but 'dirty, damned, even slavish' rather than 'clean, and without guilt':[97]

> For guilt was the existential edge of sex. Without guilt, sex was meaningless. One advanced into sex against one's sense of guilt, and each time guilt was successfully defied, one had learned a little more about the contractual relation of one's own existence to the unheard thunders of the deep.

Swift wanted 'the unheard thunders of the deep' to remain, as far as possible, unheard. Precisely for this reason, 'guilt' was *not* to be 'defied'. But he shared with Mailer a vivid sense both of guilt and of the thunders, and a fascination mixed with fear at their mutual interplay. Hence a Mailer jauntily boastful of 'his endless blendings of virtue and corruption'[98] is particularly intimately caught up (in a way which the verbal coincidence happily emphasizes, although Swift's terms have a special technical sense), in that fundamental law of the *Mechanical Operation of the Spirit*, 'That, *the Corruption of the Senses is the Generation of the Spirit*'.[99] Mailer takes to himself the term 'corruption' in a way which one suspects that Ginsberg would not wish to do. Mailer's witty speculation about the divine diarrhoea, and his easy acceptance of ecstasies which Swift would have regarded as scabrous, offer themselves to us in a way which we are free to take or leave. But there is also about them a quality of impish defiance, an edge of 'guilty' or mock-guilty self-enjoyment, a self-conscious cherishing of the 'infectious thought' and especially of the fact of having such infectious thoughts. They lack some of the full-hearted sense, found in Ginsberg, of sheer experience to be 'embraced', of vision validated wholly outside the scope of traditional normative sanctions.

Probably related to this is the fact that Mailer satirizes the things which he elsewhere supports, or to which he shows himself to be emotionally drawn, and which Swift would certainly have satirized him for supporting: some manifestations of hipsterdom, certain cults of violence, orgy, orgasm, or at least particular aspects of these cults.[100]

There is probably more satire in Mailer than in Ginsberg, and less celebration; more satire, and less denunciation in the manner of, for example, the Moloch section of 'Howl', if we define satire as in some ways more oblique and emotionally less open than denunciation (Swift likewise seldom denounces, at least in an open unironic sense, or in his own person, his nearest thing to 'Howl' being perhaps 'The Legion Club'); and more self-satire, though not necessarily more sense of humour, than in Ginsberg (not more self-satire than in Swift, however; but Swift was less coyly Shandean about it, and mocked Shandean coyness in advance).

If blasphemy means insulting 'the God of the churches', recognizing the proprieties of traditional worship and violating them as proprieties, both Mailer and Ginsberg are blasphemous. But it is also true that the force of these proprieties weighed more heavily on Swift's society than on our own, so that an 'infectious thought' about the fumes of jakes and altars would seem more deeply offensive in a Swiftian context, even though Swift merged such thoughts into his repudiation of mad 'moderns', foisting upon mere Puritans processes which Mailer, more outrageously, attributes to God. If Wotton, wilfully or otherwise, failed to distinguish the mimicked 'author' of the *Tale* from the mimicking anonymous satirist whom we know to be Swift, he is by no means the only critic, past or present, who felt that the *Tale* 'strikes at the very Root' of religion itself.[101] Swift's repudiation through irony of blasphemous notions in themselves less extreme than Mailer's, and of the activities which these notions are supposed to explain, seems shocking to many readers who understand the sectarian distinctions Swift is making, and who share his religious and political allegiances. It would not be altogether perverse to argue that whereas Swift, whatever his conscious intentions, put religious experience under satirical scrutiny, the openly 'blasphemous' Mailer and Ginsberg seek through the very 'blasphemies' to reintroduce a sense of the sacramental in a world where religious experience is largely felt to be lacking.[102] But Mailer is perhaps like Swift, and unlike Ginsberg, in courting certain frissons of offence, half-guilty pleasures of a wit indulged *as irreverent*.[103]

Swift did, however, stop short of expressing, or even of attributing to the Puritans, the notion which both Mailer and Ginsberg express, that God himself (as distinct from certain classes of his worshippers, in more or less peccant or pathological ways) has anal processes, and sexual energies, and that this is good. Mailer's God is a confused figure, whose lineaments derive, in heady mixture, from Sade, Nietzsche, Reich and various older Manichaean and Romantic sources. He has human vices and human weaknesses, is engaged in a war with the Devil which *he might lose.*[104] Unlike Swift's God, absolute and invulnerable, Mailer's is neither all-powerful nor all-good, capable of 'moral corruption'.[105] He contains the vulnerabilities and the potentialities of man, whether on a grand scale, as for example a (somewhat old-fashioned) Don Juanesque hero: 'And who was there to know that God was not the greatest lover of them all?'[106] or, in the same final paragraph of *The Prisoner of Sex* (in an even more quaintly traditional image), as one of the meek and persecuted of the earth: '(Unless dear God was black and half-Jewish and a woman, and small and mean as mother-wit. We will never know until we take the trip. And so saying realized he had been able to end a portentous piece in the soft sweet flesh of parentheses.)' On this Shandean, or *Tub*-like, note of simpering self-consciousness, *The Prisoner of Sex* closes. By a syntactical accident, it is not at once clear whether the 'he' in the final sentence refers to God, or to Mailer, who nowadays writes of himself in the Third Person. Perhaps the ambiguity is only more or less accidental, for the Mailerian God, made in man's image rather than vice versa, easily shades into Mailer's favourite Third Person, or Number One. 'Yes God is like Me, only more so', says the 'author' of 'Prologue to a Long Novel' at the end of *Advertisements for Myself*, in a climax in which wit jostles nervously and unequally with the high pitched ecstatics, as the 'author' speculates whether he is part of the divine diarrhoea, and/or a spark of the cosmic libido:[107]

> am I already on the way out? a fetor of God's brown sausage in His time of diarrhoea, oozing and sucking and bleating like a fecal puppy about to pass away past the last pinch of the divine sphincter with only the toilet of Time, oldest hag of them all, to spin me away into the spiral of star-lit empty waters.
>
> So I approach Him, if I have not already lost Him, God, in His destiny, in which He may succeed, or tragically fail, for God like Us suffers the ambition to make a destiny more extraordinary than was conceived for Him, yes God is like Me, only more so.
>
> Unless—spinning instead through the dark of some inner Space—the winds are icy here—I do no more than delude myself, fall back into that hopeless odyssey where libido never lingers, and my nature is nothing other than to search for the Devil while I carry with me the minds of some of you.

Such self-glorying and such heady terrors would, of course, have revolted Swift. But he could claim to have recognized, or, in the phrase of Eliot's Tiresias, to have 'foresuffered' it.[108] Although he does not seem to have ascribed, even to the Puritans, the notion of a God who experiences diarrhoea and orgasm, he not only accused them of experiencing both one and the other in their worship of God, but also of adorning 'their Divinity ... with all such Qualities and Accomplishments, as themselves seem most to value and possess'. In the same passage of the *Mechanical Operation* he accuses them of being unable (as Mailer professes himself to be unable) to distinguish between God and the Devil, having 'most horribly confounded the Frontiers of both', and not knowing 'whether such and such Influences come into Mens Minds, from above or below, or whether certain Passions and Affections are guided by the Evil Spirit or the Good'.[109] In a related passage in section VIII of the *Tale*, he shows the exalted visions of the Aeolists to be closely related to certain thrilling fears of the Devil, not unlike the terror of the Mailerian visionary, contemplating the icy winds of his inner space as he wonders whether he is searching for the Devil or realizing his potential Divinity:[110]

> For it is with Men, whose Imaginations are lifted up very high, after the same Rate, as with those, whose Bodies are so; that, as they are delighted with the Advantage of a nearer Contemplation upwards, so they are equally terrified with the dismal Prospect of the Precipice below.

The only essential difference is that Mailer knows he enjoys such terrors. The Puritans presumably did not know, but Swift knew it for them: that is one of the implications of the whole system of interpenetrating 'extreams of High and Low' in section VIII. And the further feeling, which Mailer's speaker finds not unwelcome, is that in his apprehensions of Godhead he might not only, in fact, be searching for the Devil, but also carrying 'with me the minds of some of you', corresponds to Swift's fears about the Mechanical Operators of the Spirit and their following of proselytes, or the atavistic Enthusiast or Innovator of the Digression on Madness, the activity of whose vapours transfers itself into others 'by a secret necessary Sympathy', and who, like Descartes, gathers them 'rapt and drawn within his own Vortex'.[111] For,[112]

> when a Man's Fancy gets *astride* on his Reason, when Imagination is at Cuffs with the Senses, and common Understanding, as well as common Sense, is Kickt out of Doors; the first Proselyte he makes, is Himself, and when that is once compass'd, the Difficulty is not so great in bringing over others; A strong Delusion always operating from *without*, as vigorously as from *within*.

We recall that Swift's Free Thinker sought to force 'all the World to think as he does, and by that means make them *Free Thinkers* too'.[113] He is like the Digression's Madman, bent on 'subduing Multitudes to his own *Power*, his *Reasons* or his *Visions*'.[114] Mailer does not talk of forcing. What he presumably means are certain titillations of empathy, interminglings of '*infectious* thought', which correspond to less extreme forms of the Swiftian transference of vapours. For Swift, as we have seen, Free Thinkers were not only tyrannical religious deviants, atheist or nonconformist, but all of us. The term 'free thinking' slides deliberately from its restricted or technical sense to that more literal and inclusive sense which covers the unregulated thoughts of every human being. The tyrant, or anarchist, is within, and if the free thoughts were allowed to emerge 'in the crude indigested manner, as they come into [even the wisest man's] head, he would be looked upon as raving mad'.[115] The excitements of a perpetual restless doubt, like the allied excitements of Enthusiasm High and Low, are things which Swift was not prepared, like Mailer, to indulge. But there is no pretence that he is immune from their dangers. Mailerian 'infectious thoughts' needed 'to be kept under the strictest regulation';[116] not trumpeted as self-exalting, but subdued or concealed with every resource of inner discipline and institutional rule. Hence part of the urgency of Swift's stress on the authority of state-religions, on a visible, established, institutionalized Church, the more firmly institutionalized the better. Mailer's attitude to institutional Churches is, as we should expect, equal and opposite. Like Swift's religious individualist, he glories in a faith which is 'personal', so that the 'churches seem like prisons of the spirit to me'.[117] He says elsewhere that 'institutionally ... the organized religions are morally dead, that their net effect is deleterious ... They're murderers of the senses.'[118] Swift would probably have accepted certain aspects of the analysis but reversed the valuations.[119]

When Mailer said that his 'infectious thought' about divine diarrhoea would be repudiated only by 'the churchly and the vicious', he was saying in part what Swift would certainly agree with, that churches forbid such thoughts, or instruct us to hold them back. Swift's position is that the churches have the right and the duty to do this. If, as we saw, his own writing sometimes came to the brink of such 'infectious thought', his defence against accusations of 'Impiety and Immodesty'[120] on his own part was to protest that he was attacking not religion but *abuses* in religion. The 'infectious thought', *taken straight*, would for Swift be every bit as blasphemous as it seemed to Wotton. Swift is *asking* us not to take it straight, though we sometimes feel that his self-involvement with his 'author' is such that he cannot simply be severed from that 'author' at moments of ironic intensity. Perhaps it is because of this self-involvement that insistent denials are called for. If what Swift satirized in Puritans and Free Thinkers was sensed as a subversive potential in himself, and if the energies of his mockery tended to blur distinctions between mock-blasphemy or satirical imputations of blasphemy and blasphemy itself, it is not surprising that Swift should seek to deny or to disguise the fact. He regarded the concealment, as well as the subduing, of subversive thoughts as a legitimate part of moral discipline,[121] and it is to be expected that some things needed to be concealed from himself as well as from others. The outer defences provided by institutions, laws and rules of behaviour, and the inner defences which formed the conscious parts of moral discipline, were reinforced by strategies of style. Any self-commitment to dangerous thoughts, any liability to their 'infection', was resisted and disguised, from himself and others, by every ironic feat available to him.

One of the functions of his 'masks' is precisely to ensure this basic submission to tradition and rule. Consider the rhetorical lists or catalogues I discussed earlier. If the lists of Rabelais, or Swift, or Mailer are energies of chaos, they are all also a kind of indecorous self-display, a copiousness of the personality which asserts itself by overwhelming the ordinary reticences and sufficiencies of discourse. Rabelais and Mailer, differ as they might from each other, make no bones about writing *Advertisements for Themselves*. But if, as I believe, self-assertion occurs on a similar scale in Swift, it can only be released at its most exuberant by Swift's hiding behind a figure who, like the *Tale*'s 'author', is *satirized* for advertising himself. Swift's 'masks', and especially Gulliver, are sometimes spoken of as fully-fledged characters, but they are all much too crude, and need to be. They have to be crude enough to permit a freedom of Swiftian self-implication without turning into rounded autobiographical figures in one direction, or independent novelistic creations in the other. Their crudeness, their heavy adaptability to the twists and turns of ironic self-expression, their transparently two-dimensional quality provide the elbow room and a kind of solid base for the complex and nervous agilities of Swift's own voice to deploy themselves. They provide also many piquancies of contrast, and a defence. The defence is against self-implication becoming *identification*.[122] A dull and lifeless figure such as Gulliver is in himself (that is, considered in abstraction from his role of ceaseless and varying interaction with the Swiftian voice), proclaims his separation from the directing intelligence of Swift through our sense of his sheer boring mediocrity. The way in which a dull figure like Gulliver makes possible some strong discharges of Swiftian feeling differs somewhat from the way in which the *Tale*'s 'author' (anything but dull, despite assertions of his dulness) performs the same function. The more vitality a Swiftian 'mask' has, the more his formal *unreality*. The 'author', as we have seen, has no name and none of the characterological accoutrements (wife, family, acquaintances, jobs) of Gulliver, nor the relatively schematic identity of the Modest Proposer. He is, as I noted earlier,[123] an anonymous mass of energies rather than any sort of 'character', and I think that the interaction between him and Swift may be correspondingly closer for this strangely vital unreality. But again, if he is anything in the formal sense, he is stupid and mad and bad, and thus, however close to Swift, cannot be identified with him. This truism means that the outrageous egotism of the 'author' cannot openly be attributed to Swift, however much Swift is 'advertising himself' by way of it. And it also constitutes an attack, on grounds both of morals and of decorum, against unruly passions and their self-regarding expression.

All Swift's speakers (Gulliver, the Modest Proposer, the *Tale*'s 'author') are thus, however different from one another, in one important sense rigidly distinguished from their creator. And although Swift is fundamentally committed to the critique contained in Gulliver's lists of disreputable human types, e.g. in IV.xii ('a Lawyer, a Pick-pocket, a Colonel, a Fool . . .'),[124] he is yet separated from the state of petulant and anti-social hysteria that Gulliver has fallen into. The Gulliver who faints at the touch of his wife and spends his time with the horses in his stable (IV.xi)[125] has reached a point where his creator is safe from literal and complete identifications with him. His inordinate list contains direct satiric power, but also a partial detachment from the desperation implied in Gulliver's crazy petulance, perhaps even an authorial superiority to the hysteria of inordinate lists. By contrast, Mailer, who begins by saying that his list in 'Prologue to a Long Novel' was found on another man's dead body, ends by assuming total responsibility for the list, and total loyalty to the mysterious, ecstatically bewildering, value of its truth:[126]

> as some of you may have sensed by now, the list I offered up to
> your amusement is from me, and I am, oh yes, now I know who
> I am or was, I am the dead man on the floor, for so I am, yes (what a
> pure moment of grief at all that has not been done), I am in the
> endless deliberate instant of the vision given by death, the million
> dying spasms of the radiating consciousness of words, this last of me,

> wailing within, turbulent with the terror that I no longer know where I am, nor if there are voices to hear me and answer back.

'I am the dead man on the floor' seems partly to belong to the idiom of Whitman's *Song of Myself*, where the poet asserts his relationship with the whole world, all mankind ('In all people I see myself'),[127] all things and all forms of experience, including death.[128] But Mailer, or his narrator, seems to go further than Whitman. In Whitman, the universal relationship is not exclusively claimed to reside in the *identity* of the poet with all other things but is also in some cases, more loosely, a matter of kinship and of sympathy. He does not say only 'I am' all other things, but sometimes says:[129]

> And these tend inward to me, and I tend outward to them,
> And such as it is to be of these more or less I am,
> And of these one and all I weave the song of myself.

Thus where Mailer's narrator says of the suicide or murder victim at the party 'I am the dead man on the floor', Whitman says 'The suicide sprawls on the bloody floor of the bedroom,/I witness the corpse . . . /I mind them or the show or resonance of them . . .',[130] or (the idiom here is beautifully relaxed and unMailerian) 'as to you Corpse I think you are good manure, but that does not offend me'.[131] The difference seems to be greater than that between varying intensities of metaphor. We know where we stand in Whitman, because *Song of Myself* is a formal celebration of relationship in a recognized rhapsodic mode. But in Mailer, the identity with the dead man is delivered with the peculiar literalness, and also with the intensity of impact, that come from its being the explanation or pay-off of what had so far been the 'mystery' (I use the word here in the special sense which pertains to tales of 'suspense', although 'mystery' in the sense in which Swift attributed it to 'dark' authors is present too) of the identity of the body: 'as some of you may have sensed by now, the list I offered . . . is from me, and I am . . . the dead man on the floor'. The sensational nature of this disclosure, as well as its apparent literalness, give it an obsessive force absent from the freer vatic utterance of Whitman. Partly for this reason, Mailer's fictional 'I', describing a house-party in Provincetown, where the real Mailer has a house, in a book of Mailer's own *Advertisements for Myself*, seems even more urgently and intimately authorial than the undisguised autobiographical 'I' of 'Walt Whitman, a kosmos, of Manhattan the son'.[132]

He is not, of course, an officially identifiable authorial figure, like

Whitman's 'I'. He has not Whitman's solidity of presence. In some ways he is like Beckett's Unnamable: 'I do not know who I am nor where I am, nor even if literally I write.'[133] One critic has called him an 'amorphous, choric presence',[134] and in many ways his floating and disorderly consciousness, lacking a clear categorizable identity, and yet maintaining an intimate closeness to his creator, resembles that of the 'author' of the *Tale*, with this proviso always that he is not a formal opposite to his creator, as in Swift, but a projection of him, somewhat as in Sterne. In a formal sense, Mailer's narrator oscillates between being pure fictional creation and a spokesman for some of his author's views. This oscillation is fundamental to Mailer's method. He says of Sergius O'Shaugnessy, who narrates the related story 'The Time of her Time'[135] but not 'Prologue to a Long Novel', 'He was not altogether different from me. But he certainly wasn't me.'[136] The 'Prologue' is classified as fiction in the volume's 'Second Table of Contents'. But it also has the sectional or alternative title of 'Advertisements for Myself on the Way Out' (the phrase is echoed by the narrator, with what seems like design, when, on the final page of the story and of the whole book, he asks: 'am I already on the way out?') Not only does its status as part of a book of collected *Advertisements for Myself*, which it shares with other pieces, inevitably cause an authorial gloss to rub off on its 'I', but its positioning at the end or culmination of the book (a deliberate and pointed positioning, and also somewhat Shandean, because it is a 'Prologue' which appears at the end, and because, as Mailer tells us, it is out of sequence in other ways too, which 'seemed more agreeable to me')[137] gives that 'I' a special prominence, a heightened and personal note of climax and of authorial valediction. These strategies, and the obvious fact that the work expresses a deep part of himself and gives voice to many sentiments which he expresses elsewhere in his own name (notably, as Mailer himself tells us, on the subject of 'Hip as a religion'),[138] are testimony to that autobiographical element whose powerful, intimate ambiguity is reflected in the following statement:

> In 'The White Negro', as in 'The Time of Her Time', and in 'Advertisements For Myself on the Way Out' can be found the real end of this muted autobiography of the near-beat adventurer who was myself. With these three seeds, let us say the book has its end.... So a hint of the best and worst of what really happened over the years of these advertisements may live in this last part which has nothing and everything to do with me.[139]

'Nothing and everything to do with me': stated thus, the relationship suggests Swiftian fluidities of convergence and divergence, without the element of formal or formulaic opposition. In *Why Are We in Vietnam?*, somewhat exceptionally, this formal opposition does exist, in something like the Swiftian sense, for the principal voice in that novel is that of an anti-speaker, expressing an ethos whose political consequences, implied in the title, are repudiated by Mailer. There are several consciousnesses in that novel, and Mailer plays pointedly on our uncertainty as to which one is being expressed at a given moment, and, as in 'Prologue to a Long Novel', as to its sheer identity, existence, namability (in a sense corresponding to Beckett's Unnamable, even though in this case the principal names are given): 'if you are really reading this and I am really writing it (which I don't know—it's a wise man who knows *he* is the one who is doing the writer's writing...).'[140] But these fluidities and uncertainties of identity are themselves tokens of a peculiar closeness to the author. When D.J., the satirized main speaker of *Why Are We in Vietnam?*, tells us that we are 'up tight with a mystery, me, and this mystery can't be solved because I'm the center of it and I don't comprehend,...',[141] the problem and the 'mystery' (the meaning of 'mystery', as in 'Prologue to a Long Novel', has overtones of mystery-novel, as well as the larger, main 'dark Author' sense) are central Mailerian ones. 'Only a dreary mind cannot bear mystery' says the more directly authorial speaker of the 'Prologue', as he refuses to introduce himself because he does not know who he is, and lacks the 'armature' of name and 'character'.[142] The word armature is of interest because in one of the formally autobiographical or confessional 'advertisements' which link the various scattered items in *Advertisements for Myself*, and which correspond in structure and style to the prefatory and digressive set-pieces of Swift's *Tale*, Mailer used the word in relation to his own personal 'character', saying that he had decided to use his autobiographical 'personality' as the 'armature' of his book of miscellaneous pieces. He notes that the writings concerned belonged to a period 'when my ideas were changing character faster than my person', so that this 'armature' may be inferred to be both imposed on the flux and part of it, both a falsification of the true fluidity of his character (if we take 'armature' in its sense of artificial stiffening, as in the final 'Prologue to a Long Novel'), yet also one of the truths of his being.[143] For, in context, 'to use my personality as the armature of this book' means not merely to make coherent the disparate material, but also and mainly to reprint the 'worst of my work' along with the rest, the parts which 'are superficial, off-balance, too personal at times', thus registering the living totality of an untidy record.[144] In the directly authorial passage, as against the quasi-authorial 'Prologue', 'armature' becomes inclusive of all the shifts and changes in Mailer himself. If the term is remembered in such a way as to incite cross-reference when we meet it again in the 'Prologue', the difference of *verbal* usage may be seen to reflect the *essential similarity* between the real author's and the quasi-author's conceptions of true 'existential' being. 'Character', in the old, traditional or Square sense, must be abandoned in favour of a Hip sense, in which it is 'seen as perpetually ambivalent and dynamic'.[145] Thus viewed, character 'enters ... into an absolute relativity where there are no truths other than the isolated truths of what each observer feels at each instant of his existence' (cf. the boast of the *Tale*'s 'author' that what he is about 'to say is literally true this Minute I am writing').[146] This item of Hip phenomenology, to which Mailer is very largely though doubtless not wholly committed, is part of the background to the 'unnamability', the non-identity of the speaker of the 'Prologue'. More generally, 'What is consequent ... is the divorce of man from his values, the liberation of the self from the Super-Ego of society ... The nihilism of Hip proposes as its final tendency that every social restraint and category be removed...'[147]

In Swift's *Tale*, the undisciplined flow of roles occurs not mainly through mystic transitions of consciousness, but through the giddiness of the hack 'author' and Swift's own shifts and modulations of ironic tone. The 'author' is pedant, Puritan, journalist, bookseller and Swiftian spokesman as the needs of Swift's irony dictate, and if he, like Beckett's Unnamable or the 'I' of Mailer's 'Prologue', has no name, this is not entirely because his identity is altogether in doubt in the same radical way as theirs, but partly because he stands for all bad authors. If he cannot be given a name, it is because many names will fit equally well. He and others are all equally able to write the same anonymous works, and he enters into an agreement with his bookseller, 'That when a Customer comes for one of these, and desires in Confidence to know the Author; he will tell him very privately, as a Friend, naming which ever of the Wits shall happen to be that Week in the Vogue...' (*Tale*, Conclusion).[148]

What is involved here is not an undeclared shifting of ironic voice, but the declared assumption of any of a set, however inexhaustible, of fixed labels. It is interesting that in Swift it should only be the undeclared process of role-changing that is in practice allowed a free and fluid intermerging, whereas the conscious act involves the simplified formality of a choice of names, crude and mendacious on the part of the 'author', and clearly categorized as such by Swift. When the speaker of Mailer's 'Prologue' announces his freedom and his intention to assume the consciousness of 'a house, a tree, a dog, a cop, a cannibal',[149] or announces his identity with the dead author of a list of mixed and interpenetrating identities,[150] or engages 'no less than the fluid consciousness of a God',[151] he means more than a liberty to adopt any of a set of clearly demarcated labels. He, and Mailer, are bestowing on themselves and on one another an omnipotence of imagination whose pretensions Swift's Digression on Madness would describe as a wild self-centredness. The final page of the 'Prologue', and of the whole book, which asserts the notion of a God in Mailer's image ('God is like Me, only more so'), speaks of 'the eye of my I at home in the object-filled chaos of any ego I choose',[152] glorying in that convergence of high insight and ecstatic charlatanism ('my I' = 'my eye'!) which Swift's *Tale* and *Mechanical Operation* recognized and repudiated as self-exalting and undisciplined delusion (but see p. 143 for a glimpse of Swift himself in the mock-role of charlatan). Swift would have rejected the Keatsian 'camelion Poet',[153] just as he rejected that other noble emblem of the Romantic imagination, the Bird of Paradise. By a teasing coincidence, the '*Camelion* sworn Foe to *Inspiration*' is mentioned in the same paragraph as the Bird in section VIII of the *Tale*.[154] (The allusion is obscure, and Swift says in a mock-note of 1710 that he does 'not well understand what the Author aims at here', but one of the 'Thoughts on Various Subjects' offers a clue: 'The *Camelion*, who is said to feed upon nothing but Air, hath of all Animals the nimblest Tongue.')[155]

The claim of Mailer's speaker to 'any ego I choose' is authorial or quasi-authorial. It is a claim infrequently made in any thorough-going or favourable sense before the Romantic period,[156] whether in poetry, as in Keats, or in the novel, as when Flaubert describes himself among the creations of *Madame Bovary*, as himself at once man, woman, horses, leaves, wind, words.[157] In Mailer, as in much Romantic writing, such operations of the sympathetic imagination are related to a neoplatonizing sense of the Oneness of the Universe.[158] But it is of interest that when a Renaissance neoplatonist like Pico della Mirandola praises man's chameleon-like power to transform himself into all other beings, he is not talking of imaginative metamorphoses but, moralistically and theologically, of man's ability to rise to spiritual heights, finally becoming 'He Himself Who made us', or to lower himself to the level of animal or plant.[159] This is a far cry from the unmoralized egotistical exaltation of Mailer's 'any ego I choose', as well as from the peculiarly immediate literalness, the ostensibly unmetaphorical nature, of the Mailerian claim. Swift repudiated not only the egotisms of proto-Mailerian 'moderns', but also those neoplatonizing and other mystiques of a harmoniously unified cosmos, ancient and modern, on which they partly rest.

Cosmos and self, system and egotism, are intimately related in Swift's satiric vision. Clothes' Philosophies and visionary Aeolism seem mad to him not only because they violate a felt sense of the actual disharmony of things, but because such systems were the products of an exalted self-importance in the human imagination. Not only does their stubborn tidy-mindedness seem a wildly falsifying self-indulgence in itself, but their assertions of universal analogy and relationship offer to the individual Ego a heady sense of being an essential part of the cosmic scheme. When the speaker of Mailer's 'Prologue', in mystic union with the stream of things, says he is 'the dead man on the floor', who wrote the catalogue of party-guests, his very assumption of another Being, or 'any ego I choose', paradoxically enacts, so Swift would certainly feel, an excessive conception of his own Ego alone. Mailer's authorial involvement with his Protean speaker would be seen as an extension, and a confirmation, of this fact. That Mailer is, as we have seen, able sometimes to view his own highpitched states satirically, and that within him there is a part which rejects the extremes of Hip (Richard Poirier says very well, 'In Mailer the Hip there is always an intellectually nice boy trying to get out and increasingly finding, as intellectually nice boys often do, that the safest way to control the merely boisterous, the local and specific pleasure, is by way of metaphysics'),[160] does not alter the argument. Indeed, as in Sterne, self-satire easily becomes yet another self-indulgence, a further coil of the solipsistic spiral. Mailer's intimacy with his various masks and speakers is more like that of Sterne, teasingly and affectionately indulgent even in moments of partial repudiation, than that of Swift, where repudiation is absolute, even in moments of partial indulgence.

For partial indulgence, in Swift, there was. A free and easy adoption of identities was part of the 'modern' muddle. But as we have seen, Swift threw himself with a deep inwardness into the mimicry of such things: inconsistency, loose transitions, changes of stance, interchanges of name, living in a frenzied present of relentless, minute-by-minute self-renewal, seeking to create states of empathy which put the reader 'into the Circumstances and Postures of Life, that the Writer was in, upon every important Passage as it flow'd from his Pen' (*Tale*, Preface).[161] Further it is the very mimicry of some of these things which turns into an essential part of his primary (as distinct from parodic or topsy-turvy) ironic strategy. This strategy unsettles precisely because of inconsistency, loose transitions, changes of stance, and endless oscillations between a direct Swiftian presence and its fictional other, the entering into and out of the roles and voices of 'Dean, Drapier, Bickerstaff, or Gulliver!'[162] The energies of satiric exposure, and those of the anarchy it mocks, come very close together. This partly accounts for that tense rigidity of discrimination which formally separates the satirist from his masks, a rigidity analogous to that with which Swift asserts the claims of discipline and rules, and which is locked in a constant tussle with energies of undifferentiated flux, the subversive nature of the inner man, satirist and satirized alike.

These feats of formal distancing are very different from anything we find in Mailer. Mailer has spoken in *Advertisements for Myself* of his difficulties with first-person narration in novels.[163] And in his more recent works of commentary or factual reportage, *Armies of the Night*, *Miami and the Siege of Chicago*, *A Fire on the Moon*, *The Prisoner of Sex*, where he writes undisguisedly in his own person, he has adopted a third-person method of referring to himself, as, for example, the Historian, the Novelist, Aquarius, the Prisoner, and most of all, plain Mailer. But this distancing turns into a paradoxically closer proximity, for it is ostentatiously selfconscious, drawing attention to itself,[164] full of Shandean simper hardly disguised by the layer of male huskiness on top.[165] The new Third Person is but old First writ large, and Swift's mimicked 'I' is in some ways further from his creator than Mailer's autobiographical 'He'. But Swift too, as we saw, works teasingly between the Third and First persons, at certain levels blurring the distinction between the two, at others preserving it hard and clean. First and Third merge into one another more easily than either does with Second, the person of the reader, the bodily and tangible other who holds the book. This figure, each of us, *mon semblable*, *mon frère*, is probably more real in Swift than in Mailer, for Swift takes his existence seriously, if only to attack him. In Mailer, the reader is shadowy, an outlet for authorial nudges and coynesses, not an active participant in a dialogue or an interplay of experience, and this may be due to the Second Person's relatively greater irreducibility to Number One.

We never really get, in Mailer, the sort of confrontation between author and reader that occurs at the end of *Gulliver's Travels*. There, First and Second Persons confront one another, as Swift involves the reader in the attack on man which he puts in Gulliver's mouth. A Third Person who is not Swift, namely Gulliver himself, is ostentatiously present, but it is with Swift and not with Gulliver that the reader is having to come to terms. At the very moment when Gulliver expresses Swift's onslaught on mankind at its greatest climax of intensity, Gulliver is, in his deranged antics with his family, his horses and the rest, furthest away from the sort of person with whom Swift can be formally identified, or whom the reader will take seriously as anything more than a satiric device.

In any event, such distinctions do not arise with the fictional narrator of Mailer's 'Prologue', because the fictional 'I' merges so thoroughly into the authorial identity. This self-identification of the actual with the fictional author asks in some ways, and vividly, to be taken straight, whether as direct autobiographical truth or as novelistic realization or a mixture of the two. It is not, like Swift's self-implication in Gulliver, satiric or rhetorical. If Mailer's rendering of factual or fictional truths seeks total apprehension of a situation in its own right, satire and rhetoric, whether in Swift or others, tend instead to *exploit* the situation for moral or persuasive purposes, selecting and formalizing rather than 'rendering'. Where Mailer 'becomes' his narrator and his dead man, with all their anguished intensities, Swift *manipulates* Gulliver's alienation so that (while it is in a sense a grotesque enlargement of genuine Swiftian feelings) it appears mainly as an example of that satiric commonplace, the angry folly of trying to mend the world. Whatever the intimacies imposed by Swift's style (and we have seen that they are considerable), all satire and rhetoric entail an element of externality and detachment. Swift may charge his satiric commonplaces with a biting fervour, but he does not, like Mailer, incorporate them totally into his own personality. They remain, identifiably and of necessity, commonplaces. Swift's lists belong to a set style; they recall, for example, Rabelais, and derive part of their strength from our sense of their difference from Rabelais; at the very least, they come as a formula we expect to find in a certain kind of prose satire. Mailer's list may in fact, consciously or not, have a similar ancestry, but it proclaims no ancestry, existing only as a moment of experience or vision in its own right.

Similarly, Swift's formula about the folly of trying to mend the world needs to be seen, partly, as a formula, a satirist's procedure, identifiable, well-tried, measurably depersonalized. It consists partly of debating points which we know that Swift 'does not mean' in a literal, as distinct from a rhetorical, sense. An example is the notion that 'mending the world' is a matter so obvious and uncomplicated that the satirist has every reason to expect that action will be taken as soon as its need has been pointed out. The formula in a way mirrors a sentiment very close to Swift's whole temperament and outlook, that virtuous conduct is a matter of superimposing on our viciously complicated natures certain simple and self-evident disciplines and truths. But when Gulliver angrily complains that, more than six months after the publication of his *Travels*, 'I cannot learn that my Book hath produced one single Effect according to mine Intentions', the surprise is all his, not Swift's nor ours.[166] Swift's self-implication exists to the extent that he commits himself, through Gulliver, to a damaging gesture against us. But he is plainly protected from *identification* with Gulliver, for whom Swift's formulaic trick is no mere formula but a (literally) maddening fact.

'Madness' formally distinguishes Swift's 'authors' from himself. Here again a feat of categorizing bids to make saving distinctions. But 'madness' is an ambiguous concept. It may mean the mental hell of Grub Street dunces, which Swift officially rejects, or the righteous misanthropy of Gulliver, through which Swift is more directly expressing sentiments of his own. And it similarly embraces both the complacent delusions of the dunces, and the harsh truths of the satirist who pierces through these delusions. In a formal sense, Mailer is much readier than Swift to merge the two together. The speaker of the 'Prologue to a Long Novel', while displaying all the mental derangements which Swift ascribes to Grub Street and the Puritan conventicle, also carries without any sense of incongruity the classic tasks of unsentimental surgery which we associate with Swift the satirist himself:[167]

> My passion is to destroy innocence, and any of you who
> wish to hold to some part [of] that warm, almost fleshly
> tissue of lies, sentimentality, affectation and ignorance
> which the innocent consider love must be prepared instead
> for a dissection of the extreme, the obscene and the unsayable.

He here resembles not the *Tale*'s glazed 'author', extolling the sentimental lies which conceal an obscene reality and thus make possible 'The Serene Peaceful State of being a Fool among Knaves',[168] but Swift himself, who pierces through the ingenuous wonder of his 'author' to reveal the hideous truth of the flayed woman and dissected beau. I argued earlier that this passage of the Digression is one of those highly-charged Swiftian moments when formulaic distinctions between satirist and butt dissolve in a dangerous and aggressive blur, taking second place to fierce universalizing intensities. The 'author' is made to transmit a Swiftian message at close range, and his bland complacencies crackle with his creator's acid fury. Nevertheless, the 'author' maintains to the last his foolish loyalty to delusion, praising the superficial man who knows how to evade the truth: 'Such a Man truly wise, creams off Nature, leaving the Sower and the Dregs, for Philosophy and Reason to lap up.'[169] This image of the cream on top occurs in a slightly different form in the Preface to the *Battle of the Books*:[170]

> There is a *Brain* that will endure but one *Scumming*: Let the Owner gather it with Discretion, and manage his little Stock with Husbandry; but of all things, let him beware of bringing it under the *Lash* of his *Betters*; because, That will make it all bubble up into Impertinence, and he will find no new Supply: Wit, without knowledge, being a Sort of *Cream*, which gathers in a Night to the Top, and by a skilful Hand, may be soon *whipt* into *Froth*; but once scumm'd away, what appears underneath will be fit for nothing, but to be thrown to the Hogs.

The passage should be compared with Mailer's prefatory 'Note to the Reader' in *Advertisements for Myself*: 'For those who care to skim nothing but the cream of each author, and so miss the pleasure of liking him at his worst, I will take the dangerous step of listing what I believe are the best pieces in this book.'[171]

The Mailer who elsewhere takes on the classical satirist's project of challenging the 'innocent' with a 'dissection of the extreme, the obscene and the unsayable', is here once again, more or less knowingly and more or less straight, adopting the classic stance of the satirist's butt. The same Mailerian Preface tells us that 'the author, taken with an admirable desire to please his readers', has interspersed 'a set of advertisements' which resemble the self-conscious prefaces and digressions which Swift parodies. Mailer coyly calls himself a 'literary fraud', admits to reading, 'on occasion', prefaces instead of the books themselves, and offers to his readers the service of making 'the advertisements more readable than the rest of his pages'.[172] Compare Swift's 'Digression in the Modern Kind':[173]

> I hold my self obliged to give as much Light as is possible, into the Beauties and Excellencies of what I am writing ... I cannot deny, that whatever I have said upon this Occasion, had been more proper in a Preface [than in a digression, or interspersed Mailerian 'advertisement'], and more agreeable to the Mode, which usually directs it there.... I do utterly disapprove and declare against that pernicious Custom, of making the Preface a Bill of Fare to the Book. For I have always lookt upon it as a high Point of Indiscretion in *Monster-mongers* and other *Retailers of strange Sights*; to hang out a fair large Picture over the Door, drawn after the Life, with a most eloquent Description underneath:

> This hath saved me many a Threepence, for my Curiosity was fully satisfied, and I never offered to go in, ... Such is exactly the Fate ... of *Prefaces*, *Epistles*, *Advertisements*, *Introductions*, *Prolegomena's*, *Apparatus's*, *To-the-Reader's*. This Expedient was admirable at first; Our Great *Dryden* has long carried it as far as it would go, and with incredible Success. He has often said to me in Confidence, that the World would have never suspected him to be so great a Poet, if he had not assured them so frequently in his Prefaces ... However, ... it is lamentable to behold ... many of the yawning Readers ... now a-days twirl over forty or fifty Pages of *Preface* and *Dedication*, ... as if it were so much *Latin*. Tho' it must be also allowed on the other Hand that a very considerable Number is known to proceed *Criticks* and *Wits*, by reading nothing else.... Now, for my self, ... having the *Modern* Inclination to expatiate upon the Beauty of my own Productions, and display the bright Parts of my Discourse; I thought best to do it in the Body of the Work ... (*Tale*, v).

Even the mockery of self-celebration, Dryden assuring his readers in his Prefaces that he is a 'great ... Poet', and the 'author' himself doing similar things 'in the Body of the Work', finds its echo in Mailer, who actually performs the exercise, largely but not entirely straight, in *both* places, Preface *and* Digression, and tells us so, and tells us that he tells us. Mailer is forever insisting on his role, actual or prospective, as the great American novelist, the consciousness of his time, or whatever; and at the same time hedging his bets, laughing at his pretensions, retreating behind coils of self-mockery.[174] Swift's starved, crazed and visionary garreteer, reporting the minute by minute 'Revolutions' of his immediate present, explaining the 'great Revolutions' of modern madness,[175] might be said to enact the 'modern' revolution, in a larger sense, by the sheer freedoms of his own self-expression. And Mailer, historian of 'the perpetual climax of the present',[176] is similarly 'imprisoned with a perception which will settle for nothing less than making a revolution in the consciousness of our time'.[177] He is even willing to describe himself as being, or having been, a starved, crazed and visionary garreteer: 'Like a starved revolutionary in a garret, I had compounded out of need and fever and vision and fear nothing less than a madman's confidence in the identity of my being ...'[178]

One might almost suppose that Mailer had Swift in mind and, like Sterne, was comically defying the parody. The self-mockery hardly pretends to subdue the solipsism, and helps to see how Swift's own mock-solipsism tends towards a primary solipsistic performance, as well as mocking that of others. Mailer the Grub Street hack, digressor, dissector, solipsist, dark author and sexual operator is all the things Swift satirized; but he is also satirist, protester, uncoverer of truth and mocker of those qualities in himself (of garreteer, solipsist, etc.) which Swift mocked in others. Where Swift's formula purports that it is the solipsistic dunce who is mad, and the satirist who is his sane mocker, Mailer overtly joins the two. In the 'crazy house' of the modern world, he argues in a striking passage in *Armies of the Night*, 'egotism may be the last tool left to History'. As the recorder of events, Mailer must set himself up as an 'ambiguous comic hero', combining an egotism 'of the most startling misproportions, outrageously and often unhappily self-assertive', with, *at the same time*, 'a detachment classic in severity'.[179] The latter quality is one which we should expect to see ascribed to Swift rather than to Mailer. It is revealing to see Mailer laying claim to such a highly unMailerian attribute. But equally important is the fact that everything we know about Swift suggests that in a deeper sense the 'detachment classic in severity' coexists in him with a passionate element of solipsistic self-involvement, and that it is Mailer's formulation *as a whole*, bringing together as it does both parts of his own personality into a single 'two-headed' egotism, which needs to be applied to Swift, satirist of a crazy world, solipsistically caught up in its craziness. It is particularly pertinent in this connection that, as I argued earlier, some of the strongest energies of Swift's *Tale* occur precisely at points where its 'author' is at his most exuberantly outrageous, in the digressions, for example, rather than in the religious allegory. And are not Swift's 'advertisements', in this Mailerian sense of self-displaying digression, sometimes so much 'more readable than the rest of his pages', that one scholar has been led, partly by stylistic evidence, to dispute Swift's authorship of the rest?[180] Mailer ascribes his blend of solipsism and classic detachment to the fact that he is 'a novelist and so in need of studying every lost lineament of the fine, the noble, the frantic, and the foolish in others and in himself'.[181]

Swift was in no position, historically, to make the claim, and had he been able to predict the history of the novel, he would almost certainly have repudiated any notion of being identified with any of its stages. Nevertheless, if an impetuous egocentricity of Swift's own is projected through the *Tale*'s 'author', whilst an egocentric Mailer lays claim to 'a detachment classic in severity', it is possible to feel that the polar opposition of the two authors on many central issues brings them close to one another in some ways, and closer than either of them is to an intermediate or more moderate figure, a 'liberal' novelist, for example, of the Jamesian or Conradian school, ironists of modulation and sceptical hesitancy rather than of sharp oppositions thrust together.[182]

This play of oppositions, in Swift, is very complex. But the complexity consists of a multitude of paradoxical opposites, rather than a fine shading of nuance and qualification. His mad 'moderns' are simultaneously noted for their resolute superficiality *and* for forays into the uncharted depths of their nature.[183] They combine a complacent devotion to prettified appearances, 'Artificial *Mediums*, false Lights, refracted Angles, Varnish, and Tinsel',[184] with a confessional urge of indecent proportions. As an amateur of dissections, the 'author' of the *Tale* both recoils from and likes to dabble in the horrors of the inner ugliness. By a related paradox, he is both a Royal Society virtuoso performing foolish and cruel experiments, and a mouthpiece for the satirist whose surgical operations enable him to expose or extract the filthy truth.[185] The latter role, with all its imagery of dissection and surgery, is one in which Swift himself frequently saw himself, in a more direct and straightforward sense than we find in the paradox-ridden world of the Digression on Madness. In the fourth of the *Drapier's Letters* he speaks of some threats by William Wood as 'the last Howls of a Dog dissected alive, as I hope he hath sufficiently been';[186] in the *Answer to ... A Memorial*, he asserts the usefulness of exposing to view the rotten corpse of the late Lord Chief Justice Whitshed's reputation and those of other political malefactors;[187] in the *Vindication of ... Lord Carteret* he speaks of himself as 'an incensed political *Surgeon*' who will take the 'miserable Creature *Traulus* ... without waiting for his Death', and 'will *flay*, and *dissect* him alive; and to the View of Mankind, lay open all the disordered Cells of his Brain, the Venom of his Tongue, the Corruption of his Heart, and Spots and Flatuses of his Spleen.—And all this for *Three-Pence*.'[188] The allusion is to Swift's poem against Lord Allen (*Traulus*), which appeared in two parts in 1730.[189] The phrase 'And all this for *Three-Pence*' also, however, carries a note of gay charlatanism, the high spirits of a cheap, bargain-vending quack. Swift's fondness for appearing in the role of mountebank and projector does not here undercut the earnestness of the hostile feeling, but coexists with it. And Traulus is a mad 'modern' too, who once exposed by the surgeon's dissection will unavoidably be confined 'for some Months *more* to his Garret', there to be 'fed like a wild Beast through a Hole'[190] just like the inmates of that related political madhouse, the Legion Club.[191]

Who, then, is mad? Dissector or dissected or both? Is the righteous satirist mad in a bad world, or the bad man mad by righteous standards?

Two traditional formulae of satire, parallel and opposite, coexist in a paradoxical confrontation which might itself be called formulaic. But as so often in Swift, this formulaic effect is itself *exceeded*. The good madness of the castigator is allowed to curdle into the bad madness of the world. When a righteous and rational programme, despite all its moral obviousness, is ignored by an incurably bad world, its proponents come to seem mad not merely in the rhetorical sense but in a more primary sense that Swift himself would label as mad, and in turn, by that fact, antisocial and bad. The righteous 'project' of mending the world becomes a vicious insanity. The crazed political projectors who propose 'Schemes for persuading Monarchs to chuse Favourites upon the Score of their Wisdom, Capacity and Virtue; of teaching Ministers to consult the publick Good; of rewarding Merit, great Abilities, and eminent Services', belong to the very same research establishment whose other projects include the refinement of totalitarian methods for discovering political subversives, for example by prying into 'the Dyet of all suspected Persons; their Times of eating; upon which Side they lay in Bed; with which Hand they wiped their Posteriors...' (*Gulliver's Travels*, III.vi).[192]

Gulliver carries the two kinds of madness in himself. So does the modest proposer, who once saw his sensible and humane schemes ignored, and who, crazed by this failure, now preaches cannibalism. There is in neither case any simple reversal of praise and blame, nor any comfortingly straightforward sarcasm about the righteous madness of the wise and good in an upside-down world. Gulliver's mean and arrogant fulminations, or the proposer's ghastly lucidity, both intensify the force of the rhetorical madness in a gratuitously violent way, and also generate an insecure scepticism even as to its righteousness. The formula, with its tendency to point-making simplification and to detachment, survives in each case, though under great strain. It is a characteristically Swiftian painfulness that the madness goes beyond the formula. But it is nevertheless framed by the formula. There is a framework for it to overspill. And when it overspills into what is in effect a second formula, that the world is so bad that a man can preach cannibalism to it in the calmest possible way, there remain such ultimate certainties as that, granted all possible scepticisms, cannibalism is bad. The proposition can be taken sufficiently for granted to be used formulaically, with detachment.

We are here at an opposite pole from Mailer (or Sade, or Artaud, or Genet), who are seldom formulaic or detached; in whom the imaginative contemplation of 'forbidden' acts no longer primarily implies that they are bad; and in whose writings cannibalism comes into its own as a potentially valid way of asserting one's 'vitalité intégrale',[193] one's personal, sexual, racial or political authenticity. When Artaud says that the theatre of cruelty must in some sense realize the audience's criminality, its erotic drives, its savagery and even its cannibalism, he is not saying that he wants the audience to commit criminal or cannibalistic acts. But he also insists that the bringing into play of these impulses is not merely imaginary or illusory, but what he calls *interior*: 'non pas supposé et illusoire, mais intérieur'.[194] Thus where for Swift an extreme act like cannibalism is turned into a satiric formula for allegorizing and scourging a vicious immorality, for Artaud it is an atavistic potential which the artist must release. For Swift, literature is therapeutic, if at all, by its direct imposition of moral restraints upon our disruptive buried instincts; for Artaud, by its liberation of buried instincts. These instincts the Swiftian satirist seeks to repress, and the Mailerian dissector to release.

It is not always clear, in Mailer or in other theorists of the extreme situation, to what extent this liberation is envisaged through the imaginative (i.e. 'interior', as opposed to merely imaginary) experience, or through actual performance. A powerful ambiguity often, and perhaps necessarily, hovers over the question of how to set about that self-authentication which is said to come from the freeing of 'cruel' instincts. But it is certain that when the narrator of Mailer's 'Prologue' proposes to enter the consciousness of 'a house, a tree, a dog, a cop, a cannibal',[195] he is claiming the right to an imaginative state untrammelled by moral inhibitions. This is a right which Swift would refuse. But he did avail himself tacitly of some of its satisfactions. The *Modest Proposal* depends on our recognizing that the wrongness of cannibalism is self-evident and overriding. Yet we have seen that the critique of mass-extermination was not unmixed with some 'cruel' extermination-velleities on Swift's own part; and the horrors of the *Modest Proposal* have been felt by many readers to contain an element of unmoralized 'black humour' which exists beyond the overt satiric purposes.[196] The 'infectious thought' is clearly being indulged with a certain grim gusto not wholly accounted for by the formulaic intentions.

Marshall McLuhan noted in a striking phrase that the *Dunciad*'s world of Chaos and of Night was an exposure of 'the Africa within'.[197] 'The new collective unconscious Pope saw as the accumulating backwash of private self-expression.'[198] His remarks are to some degree extended also to the Swift of the *Tale* and the *Battle of the Books*.[199] The cannibal-velleities of the *Modest Proposal* reinforce the connection, not least because of the element of Swiftian participation which exists in the treatment of this primitive 'cruelty', as in that of the other atavistic 'modernisms' of scribbler and sectarian. The primitive tribalism (the terms are McLuhan's) which paradoxically emanates from the forms of self-expression of 'modern' literary and religious subcultures[200] comes out openly in a later age, when Mailer, reviewing Genet's *Blacks*, says 'it is possible that Africa is closer to the root of whatever life is left than any other land'.[201] A few lines earlier, after quoting the famous speech by Genet's Archibald, in which the Blacks are exhorted to 'negrify' themselves, to realize their full blackness, including their 'cannibal tastes', Mailer asks, jauntily 'Who is to say the gates of heaven are not manned by cannibals mumbling: Lumumba!'[202] Mailer relishes the notion of this 'nightmare' to the liberal conscience:[203]

> 'The Blacks' gives life because it is a work of perceptions which slice like razors ... It is a scourge to liberal ideology, vomitorium for the complacent ... The play entertains the forbidden nightmare of the liberal: what, dear Lord, if the reactionary is correct, and people *are* horrible?

Mailer's talk about 'nightmares' echoes a key-term of Conrad's *Heart of Darkness*,[204] and it is a teasing fact that Mailer's Lumumbist Heaven should emanate from the same Congo as the Inferno of Conrad's tale. But Mailer, like Genet (*and* Swift), is far removed from the awed and questioning hesitancies of Conrad's exploration of 'the Africa within', with its imagery of 'peeping over the edge',[205] and its conscientious discriminating between a 'choice of nightmares'.[206] The dream-like call of primitive horror, the sense that the evil Kurtz's discourses 'had behind them ... the terrific suggestiveness of words heard in dreams, of phrases spoken in nightmares',[207] does not mean, in *Heart of Darkness*, that the dreams are 'unreal', but that on the contrary they have a force which is more than that of the merely real; able to penetrate civilized defences all the more for having melted them into the sensitized magic of a trance-like state.[208] Conrad would have understood Artaud's notion that the imaginative, dream-like fulfilments of the theatre of cruelty are more, not less, powerful than a spectacle of the same cruelties and crimes *actually* committed.[209] It would be a gross misrepresentation to say that Conrad was given to sentimental evasion, or was ignorant of 'the Africa within'. He is openly exploring the 'civilized' man's response to its call, and registering the doubts, and the conflicts of loyalty, which are included in this response.[210] It is not he who draws back from the abyss, but his narrator Marlow, and even then not without at least once going through 'to dream the nightmare out to the end'.[211] But this drawing back of Marlow's 'hesitating foot'[212] is something Conrad plainly respects, whilst taking care to distance his own involvement in the whole drama by retreating behind not one narrator only but two. The novel is a clearsighted tribute to the call of the wild and its powers, but remains well outside the domain of polarizing commitments, whether of self-abandonment to the lure or of total suppression from within. The only character who has taken an absolute step in either direction is Kurtz,[213] and, despite his immense symbolic importance, he is a shadowy figure in the novel, and relatively little seen.

By contrast, Swift and Mailer impose a kind of absolute simplification. Swift's cannibal satire speaks uncompromisingly and painfully of man's inhumanity to man, and Mailer's half-funny heavenly scene suggests that cannibalism may yet in some sense embody our best or truest authenticity. There are many ways in which Mailer reads like Swift stood on his head. But it is also true that each often reaches towards the position of the other, Swift in unacknowledged commitment to what he satirizes, Mailer sometimes in entertaining the frissons of guilt provided by the offended Super-Ego, or in claiming 'a detachment classic in severity', or in maintaining that his Marxist radicalism is blended with an eighteenth-century Anglo-Irish conservatism: 'Mailer was a Left Conservative ... he tried to think in the style of Marx in order to attain certain values suggested by Edmund Burke.'[214] Mailer insists that his Left Conservatism is not a 'liberal' compromise between Left and Right, but that he is *radical*, so to speak, at both ends: 'Since he was a conservative, he would begin at the root ... Since he was also a *Left* Conservative, he believed that radical measures were sometimes necessary to save the root.'[215] Mailer names Burke rather than Swift, but Swift and Burke have come down together in some political mythologies of our time, as rebellious upholders of tradition, conservative libertarians, men who, in Yeats's famous phrase, 'hated Whiggery'.[216] Swift is in fact a great deal closer to what Mailer describes than Burke, that anti-revolutionary Whig gradualist and moderation-man, ever was. Both Mailer and Swift (the latter a conservative whose satire is 'radical' in the sense that it pierces beyond specific culpabilities to the very nature of man) hate what Mailer, in a *Partisan Review* note on Black Power, calls the 'liberal with a psychotic sense of moderation'.[217] Swift, in the voice of the most genuinely moderate of all his spokesmen, wrote in the *Sentiments of a Church-of-England Man* of the callous violence that lies hidden behind the self-styled moderates of the party-political scene;[218] and, despite his own official commitment to moderation in human affairs, had a deep and instinctive dislike of those 'whom the World calls *moderate Men*, and I call *Men of Discretion*'[219] (Mailer calls them 'the churchly and the vicious').[220] Not only does Swift's allegiance to the 'common Forms', and to the associated disciplines and restraints of the Super-Ego (restraints which the Mailerian hipster explicitly rejects),[221] contain a powerful presence of their opposite, but there is a sense in which the Houyhnhnms, that monument to the triumphant Super-Ego, come close to certain ideals of anarchy. If Orwell found Houyhnhnmland totalitarian,[222] Godwin saw it as an anarchist Utopia, and modelled his ideology upon it.[223] The Houyhnhnms exist, at least, at that point where reason comes so completely into its own, that the drives and impulses of any individual can be trusted to be spontaneously virtuous and undisruptive, so that only a minimum of formal government is necessary. The result is a cool and graceful self-possession in personal behaviour which flows from complete social cohesion, and from the elimination of false needs and passions. It is possible to relate this easy self-control to the emphasis on 'coolness' and emotional containment in the hipster code. Of course, hipster coolness differs radically in its sources from its Houyhnhnm counterpart. It is rooted in the senses, in an essentially sexual religion of the life-force, and in the cleansing or cathartic power of violent acts,[224] whereas the Houyhnhnms' self-control proceeds from an unquestioned supremacy of the Super-Ego. It is a control that comes from a wisdom of emotional daring ('to be in control of a situation because you have swung where the Square has not, or because you have allowed to come to consciousness a pain, a guilt, a shame or a desire which the other has not had the courage to face'),[225] from individual victories of the sensibility, whereas Houyhnhnm reason dispenses with singular or disturbing emotional experiments and is essentially conformist. The hipster's self-control is a cool containment of energy, an availability to further feats of 'making it', not a subduing or ironing-out of the tyrant passions.

But underlying these differences between the hipster or White Negro and the Houyhnhnm is a sort of authoritative and stylish calm, proceeding from the elimination of what Swift would see as false needs, and what Mailer calls 'bad and energy-wasting habits'.[226] Even this hipster formulation will remind us of the distinction between Swift's emphasis on 'conventional moral responsibility' and the hipster's 'abdication' of it.[227] But if anyone doubts the applicability of 'coolness' to the Houyhnhnm world of calm wisdom, readiness to meet death, instinctive mutual collaboration and government, he should consider Mailer's remarks, in the *Partisan Review* symposium of 1968 on 'Black Power',[228]

> on the superior cool of the Negro in public places.
> For the cool comes from a comprehensive vision, a
> relaxation before the dangers of life, a readiness
> to meet death, philosophy or amusement at any turn.
> Commend us, while we are on lists, to the
> ability of the Negro to police himself, as opposed
> to the ability of the White to police others. At
> the Civil Rights March on Washington in 1963 with
> over a hundred thousand Negroes in town, no episodes
> of violence were reported—in the riots in the years
> which followed, fascinating patterns of cooperation
> among the rioters emerge. One may look, as Government
> commissions do, for patterns of a plot; or one may do
> better to entertain the real possibility that the Negroes
> have psychic powers of mass impromptu collaboration which
> are mysterious, and by that measure, superior to the White.

This account envisages not only a spontaneously well-knit form of anarchic order in non-violence, but also a peculiar cohesiveness, a mysterious 'mass impromptu collaboration' in the use of force. The mysterious primal bond of the Negro thus meets what is surely its polar opposite, the instinctive *rational* bond between Houyhnhnms, in an essentially similar combination of calmness, self-assurance, authority and spontaneous cohesion (even the 'readiness to meet death' may be felt to link the two together). Is there not the same anarchist vision of spontaneously and instinctively developed collaborative organizations (for reason in the Houyhnhnms is so absolute as to be instinctive), the same collective non-violence, able to turn to violence, but only against the radical enemy, whether white man, foreign invader or Yahoo? Gulliver warns his fellow countrymen not to try to colonize Houyhnhnmland:[229]

> The *Houyhnhnms*, indeed, appear not to be so well prepared
> for War, a Science to which they are perfect Strangers, and
> especially against missive Weapons. However, supposing
> myself to be a Minister of State, I could never give my
> Advice for invading them. Their Prudence, Unanimity,
> Unacquaintedness with Fear, and their Love of their Country
> would amply supply all Defects in the military Art. Imagine
> twenty Thousand of them breaking into the Midst of an *European*

> Army, confounding the Ranks, overturning the Carriages, battering the Warriors Faces into Mummy, by terrible Yerks from their hinder Hoofs ... (*Gulliver's Travels*, IV.xii).

Gulliver continues with a suggestion which finds an important echo in Mailer: 'But instead of Proposals for conquering that magnanimous Nation, I rather wish they were in a Capacity or Disposition to send a sufficient Number of their Inhabitants for civilizing *Europe*.'[230] Mailer says, near the end of his passage: 'The irony is that we may even yet need a black vision of existence if civilization is to survive the death chamber it has built for itself.'[231] And Gulliver's contrast between the Houyhnhnms' ability to govern themselves and the cruel disorders of European colonization[232] is close to Mailer on 'the ability of the Negro to police himself, as opposed to the ability of the White to police others'.[233]

What Swift (or rather Gulliver: but Gulliver is here very close to Swift) says the Houyhnhnms can teach Europe are 'the first Principles of Honour, Justice, Truth, Temperance, publick Spirit, Fortitude, Chastity, Friendship, Benevolence, and Fidelity', the high virtues of a traditional and civilized moral code.[234] Mailer is talking instead, at an opposite pole, of primitive regeneration. But it is interesting that some of the notions of racial self-authentication among Black Power leaders (or Mailer's conception of these notions) directly resemble the more primitivistic elements of the Houyhnhnm Utopia. Thus it is stated that the Negro's superiority over the white man rests partly on the fact that the Negro is physically healthier, even though (among other disadvantages) he gets 'less medical care', and lives in less hygienic circumstances: the Houyhnhnms 'are subject to no Diseases, and therefore can have no Need of Physicians' (IV.ix). Whatever the medical facts, the Utopian ideals match. Living 'according to nature' in the Houyhnhnm sense (i.e. by reason's laws) and in the opposite primitivist sense (i.e. by closeness to one's authentic primitive self) are thrust into a surprising congruence. Second, the 'Negro's relatively low rate of literacy seems to be in inverse relation to his philosophical capacity to have a comprehensive vision of his life': the Houyhnhnms, also superior in what Mailer calls 'actual culture', explicitly 'have no Letters' at all (IV.ix). Again, genuine opposites resolve themselves into a similar primitivist ideal. Among possible developments in a 'Black Power' culture, elements of white civilization would be avoided, and there would for example be 'an opportunity to explore Black medicine, herbs in place of antibiotics'; or again, 'not housing projects, but a new way to build houses'. It is a pleasant and arresting coincidence, that the Houyhnhnms, without conventional medicines, 'have excellent Medicines composed of Herbs' (IV.ix); and that their buildings, clearly deficient in many European features, are 'very rude and simple, ... not inconvenient, ... well contrived to defend them from all Injuries of Cold and Heat' (IV.ix).[235]

There is among all these paradoxical identities, reversals and counter-reversals, another yet to be noted, although it has been implicit all along. What so strikingly develops in Mailer as the sketch of a Houyhnhnm Utopia, has its roots precisely in what Swift identified with the Yahoos: the human creature in a more authentic, primitive state, fiercely impulsive in its energies, passionate rather than rational. Mailer's protesting procession of 'armies of the night' (hipsters, Negroes and the rest) would, moreover, be identified by Swift or by Pope not only with the Yahoos but with what McLuhan called the 'armed horde of nobodies', sons 'Of *Night* Primaeval, and of *Chaos* old', who people the mock-epic world of the *Dunciad*, turning into pageantry and procession the subliterate glories of Dulness, 'the Africa within'.[236] Grub Street and the Yahoo beast spell out a nightmare of spontaneous expression which is poles apart from the 'sweetness and light' of the Houyhnhnms, their easy strength, their racial superiority.[237] But it is this easy strength and this sense of racial superiority that Mailer attributes to the Black revolutionaries,[238] along with some of the primitive energies, now affirmed as life-giving, of the Yahoos. A fact which may account for some of the differences between the Houyhnhnms and the Black revolutionaries of the later neo-primitivist vision is that the former are already a ruling class, the established and institutional power in the land, while the Black Power Negro is still an outsider. The somewhat more codified behaviour of the Houyhnhnms, their more *formally* organized institutions, the regularity of their responses are partly due to the fact that they already exist in an achieved Utopia, whereas the others are engaged in all the uncertainties of a struggle for Utopia. However that may be, Mailer, and perhaps some Black thinkers too, have envisaged the future Black Utopia in terms of some of the most traditional images of the White Man's dream of perfectibility through primitive reversion, a New Houyhnhnmland—but (as Swift would certainly qualify it) for Yahoos. White myths pervade the Negro image of release from White domination, and Mailer, reporting this, seems himself to slide from calling the hipster a White Negro to seeing the Negro as a Black hipster.

If, therefore, Mailer sets up for many of the things Swift mocks, he also sets up for some of the things with which Swift is most deeply identified. But the specific resemblances, important as they are, take second place to the manner in which both authors tend, from opposite positions, towards one another. The tendency, in both authors, is to reach out towards a stark antithetical counterpart. It is not a matter of subtle hesitancy, of exploratory and fastidious nuance, of delicate accommodation and reserved judgments, of a questioning, inclusive, ironic tolerance. In both authors we are far away from the oscillations of a 'liberal' novelist like the Conrad of *Heart of Darkness*, exploring the choices between a traditional 'European' morality and the teasing atavistic appeal of savagery. Such things, triumphs of the highly developed novel-form, the history of 'fine consciences', Swift and Mailer would equally set aside, however unfairly, as cultivated evasions, lazy luxuries of analysis and doubt.[239] Between Swift's repudiation of the friendly complacencies of 'a very refined Age' (*Tale*, x),[240] and Mailer's description of *The Blacks* as 'a scourge to liberal ideology, vomitorium for the complacent',[241] lie more than two and a half centuries of Augustan urbanity, bourgeois gentility, and liberal novelists. That these intervening phenomena, and especially the last, help to account for certain differences between Mailer (or other explorers of violence and the extreme situation) and Swift, is to be expected; and the gap in literary distinction between the two writers is surely very wide. A full analysis of the whole question belongs at the very centre of the literary and cultural history of the modern world, and would require a separate study to itself.

NOTES

CHAPTER I GULLIVER AND THE GENTLE READER

1. *Works*, I.29. See also I.32.
2. Herbert Read, *Selected Writings* (London, 1963), p.127.
3. *Works*, I.42n.
4. See Edward W. Rosenheim, Jr, *Swift and the Satirist's Art* (Chicago and London, 1963), p.62.
5. *Tristram Shandy*, IV.x; IX.viii.
6. For a most useful survey of this 'self-conscious' mode of writing, see Wayne C. Booth, 'The self-conscious narrator in comic fiction before *Tristram Shandy*', *Publications of the Modern Language Association of America*, LXVII (1952), 163-85. There is a good deal of this kind of writing shortly before Sterne, not necessarily derived from Swift, and my point does not *primarily* concern an 'influence'. See also Booth, *The Rhetoric of Fiction* (Chicago and London, 1965), p.229.
7. Norman Mailer, *Advertisements for Myself* (London [Panther Books], 1970), p.7.
8. See pp.140 ff., and chapter V, *passim*.
9. It is noteworthy that in some of his *private* correspondence with Stella, Swift frequently used what we now recognize as Shandean mannerisms: coy spontaneities of self-reference, playfully affectionate bits of private nonsense and of intimate double-entendre, broken sentences and even the sort of non-verbal and sub-verbal communication ('little language', grunts and cries) which is part of the everyday world of Tristram and Walter Shandy and Uncle Toby, but which Swift was quick to satirize in its more public manifestations (e.g. the sub-verbal communion, through looks and sighs and belches, of the worshippers in the *Mechanical Operation of the Spirit*, *Works*, I.183, etc.). See the examples from the *Journal to Stella* cited in Herbert Davis, *Jonathan Swift: Essays on his Satire, and Other Studies* (New York, 1964), pp.82 ff., and Davis's pertinent comment on p.93 'that the letters of Swift from which I have been quoting, were first published at various times between 1745 and 1767, that the account of the life and character of Stella first appeared in 1765, and the *Journal to Stella* partly in 1766, and partly in 1768; they were all therefore first read by those who had delighted in the novels of Richardson and Sterne, and who were enjoying the sentimental comedies of Kelly and Cumberland.'

10. *Works*, I.22. Here again Swift is prepared privately to practise the things whose *public* manifestation he reproves. A. B. England has recently shown how in the private *Journal to Stella* Swift is concerned that his writing should suggest 'that nothing which comes into his consciousness is irrelevant', and that the moment by moment reporting of facts and feelings, even if they turn out to be erroneous, must stand as the true record of 'the incoherent, discontinuous movement of his experience and his thoughts', citing comments like 'I must say every sorry thing that comes into my head', 'Mr. Lewis's man came in before I could finish that word beginning with a W ...', etc. ('Private and public rhetoric in the *Journal to Stella*', *Essays in Criticism*, XXII (1972), 133; *Journal to Stella*, II.568, 371). Like other critics, Mr England rightly argues that the spontaneities and discontinuities are themselves part of a deliberate rhetoric. So, of course, were Sterne's. The points of interest in the present context are that Swift was both drawn to a proto-Shandean style and at the same time reserved his non-satiric uses of it for his *private* writings.

Compare Swift's narrator's claim that his statements are 'literally true this Minute I am writing', whatever the next moment may bring, with the Mailerian hipster's doctrine that 'there are no truths other than the isolated truths of what each observer feels at each instant of his existence ... the truth is not what one has felt yesterday or what one expects to feel tomorrow but rather truth is no more nor less than what one feels at each instant in the perpetual climax of the present' (*Advertisements for Myself*, pp.285-6; see also above, pp.69, 133 f.).

11. Richardson, Preface to *Sir Charles Grandison*.

12. *Works*, I.27.

13. *Tristram Shandy*, I.vi.

14. *Works*, I.131, 133.

15. F. R. Leavis, 'The irony of Swift', *The Common Pursuit* (Harmondsworth, 1962), p.80.

16. H. W. Sams, 'Swift's satire of the Second Person', *ELH. A Journal of English Literary History*, XXVI (1959), 36-44.

17. C. S. Lewis, 'Addison', in *Essays on the Eighteenth Century Presented to David Nichol Smith* (Oxford, 1945), p.1; Irvin Ehrenpreis, *The Personality of Jonathan Swift* (London, 1958), p.39, on *A Beautiful Young Nymph Going to Bed*. Ehrenpreis also lists parallels from other writers. See also Roland M. Frye, 'Swift's Yahoo and the Christian symbols for sin', *Journal of the History of Ideas*, XV (1954), 201-17, and Deane Swift's *Essay* (1755), pp.221 ff.

18. This notation gives the book and chapter reference to *Gulliver's Travels* and the page in *Works*, XI. It is used in this chapter, where quotations from *Gulliver's Travels* are particularly frequent. In the rest of this book, I shall revert to the convention I have adopted for all other works by Swift throughout, of giving references to volume and page of *Works* in the notes, leaving references to chapters, sections or lines, where convenient, in brackets in the text.

19. For an amusing passage about indoor as against outdoor defecation, see

'A Panegyrick on the D—n', ll.229 ff. (*Poems*, III.894 ff.).
20. William King, *Some Remarks on The Tale of a Tub* (1704) cited by Ricardo Quintana, *The Mind and Art of Jonathan Swift* (New York and London, 1936), p.75; William Wotton, *A Defense of the Reflections upon Ancient and Modern Learning ... With Observations upon The Tale of a Tub* (1705), in *A Tale of a Tub*, ed. A. C. Guthkelch and D. Nichol Smith, 2nd edn (Oxford, 1958), pp.322, 323, 326; *Works*, I.5. Swift was not at first known to be the author.
21. The tartness of these jokes in *Gulliver* may be contrasted with the protracted and elaborate geniality with which Norman Mailer describes 'an overwhelming urge to micturate' in *Armies of the Night* (New York, 1968), pp.42-4, with its vacuous mock-concern about what people would think of his 'pissing on the floor' if the attendant reported it to the police or the press got hold of the news (p.43), and with its fussily self-delighting returns to the episode, and to Mailer's coy feelings of guilt, later in the book (pp.63, 71).
22. Thackeray, *The English Humourists of the Eighteenth Century*, Everyman's Library (London and New York, 1949), p.32.
23. For other satirical treatments of the papal ceremony, see *Tale*, IV (*Works*, I.71), and Rabelais I.ii; I.xxxiii; II.xxx.
24. *English Humourists*, pp.34-5.
25. Edward Stone, 'Swift and the Horses: Misanthropy or Comedy?', *Modern Language Quarterly*, x (1949), 374n.
26. Real concealment seemed a necessity, with such a subversive book, though Pope told Swift on 16 November 1726 that people were not worried by 'particular reflections', so that he 'needed not to have been so secret upon this head' (*Correspondence*, III.181). In any case, *simple* anonymity or pseudonymity would have served the practical purposes. Swift's authorship soon became fairly well known anyway.
27. Horace, *Odes*, III.xi.35.
28. *Correspondence*, III.180, 189. See also Mario M. Rossi and Joseph M. Hone, *Swift or the Egotist* (London, 1934), pp.330, 411.
29. See Ricardo Quintana, *Swift: An Introduction* (London, 1962), pp.53 ff., 158 f.
30. Rabelais, II.xxviii, *et passim*; Lucian, *True Story*, I.2 ff.; Butler, *Erewhon*, ch.ix, *ad fin*.
31. 'Democritus Junior to the Reader', *Anatomy of Melancholy*, Everyman's Library (London and New York, 1932), I.15, 123.
32. Contrast Gulliver's use of this convention: 'I never suffer a Word to pass that may look like Reflection, or possibly give the least Offence even to those who are most ready to take it. So that, I hope, I may with Justice pronounce myself an Author perfectly blameless; against whom the Tribes of Answerers, Considerers, Observers, Reflecters, Detecters, Remarkers, will never be able to find Matter for exercising their Talents' (IV.xii.293). This hardly pretends to be a friendly, or even a plausible, gesture from Swift, though it is, of course, amusing.
33. For both these uses, see *Oxford English Dictionary*, 'Thou', *pers. pron.*,

1b, and 'Thou', *verb*.

34. Swift, *Epistle to a Lady*, ll.139ff. (*Poems*, II.634-7).

35. *Correspondence*, III.179.

36. Ibid., 120.

37. Ibid., 181, 182.

38. The clinching joke, though not the passage as a whole, is Swift's. See R. W. Frantz, 'Gulliver's "Cousin Sympson"', *Huntington Library Quarterly*, i (1938), 331-3.

39. Boswell, *Life of Johnson*, ed. G. B. Hill and L. F. Powell (Oxford, 1934), II.319.

40. *Correspondence*, III.257-8.

41. *Jonathan Swift and the Anatomy of Satire* (Cambridge, Mass., 1961), p.7.

42. *Epistle to a Lady*, ll.164-70 (*Poems*, II.635).

43. *Correspondence*, III.103, 117.

44. Irvin Ehrenpreis, 'The meaning of Gulliver's last voyage', *Review of English Literature*, iii (1962), 35.

45. The passage seems to some extent to conform to Erasmus's prescription for amplifying a description with appropriate graphic detail: see *De Copia*, Book II, Fifth Method, especially the examples from Quintilian, VIII.iii.67-69, and Lucan, III (*On Copia of Words and Ideas*, trs. and ed. Donald B. King and H. David Rix (Milwaukee, 1963), pp.47-50). Quintilian is describing how to make vivid the capture of a city, Lucan is describing a particular battle. Neither passage has nor seeks the crazy and generalized exuberance of Gulliver's headlong list. Swift's lists are further discussed in chs IV and V.

46. George Orwell, *Nineteen Eighty-Four*, part I, ch.i (Harmondsworth, 1954), pp.10-11.

47. See pp.50-2.

48. A. E. Case, *Four Essays on Gulliver's Travels* (Gloucester, Mass., 1958), p.110.

49. Thomas Sheridan, *The Life of the Rev. Dr. Jonathan Swift*, 2nd edn (1787), p.433.

50. Joseph Horrell, 'What Gulliver knew', *Sewanee Review*, li (1943), 492-3; Case, *Four Essays*, p.121; Samuel H. Monk, 'The pride of Lemuel Gulliver', *Sewanee Review*, lxiii (1955), 56.

51. More, *Utopia*, trs. Ralph Robinson, Everyman's Library (London and New York, 1951), p.85. For an excellent discussion of More and Swift, see John Traugott, 'A voyage to Nowhere with Thomas More and Jonathan Swift: *Utopia* and *The Voyage to the Houyhnhnms*', *Sewanee Review*, lxix (1961), 534-65. A somewhat different comparison is made by Brian Vickers, 'The satiric structure of *Gulliver's Travels* and More's *Utopia*', *The World of Jonathan Swift*, ed. Brian Vickers (Oxford, 1968), pp.233-57.

52. *Tom Jones*, III.iii. I hasten to say that I do not believe that the Houyhnhnms are therefore a satirical skit on the deists (or that Square, as one might just as easily 'prove', was a skit on the Houyhnhnms), though the rationalisms have points in common. A. O. Lovejoy's 'The parallel of Deism and Classicism', *Essays in the History of Ideas* (New York, 1960), pp.78-98, makes abundantly clear that many basic assumptions about Nature and

Reason were the common property of deists and non-deists alike. (My discussion here is indebted to this and other essays in Lovejoy's book.) This may be the place to say categorically that in my view Swift treats the Houyhnhnms mainly seriously and not mockingly, and that the recent arguments to this effect by Sherburn, Crane, Rosenheim, W. B. Carnochan, and others have put criticism of *Gulliver's Travels* back on the right lines.

53. These wonderfully apt examples are adapted from Rabelais, v.xxii, as is noted in W. A. Eddy, *Gulliver's Travels: A Critical Study* (New York, 1963), pp.161-2. Jean Plattard's notes to the *Cinquiesme Livre* (Paris, 1948), pp.324-5, show that Rabelais was literalizing a series of adages of Erasmus. See also the account of Lucian's *True Story* in Eddy, p.16.

54. Pope, *Dunciad*, III.6.

55. See for example Roland M. Frye (above, n.17), pp.208-9.

56. This is an illuminating parallel to Swift's remark to Pope on 26 November 1725 about the kite (*Correspondence*, III.118). I have briefly discussed interpretations of this controversial letter in a review in *Notes and Queries*, ccix (1964), 316-17.

57. There are certain analogies between this mode of attack, and those strategies of aggression *either way*, of putting one's victim in an 'untenable position' or 'double bind', some of whose manifestations in the domain of psychopathology are described in R. D. Laing, *Self and Others* (Harmondsworth, 1971), ch. ix, esp. pp.141 ff., 147. And see Peter Sedgwick in *Laing and Anti-Psychiatry*, ed. Robert Boyers and Robert Orrill (Harmondsworth, 1972), pp.22-4.

58. The passage runs pointedly against the Lilliputian (I.vi.60) and English (III.vii.201-2) examples. All rather strikingly have grandfather-grandchildren references. The contrast may reflect Swift's interest, noted by some critics, in a cyclical theory of history (e.g. III.x.210), but such force as it has on the reader *as a contrast* is simply to the discredit of England.

59. R. S. Crane, 'The Houyhnhnms, the Yahoos, and the history of ideas', *Reason and the Imagination*, ed. J. A. Mazzeo (New York and London, 1962), pp.231-53.

60. See Ehrenpreis, op. cit., *Review of English Literature*, iii (1962), 34. In some ways, *animal rationis capax* is not really very different from *animal rationale* in the low-pitched textbook sense. Bolingbroke may have this partly in mind when he says the distinction 'will not bear examination' (*Correspondence*, III.121).

61. *Works*, IX.166.

62. Physicians provide a monstrously concrete example of Nature turned upside down. The basis of the reversal is the perfectly fair notion, discussed earlier, that health is the 'natural' state of the body: 'these Artists ingeniously considering that in all Diseases Nature is forced out of her Seat; therefore to replace her in it, the Body must be treated in a Manner directly contrary, by interchanging the Use of each Orifice; forcing Solids and Liquids in at the *Anus*, and making Evacuations at the Mouth' (IV.vi.254).

63. But this parenthesis may refer to the word 'degrading', and not to the phrase 'human Nature'.

64. Lucian, *Timon, or the Misanthrope*; Plutarch, *Life of Antony*, LXX; Shakespeare, *Timon of Athens*. Or it may be that when Swift professed his misanthropy in *Gulliver's Travels* to be 'not [in] Timons manner' (*Correspondence*, III.103) he was merely saying that he was just as misanthropic, but would avoid Timon's 'manner' only, i.e. his style of ranting grandiloquence, a version of that 'lofty Stile' (*Epistle to a Lady*, ll.140, 218, *Poems*, II.634, 637), which Swift almost invariably refused to use.
65. Robert C. Elliott, *The Power of Satire* (Princeton, 1960), pp.225-6.
66. *Correspondence*, III.117. See W. B. Carnochan, 'The complexity of Swift: Gulliver's fourth voyage', *Studies in Philology*, lx (1963), 32 ff.
67. 'O, if the World had but a dozen Arbuthnetts in it I would burn my Travells' (*Correspondence*, III.104). Don Pedro may, in this sense, be an Arbuthnot.
68. Traugott, op. cit., *Sewanee Review*, lxix (1961), 562. For another useful perspective, see R. S. Crane, 'The rationale of the fourth voyage', *Gulliver's Travels. An Annotated Text with Critical Essays*, ed. Robert A. Greenberg (New York, 1961), pp.305-6.
69. See also George Sherburn, 'Errors concerning the Houyhnhnms', *Modern Philology*, lvi (1958), 94-5, and Carnochan, op. cit., *Studies in Philology*, lx (1963), 25-6.
70. Carnochan, op. cit., p.27.
71. *Reason and the Imagination*, pp.247 ff.
72. *Hudibras*, I.i.65, 71-2. See Ehrenpreis, op. cit., *Review of English Literature*, iii (1962), 23 ff., for further illustration of the relevance of logic books. Another specified example of the non-rational animal was the ape. That Gulliver should have been taken by a Brobdingnagian monkey for one of its kind (II.v.122) gains an additional piquancy from this. Swift uses the horse, unlike the monkey, as an opposite, not as a parallel, but man is the loser both ways.

CHAPTER II ORDER AND CRUELTY

1. *Works*, I.109-10.
2. *Poems*, II.581-3.
3. See Irvin Ehrenpreis, *The Personality of Jonathan Swift* (London, 1958), pp.43 ff.
4. André Breton, *Anthologie de l'Humour Noir*, new edn (Paris, 1966), pp.25, 17.
5. *Works*, XI.236, 276, 281. Cf. the passage in the *Modest Proposal* about the use of the 'flayed' skins of the cannibalized children to 'make admirable *Gloves for Ladies*, and *Summer Boots for fine Gentlemen*' (*Works*, XII.112).
6. For other collocations of Swift and Sade by Breton, see the passages from the Surrealist manifestos cited by Denis Donoghue, *Jonathan Swift: A Critical Anthology* (Harmondsworth, 1971), p.130. Swift has no elaborate cannibal extravaganzas in Sade's manner, but it is probable that Sade took some of his inspiration from Swift, whom, according to Simone de Beauvoir,

Sade 'used and even copied' (*Must We Burn de Sade?* trs. A. Michelson (London and New York, 1953), p.62).

7. See William Frost, 'The irony of Swift and Gibbon: a reply to F. R. Leavis', *Essays in Criticism*, xvii (1967), 44-5: 'Swift alludes ... to a well-known public sight visible in his London, the bloody back of a prostitute whipped at the end of a cart on the way to the Fleet Prison ... [and comments on] the widespread callousness to the sufferings of not very advantaged groups in Augustan England'. I agree that Swift is probably referring to a whore, or other malefactress, but believe that it is more correct to say, with E. W. Rosenheim, that she 'would, for eighteenth-century readers, be recognizable as someone who deserved flaying' (*Swift and the Satirist's Art* (Chicago, 1963), p.202), and that Swift himself thought so too. Swift was not notably soft-hearted in his ideas about the treatment of 'not very advantaged groups'. In his *Proposal for Giving Badges to the Beggars* and in several other writings, for example, he recommended the whipping of certain classes of beggars, drunkards, whoremongers and others, and did not think that 'those profligate, abandoned Women, who croud our Streets with their borrowed or spurious Issue' deserved any charity (*Works*, XIII.131-40; IX.202). For some disagreements between myself and others about the flayed woman, see *Essays in Criticism*, xx (1970), 496-7; xxi (1971), 115-16 and 417-18. The last of these discussions contains a suggestion by Mr Philip Drew 'that "a woman *flay'd*" may mean "a woman without her make-up on"', which seems to me wholly improbable. It is partly based on a passage in *The Way of the World* where the use of the term to suggest lack of make-up is manifestly metaphorical and mock-violent.

8. William S. Burroughs, *Naked Lunch* (New York, 1966), p.xliv. I find it difficult to accept suggestions that this is not what the passage means.

9. *Works*, XII.114.

10. See G. W. Ireland, *Gide* (Edinburgh and London, 1963), pp.46-50.

11. *Works*, I.140.

12. Ibid., 77.

13. *Tale of a Tub*, ed. A. C. Guthkelch and D. Nichol Smith, 2nd edn (Oxford, 1958), p.123n.; Ronald Paulson, *Theme and Structure in Swift's Tale of a Tub* (New Haven, 1960), pp.53 ff.

14. *Works*, I.31.

15. Something of the same shock may be felt in Blake's juxtaposition of these two aphorisms in the 'Proverbs of Hell', nos 18-19: 'If the fool would persist in his folly he would become wise./Folly is the cloke of knavery.' Blake's first aphorism belongs straightforwardly to the traditional paradoxical exaltation of wise folly. Swift, too, as I shall argue, is invoking that tradition, although his relationship to it is even more elusive than Blake's.

16. W. B. Ewald, *The Masks of Jonathan Swift* (Oxford [Blackwell], 1954), p.39, n.73. Actually, Ewald's remark is not only irrelevant to the real feeling of the passage, but also wrong on its own terms. There actually *is* 'consistency', if one wants it, in the fact that the 'author' is the sort of fool who performs experiments in order to discover the obvious.

17. *Works*, I.114.

18. Ibid., XII.110.
19. Ibid., I.140.
20. Pope, *Essay on Criticism*, l.507.
21. *Paradise Lost*, I.254-5; IV.20-3, 75 ff. For the literary and theological background, see Helen Gardner, 'Milton's "Satan" and the theme of damnation in Elizabethan tragedy', *Essays and Studies*, N.S., i (1948), 58 & n.; and Merritt Y. Hughes, '"Myself am Hell"', *Modern Philology*, liv (1956), 80-94.
22. *Rasselas*, ch. xxxi [i].
23. *Paradise Lost*, IV.75 ff.
24. Donne, 'Batter my heart, three person'd God'. On this poem, and on paradoxes of psychological self-entrapment and infinite regression in Donne generally, see Rosalie L. Colie, *Paradoxia Epidemica. The Renaissance Tradition of Paradox* (Princeton, 1966), esp. pp.139, 413 ff., 495-507. For a modern example of psychological impasse, and of infinite regression, to be resolved by an all-cancelling religious solution, see Eliot's *Ash-Wednesday*, II:

> The single Rose
> Is now the Garden
> Where all loves end
> Terminate torment
> Of love unsatisfied
> The greater torment
> Of love satisfied
> End of the endless
> Journey to no end
> Conclusion of all that
> Is inconclusible ...
> (*Collected Poems 1909-1935* (London, 1951), p.96).

The torments of love satisfied and unsatisfied in Eliot's poem may be compared with Donne's 'queasie paine/Of being belov'd, and loving' ('The Calme', ll.40-1), and with Shakespeare's Sonnet 129, in that all three suggest the psychological impasse of torment *either way*. The suggestion of infinite mental regress, and the wording of the last two lines of the quoted passage, also recall *Rasselas* and its 'conclusion, in which nothing is concluded', which has a recurrent importance in my argument.
25. *Paradise Lost*, IV.81-2.
26. James Boswell, *Life of Johnson*, ed. G. B. Hill and L. F. Powell (Oxford, 1934), I.342 (on the moral of *Rasselas*).
27. See *Works*, IX.261-2: 'The want of belief is a defect that ought to be concealed when it cannot be overcome ... I am not answerable to God for the doubts that arise in my own breast, since they are the consequence of that reason which he hath planted in me, if I take care to conceal those doubts from others, if I use my best endeavours to subdue them, and if they have no influence on the conduct of my life.' Compare Johnson's prayer of 12 August 1784, *Diary, Prayers, and Annals*, ed. E. L. McAdam,

Jr, and D. and M. Hyde (New Haven and London, 1958), pp.383-4: 'teach me by thy Holy Spirit to withdraw my Mind from unprofitable and dangerous enquiries, from difficulties vainly curious, and doubts impossible to be solved.' These and other resemblances between Swift and Johnson are discussed more fully in my essay 'The character of Swift's satire', *Focus: Swift*, ed. C. J. Rawson (London, 1971), pp.21, 17 ff.
28. *Life of Johnson*, II.350-1. The Hill-Powell edition aptly cites, against this passage, Swift's '*perpetual Possession of being well Deceived*'.
29. *Vanity of Human Wishes*, ll.7, 10; *Rasselas*, chs. xi, xxvi.
30. *Vanity of Human Wishes*, ll.5-10.
31. Pope, *Epistle to a Lady*, ll.95-100.
32. Ibid., 2, 41, 270.
33. *Epistle to Bathurst*, ll.103-4; *Epistle to a Lady*, ll.119-20.
34. As in the previous chapter, my phrasing alludes to H. W. Sams's good essay, 'Swift's satire of the Second Person', *ELH. A Journal of English Literary History*, xxvi (1959), 36-44.
35. *Epistle to a Lady*, ll.21-4. The sentence does not in fact end at this point. I refer to a *conclusiveness* of feeling, rather than to a syntactical *conclusion*.
36. *Windsor-Forest*, l.15.
37. *Epistle to a Lady*, ll.41-2.
38. *Poems*, II.530. Swift's lines may also be compared with ll.27-8 of Pope's *Epistle*, which are more severe than the couplet about tulips and charms, but which have a mock-heroic grandiloquence (echoing, as Peter Dixon pointed out in *Notes and Queries*, ccxi (1966), 460-1, Dryden's *Aureng-Zebe*, II.125-7) in sharp contrast to Swift's brisk, light flatness.
39. *A Short Character of ... Thomas Earl of Wharton* (*Works*, III.179).
40. Aspects of Augustan couplet-rhetoric are further discussed in my *Henry Fielding and the Augustan Ideal Under Stress* (London, 1972), chs ii and iii. For a good account of the range and variety of Pope's couplet styles, see John A. Jones, *Pope's Couplet Art* (Athens, Ohio, 1969). William Bowman Piper, *The Heroic Couplet* (Cleveland and London, 1969) is a very full historical and analytical study of the couplet, from the beginnings to Pope and after, and contains much that is pertinent to my discussion.
41. *Tom Jones*, III.x.
42. *Works*, XI.255.
43. Ibid., 246. This and the preceding passage are also discussed in *Henry Fielding and the Augustan Ideal Under Stress*, pp.46-7.
44. See above, pp.15-17.
45. *Works*, XI.247.
46. Ibid., 258 ff.
47. Ibid., 134.
48. Ibid., 245. For further discussion of the chaotic cataloguing, see also chs IV-V, *passim*, esp. p.104.
49. Yeats, *Collected Poems* (London, 1952), p.268; Mailer, *An American Dream*, ch. ii (London, 1966), p.43. For spirals in Mailer and Laing, see above, pp.66 ff. Images of the endless flight of stairs, the infinite regression,

the bottomless drop into a gaping void, are not, of course, confined to twentieth-century authors, though they probably appear most commonly as images of stark anguish in Romantic and post-Romantic times. For some examples from Piranesi, De Quincey and Poe, see Robert M. Adams, *Nil. Episodes in the Literary Conquest of the Void during the Nineteenth Century* (New York, 1966), pp.35-8, 44, 50.

50. Pope, *The First Satire of the Second Book of Horace Imitated*, l.140; *Epilogue to the Satires*, II.208-9.

51. A suggestive recent comment by W. B. Carnochan is apt in this connection: 'irony, Swift's especially, is the satirist's rhetorical victory in the presence of self-defeat' ('Swift's *Tale*. On satire, negation, and the uses of irony', *Eighteenth-Century Studies*, v (1971), 124).

52. *Works*, XI.187-92. See above, pp.21, 144.

53. Ibid., I.71.

54. See above, pp.13-14, 35-6.

55. A more fully documented discussion of this point is given in *Focus: Swift*, pp.43, 47 ff., and *Henry Fielding and the Augustan Ideal Under Stress*, pp.44 ff.

56. See *Focus:Swift*, pp.50-7. Many of the points in this paragraph are considered in greater detail in the essay on 'The character of Swift's satire' in *Focus:Swift*.

57. See *Focus:Swift*, pp.18 ff. Swift's sense of his own turbulent restlessness of spirit comes out very strongly in a famous passage of his letter to the Rev. John Kendall, 11 February 1692, in which he cites the comment of a distinguished man who 'us'd to tell me, that my mind was like a conjur'd spirit, that would do mischief if I would not give it employment ...' (*Correspondence*, I.4).

58. *Works*, XI.131.

59. Ibid., IV.49.

60. Ibid., IX.261-2; see above, n.27.

61. The phrase 'human condition', in various senses, had long been in common use, and I note here what seem to me the three best-known examples of the usage most closely pertinent to the present discussion. Pascal's '*Condition de l'homme:* inconstance, ennui, inquiétude' is no atheistic void, but the reflexion of a man who, like Swift and Johnson (with both of whom he has from time to time been interestingly compared), is convinced of the 'Misère de l'homme sans Dieu' and of the corresponding 'Félicité de l'homme avec Dieu' (*Pensées*, nos. 61, 29; ed. Louis Lafuma (Paris, 1960), pp.122, 117). See Chester F. Chapin's brief recent rebuttal of the notion of an 'existentialist' Pascal, depicting 'the human condition as absurd' ('Johnson and Pascal', in *English Writers of the Eighteenth Century*, ed. John H. Middendorf (New York and London, 1971), pp.7-8; and see the whole essay, pp.3-16, for a valuable discussion of Pascal and Johnson on the subject of human 'restlessness'). The well-known lines about the 'wearisome Condition of Humanity' in the Chorus at the end of Fulke Greville's *Mustapha*, according to Geoffrey Bullough, should be read as meaning that peace is to be found neither in Nature, nor in ritual and

dogma, but in 'the knowledge of God within the heart' (Fulke Greville, *Poems and Dramas*, ed. Bullough (Edinburgh and London, n.d.), II.136-7, 251). For a more recent discussion of the play, and its religious orientation, see Joan Rees, *Fulke Greville* (London, 1971), pp.139-81, esp. 169, 171, 181. Mrs Rees, p.181, notes the ironic fact that Archbishop Tillotson felt obliged to refute the opening lines of Greville's Chorus, which were 'so frequently in the mouths of many who are thought to have no good will to Religion' (John Tillotson, *Works*, 1704, p.329). C. S. Lewis, citing the lines from *Mustapha*, compares Greville to Pascal (*English Literature in the Sixteenth Century* (Oxford, 1968), pp.524-5).

Hobbes presents a somewhat different picture. Religion is prominent in his system, but primarily in its functional, i.e. psychological and political, aspects; and God's nature and existence are much more problematic in him than in Fulke Greville or Pascal. But even Hobbes's 'Natural Condition of Mankind' is defined as a condition of war only so long as it is understood that man is placed in it by 'mere nature': the condition is remediable by government ('a common power to keep them all in awe'), by various operations of the passions and the reason, etc. (*Leviathan*, I.xiii, ed. Michael Oakeshott (Oxford [Blackwell], n.d.), pp.80-4). The actual state of social man in an adequately organized society is by definition different from the state of nature, and does not seem to be open to the kind of radically absurdist view of the 'human condition', whatever the social arrangements, which is frequently met in thinkers of more recent times.

62. Pope, *Epistle to Cobham*, ll.208-9; Johnson, *Rasselas*, *ad fin.*

63. F. R. Leavis, 'The irony of Swift', *The Common Pursuit* (Harmondsworth, 1962), pp.79, 86, etc.

64. Ibid., p.84.

CHAPTER III 'TIS ONLY INFINITE BELOW

1. Wallace Stevens, *Collected Poems* (London, 1959), p.78.
2. Ibid., pp.17, 192-3, 400.
3. Ibid., pp.373, 527.
4. Ibid., p.171.
5. See the poem entitled 'Mud Master' (ibid., pp.147-8). 'Mud Master' seems characteristically to pun on the notions that mud is the master and also that the 'shaft of light' which will release spring is master of the mud.
6. Ibid., pp.227-8. On some creative circularities of Narcissism, see Stevens's *The Necessary Angel* (London, 1960), pp.79-80.
7. *Collected Poems*, p.405.
8. Ibid., p.168.
9. Ibid., pp.68-9, 192-3.
10. *Poems*, II.642.
11. Ibid., 644.
12. *Journal to Stella*, ed. Harold Williams (Oxford, 1948), I.90. Swift had a penchant, notably at the time of the *Journal to Stella*, for identifying himself,

more or less ironically, with Grub Street activity (see Pat Rogers, *Grub Street: Studies in a Subculture* (London, 1972), pp.236 ff.).
13. *Poems*, II.651.
14. Stevens, *Collected Poems*, p.427.
15. *Poems*, II.652.
16. Ibid., 653-4.
17. Ibid., 652, 657.
18. Ibid., 654.
19. *Works*, I.99.
20. See *Tale of a Tub*, ed. A. C. Guthkelch and D. Nichol Smith, 2nd edn (Oxford, 1958), p.158n., citing *Rehearsal Transpros'd*, 1672, p.206.
21. *Works*, I.99.
22. Bacon, *Works*, ed. J. Spedding *et al.* (London, 1857-74), XII.43. Cited by Brian Vickers, *The World of Jonathan Swift* (Oxford [Blackwell], 1968), p.121.
23. R. D. Laing, *The Politics of Experience and The Bird of Paradise* (Harmondsworth, 1967), p.156.
24. Ibid., p.140.
25. The notion of Swift's *exploration through wit* of the psychological condition of man is adapted from Norman O. Brown, *Life Against Death. The Psychoanalytical Meaning of History* (London, 1968), p.168.
26. R. D. Laing, *The Divided Self* (Harmondsworth, 1967), pp.92-3, 162.
27. Ibid., pp.52, 81-2. See 81-2, and next note, for circles and spirals which are not vicious.
28. Ibid., pp.24, 93, 51: in the last example the notion of psychological cannibalism and of self-devouring figures prominently. For further spiral images in Laing, see also *Self and Others* (Harmondsworth, 1971), pp.43, 138, 157, 178. The 'openness' of spirals can of course also be an image of liberation, see above, pp.75 ff.
29. Yeats, *Collected Poems* (London, 1952), pp.280-1.
30. Yeats, 'Vacillation', ibid., p.282.
31. Yeats, 'Byzantium', ibid., p.280. My italics.
32. *Divided Self*, p.53.
33. R. N. Carew Hunt, *The Theory and Practice of Communism* (Harmondsworth, 1966), pp.42-3; R. D. Laing and D. G. Cooper, *Reason and Violence. A Decade of Sartre's Philosophy 1950-1960* (London, 1964), pp.15-16. See also K. R. Popper, *The Open Society and its Enemies*, vol. I: *The Spell of Plato* (London, 1963), pp.16-17 and notes pp.204 ff., for very early conceptions of the relationship of 'flux' to a 'doctrine of the identity of opposites', in Heraclitus.
34. *Theory and Practice of Communism*, pp.43-5; *Reason and Violence*, pp.11-12.
35. Joseph Conrad, 'Henry James, an appreciation', *Notes on Life and Letters* (London, 1949), esp. pp.15-19. For further discussion of the differences between the Jamesian or Conradian novel, and the writings of both Swift and some modern writers who explore 'extreme situations', see above, and below, pp.142-3, 146-52, 182-3.

36. Norman Mailer, *Cannibals and Christians* (New York, 1967), pp.209, 212, 216. Yeats, for different reasons, also believed 'that the definition of character and individuality pertains to the surface of life; being in itself a kind of "mechanical specialisation", it often hinders access to the archetypal "life" beneath' (Peter Ure, *W. B. Yeats and the Shakespearian Moment* (Belfast, 1969), p.12).
37. Mailer, *Advertisements for Myself* (London [Panther Books], 1970), pp.425, 426. See also p.436, 'the spiral spinning a blind spider's path'. For the spiral as one of Mailer's favourite images, see Richard Poirier, *Mailer* (London, 1972), p.59.
38. Conrad, *Notes on Life and Letters*, p.17.
39. Mailer, *The Presidential Papers* (Harmondsworth, 1968), p.198.
40. *Advertisements for Myself*, pp.426-7.
41. D. H. Lawrence, *Fantasia of the Unconscious, and Psychoanalysis and the Unconscious* (Harmondsworth, 1971), p.144.
42. See above, ch. II, *passim*.
43. On Mailer's tendency 'to think in "couples"', see Tony Tanner, 'On the Parapet. A study of the novels of Norman Mailer', *Critical Quarterly*, xii (1970), 160-1. See also Richard Poirier's remarks on Mailer's tendency to think exclusively in terms of polarized oppositions: '"War" is so much the prior condition of experience for Mailer that any elements not in opposition are treated as mere contingencies. One often has the feeling that what gets left out of his work is a lot of the ordinary stuff of life, which he cannot very easily assign to one side or another of an opposition' (*Mailer* (London, 1972), p.25). The phrase 'mere contingencies' recalls Yeats's 'mere complexities'. That there is a relationship between this mode of thinking, and the notion that old-fashioned conceptions of 'character' are no longer applicable, is confirmed not only by Yeats (see above, n.36), but also by a conversation in one of Ionesco's plays, *Victimes du Devoir*: Nicolas and the Policeman discuss the need in the theatre to replace the old psychology, based on the principle of unified 'identity' and 'character', by a new 'dynamic psychology' capable of rendering not static being, but the complexity and formlessness of becoming, and which is at the same time a psychology based on 'antagonism' and polarized 'contradiction' (*Théâtre*, vol. I (Paris, 1954), pp.225-7).
44. For Mailer's dislike of 'the moribund liberalities of the Left', his view that 'the hipster is equally a candidate for the most reactionary and most radical of movements', his notion that the radical and the reactionary see 'the reality more closely than the liberal', his description of himself as a Left Conservative (or radical of both left *and* right), see *Advertisements for Myself*, pp.304, 287-8; *Armies of the Night* (New York, 1968), pp.208-9; and above, pp.146 ff. For the concept of a radicalism, whether of the left or the right, which is the antithesis of 'liberal progressivism', see the comments on Plato and Marx in Popper, *Open Society*, I.164, 167-8. A related conception of political process as a 'polarized circuit', with renewals envisaged as following upon death by self-devouring ('The serpent shall swallow itself ... Then we can have a new snake') may be found in D. H. Lawrence's

Kangaroo, ch.xvi (Harmondsworth, 1968), pp.333-4. Lawrence's hero desires liberation from some specific contemporary manifestations of this circuit, in 'a new recognition of the life-mystery'.

45. I use this phrase in preference to the better-known Trotskyite technical term, 'permanent revolution', in order to avoid confusion. The view held by Marx and by Trotsky that the revolution must continue throughout the world in a continuous process until universal victory is achieved, instead of being allowed to stabilize itself in 'clearly defined stages, each of which was valid for a particular period' is germane to my meaning; but the doctrinal wrangle as between 'permanent revolution' and 'socialism in one country', and other related items of ideology, are marginal to the present argument (see Hunt, *Theory and Practice of Communism*, pp.220 ff.). But I wish more particularly to include the unprogrammatic concepts of continuous rebellion current in various revolutionary youth movements in our time; what Mailer described when he said in *Armies of the Night* that 'the New Left and the hippies were coming upon the opening intimations of a new style of revolution – revolution by theater and without a script' (p.249), the hippies in particular dedicated, in politics as well as in life-style, 'to every turn of the unexpected' (p.251), opposed to programmatic ideologies and strategies ('Communist, Trotskyist, . . . plain Social Democrat' or any other kind) and to the philosophy of the carefully predicted 'next step' (pp.101, 248).

46. *Theory and Practice of Communism*, p.46.

47. *Advertisements for Myself*, pp.286, 284.

48. *An American Dream* (London, 1966), p.43.

49. *The Divided Self*, p.77. In Laing's more recent writings, there is a rejection of the concept of 'schizophrenia', as an artificial and not meaningful classification imposed by society in its own political interests. But the mental predicaments described in *The Divided Self* are not invalidated as facts: Laing's descriptions survive his change of terminology, and the same mental predicaments are recurrently featured in his later writings.

50. Samuel Beckett, *Molloy, Malone Dies, The Unnamable* (London, 1959), pp.318-9. See also Richard N. Coe, *Beckett* (Edinburgh and London, 1964), pp.71, 85-6.

51. *Poems*, II.653-4.

52. *Molloy etc.*, p.303. Examples of the *Tale*'s 'author' and of other 'moderns' using their writings to talk about their sufferings, the severe and unhealthy conditions in which their works were written, etc., occur in the 'Apology' and 'Preface' to the *Tale* (*Works*, I.3, 27). Laing's *Bird of Paradise* also has a quasi-Swiftian 'self-consciousness': see, for example, at *Politics of Experience etc.*, p.152, the reference within the work to the work itself as being 'like all writing an absurd and revolting effort to make an impression on a world that will remain as unmoved as it is avid' (which recalls Gulliver or the Modest Proposer on their failure to persuade a bad world to mend its ways), and the immediately following paragraph, beginning 'Who is not engaged in trying to impress, to leave a mark, to engrave his image on the others and the world' (which, in addition to the

Tub-like 'self-consciousness', may be compared with the opening of section I of the *Tale* and its advice to those who wish 'to be heard in a Crowd', *Works*, I.33). Such 'self-conscious' writing shows that 'infinite regress of self-regard' which Rosalie L. Colie has shown to be traditional in the literature of paradox, and which she finds, notably, in Montaigne (*Paradoxia Epidemica. The Renaissance Tradition of Paradox* (Princeton, 1966), p.519). It would be fair to say that in Beckett or Laing, as in Swift, such things are carried to extremes not often found in other writers, and are fraught with an intensity of excitement or of painfulness which are fairly uncommon.

53. *Molloy etc.*, pp.305, 316.

54. Pat Rogers, in a review of Howard Erskine-Hill's *Pope: The Dunciad* (London, 1972) in *Scriblerian*, v (1972), 43, warns against seeing either Swift or Pope 'as a secret sharer of the duncely agonies'. He adds: 'My own view is that mock sympathy with the hack is simply part of the Scriblerian fiction: a dramatic pose, not an identity crisis.' Both statements seem right and important, especially if the secret sharing of agonies implies sympathy in sorrow. But the fact that there is no sorrow, and that the 'mock sympathy' has satiric and parodic purposes, does not in my view imply that no self-implication of author with parodied hack takes place. It is one of the arguments of this book that some 'secret sharing' (and some not so secret) does take place between Swift and his satiric butts, however complex and elusive this sharing may be.

55. 'A Letter from Capt. Gulliver, to his Cousin Sympson' (*Works*, XI.6); *Modest Proposal* (*Works*, XII.116-7).

56. See above, pp.13-14, 35-6, 57.

57. *Poems*, II.649.

58. *Works*, I.77.

59. *Poems*, II.657. By an ironic coincidence, some cancelled fragments of the actual poem have survived, and are sometimes printed by editors immediately after the final words, *Caetera desiderantur* (*Poems*, II.639, 658-9). See also George P. Mayhew, *Rage or Raillery. The Swift Manuscripts at the Huntington Library* (San Marino, California, 1967), pp.97-100, 109 ff.

60. *Works*, I.135.

61. Ibid., 133. See also the practitioner of 'the Famous Art of *whispering Nothing*' in the Academy of Modern Bedlam, *Tale*, IX (*Works*, I.112), and W. B. Carnochan, 'Swift's *Tale*. On satire, negation, and the uses of irony', *Eighteenth-Century Studies*, v (1971), 122-44, esp. 125-7. Cf. Beckett's Unnamable: '... I had nothing to say and had to say something ...' (*Molloy etc.*, p.400). On the question of writing about 'nothing' in Beckett, see John J. Mood, '"The Personal System" – Samuel Beckett's *Watt*', *Publications of the Modern Language Association of America*, lxxxvi (1971), esp. 258, 263. For some suggestive insights into the relation of madness to configurations of limitless nothingness, see Michel Foucault, *Madness and Civilization. A History of Insanity in the Age of Reason*, trs. Richard Howard (New York and Toronto, 1967), pp.224 ff., esp. 227-8; and p.100. Many discussions of 'nothing' in Rosalie L. Colie, *Paradoxia Epidemica*, are pertinent to my argument, and see also Robert M. Adams, *Nil. Episodes in*

the Literary Conquest of the Void during the Nineteenth Century (New York, 1966).
62. *Dunciad*, I.118-20. On the Miltonic elements of this, see the note in the Twickenham edition (ed. James Sutherland, 3rd edn (London and New Haven, 1963), p.77), and Arthur Sherbo in *Modern Language Review*, lxv (1970), 505.
63. *Paradise Lost*, IV. 75-7.
64. *Notes from Underground*, I.iii, v; trs. A. R. MacAndrew (New York, Toronto and London, 1961), pp.97, 103. See R. D. Laing, *Politics of Experience*, p.33: 'We are afraid to approach the fathomless and bottomless groundlessness of everything. "There's nothing to be afraid of." The ultimate reassurance, and the ultimate terror.'
65. *Works*, IV.38.
66. Ibid., 36.
67. Ibid., IX.262.
68. Ibid., IV.49.
69. *Correspondence*, ed. Harold Williams (Oxford, 1963-5), v.89. For a discussion of patterns of 'infinite regress' in self-consciousness in the literature of paradox, see Colie, *Paradoxia Epidemica*, esp. ch.xii, '"I am that I am": problems of self-reference'. See also Carnochan, 'Swift's *Tale*', pp.131-3, on the 'circle without limits' and 'the vortex of self-reference' in the *Tale of a Tub*.
70. *Works*, I.112-3. See also the researcher in *Gulliver*, III.v, whose project is 'to reduce human Excrement to its original Food' (*Works*, XI.180), and cf. above, chapter 1, n.62.
71. *Rasselas*, ch.xxxi [i]. In the last chapter, or 'conclusion, in which nothing is concluded', the prince's imaginary kingdom gets bigger the more he thinks of it. This is but the final instance in a whole series of unfulfilled aspirations in the tale as a whole. The official moral of *Rasselas*, as Boswell describes it, is to end these infinitely extending desires by fixing men's hopes on 'things eternal' (*Life of Johnson*, ed. G. B. Hill and L. F. Powell (Oxford, 1934), I.342). But Johnson knew that this exercise was itself very difficult, given the restless nature of man, and it is the unfulfilled longings, not the ultimate divine resting-point, which are vivid in this work. In Mailer's 'White Negro', that divine resting-point has itself become an infinitely receding part of the unceasing aspiration, when the hipster's God is described as 'the paradise of limitless energy and perception just beyond the next wave of the next orgasm' (*Advertisements for Myself*, p.283).
72. *The Divided Self*, p.49; and see the chapter on 'Food' in Norman O. Brown's *Love's Body* (New York, 1966), which also cites related passages from more ancient (especially religious) symbolisms.
73. Stevens, *Opus Posthumous* (London, 1959), p.66.
74. Stevens, *Collected Poems*, p.194.
75. *Paradoxia Epidemica*, p.40.
76. Fulke Greville, *Mustapha*, Chorus Tertius, ll.85-6 (*Poems and Dramas*, ed. G. Bullough, II.107), cited Marjorie Hope Nicolson, *The Breaking of the Circle*, rev. edn. (New York and London, 1965), p.47; see Nicolson,

pp.47-8n., and, for a modern image of the snake swallowing itself, see the quotation from Lawrence in n.44 above.

77. Popper, *The Open Society*, I.210: 'Apart from [some] scanty allusions, there is hardly anything to indicate that Plato took the upward or forward part of the cycle seriously. But there are many remarks ... which show that he believed very seriously in the downward movement, in the decay of history'. See Popper's discussion, pp.19 ff., 208 ff., and J. B. Bury, *The Idea of Progress* (New York, 1955), pp.10 ff., 13n. On Swift's 'deteriorationism', see Z. S. Fink, 'Political theory in *Gulliver's Travels*', *ELH. A Journal of English Literary History*, xiv (1947), 151-61, esp. *ad fin.*; Ricardo Quintana, *Swift. An Introduction* (London, 1962), pp.79-80, 153-6; and see above, ch. I, n.58.

78. Mircea Eliade, *The Myth of the Eternal Return* (New York, 1965), *passim*.

79. *The Breaking of the Circle*, p.167.

80. Andrew Marvell, 'On a Drop of Dew', ll.25-6.

81. See *Paradoxia Epidemica*, pp.40, 228 *et passim*.

82. John Donne, 'A Jeat Ring Sent', l.4, cited Nicolson, *The Breaking of the Circle*, p.123.

83. Eugène Ionesco, *La Cantatrice Chauve*, scene XI, *Théâtre*, I.52.

84. Vladimir Nabokov, *Speak, Memory* (London, 1967), p.275.

85. Ibid., p.301.

86. Stevens, *Opus Posthumous*, p.66.

87. Stevens, *Collected Poems*, p.24.

88. Jorge Luis Borges, *Fictions*, ed. Anthony Kerrigan (London, 1965), pp.72-80.

89. Ibid., p.72. In the version printed in the Penguin selection, *Labyrinths*, ed. Donald A. Yates and James E. Irby (Harmondsworth, 1970), p.78, the phrase is 'represent and promise the infinite'. The Spanish text reads 'figuran y prometen el infinito' (*Ficciones* (Buenos Aires, 1967), p.85).

90. *Fictions*, p.80. The version in *Labyrinths*, p.85, gives *'unlimited and cyclical'*. The Spanish text reads *'ilimitada y periódica'* (*Ficciones*, p.95).

91. *Gulliver's Travels*, III.v (*Works*, XI.184). Borges's 'Book' is a revelation of religious mysteries, whereas the projector's 'compleat Body' is in the main, presumably, a secular work of pseudo-science, but Swift's projectors and his mystery-mongering 'dark Authors' are never far apart from one another: see the 'compleat Bodies' in *Tale*, V, X, etc. (*Works*, I.78 9, 118-19; also I.23).

92. *Works*, I.93.

93. Richard N. Coe, *Beckett* (Edinburgh and London, 1964), pp.59, 69.

94. Hugh Kenner, *Flaubert, Joyce and Beckett. The Stoic Comedians* (London, 1964), p.105. On Beckett's 'paradoxical fecundity', see p.81. A recent study of *Watt* has shown that Beckett's lists and permutations are not as complete and unflawed as has been supposed; see John J. Mood, '"The Personal System"—Samuel Beckett's *Watt*', *Publications of the Modern Language Association of America*, lxxxvi (1971), 255-65.

95. Foucault, *Madness and Civilization*, p.21.

96. Ibid., pp.83, 159-60, 199-200 etc.

97. Ibid., pp.173-4.

98. An interesting small example concerning the role of physical confinement in the treatment of mental cases occurs in an interview with Theodore Lidz on 'Schizophrenia, R. D. Laing and the Contemporary Treatment of Psychosis'. Dr Lidz (who is, as it happens, critical of Laing) shows a pragmatic recognition of the paradox that mental patients desire the reassurance but not the imprisoning aspect of confinement. He says that his hospital has 'a closed floor', which, however, is 'only symbolically closed. Anybody who wants to put his mind to it can run off almost any day he chooses. The floor has to be at least symbolically closed to give the patient a sense of a limited area to live in' (*Laing and Anti-Psychiatry*, ed. Robert Boyers and Robert Orrill (Harmondsworth, 1972), p.127).
99. *Reason and Violence*, p.7.
100. *Politics of Experience*, p.95.
101. Ibid., p.110.
102. *Works*, IV.36, 38.
103. *Politics of Experience*, pp.68-9.
104. *Works*, IV.49.
105. Pope, *Essay on Man*, II.121-2; I.291.
106. See A. O. Lovejoy's comment on Swift in *The Great Chain of Being* (New York, 1960), p.239.
107. Martin Price, *To the Palace of Wisdom* (Garden City, New York, 1965), pp.136-7.
108. *Poems*, II.652.
109. See above, ch. II, esp. pp.42 ff., and *Henry Fielding and the Augustan Ideal Under Stress*, pp.44 ff.
110. See *Henry Fielding and the Augustan Ideal Under Stress*, pp.55 ff., 67 ff.

CHAPTER IV CIRCLES, CATALOGUES AND CONVERSATIONS

1. Marjorie Hope Nicolson, *The Breaking of the Circle. Studies in the Effect of the 'New Science' upon Seventeenth-Century Poetry*, rev. edn (New York and London, 1965), p.7.
2. Ibid., p.167.
3. Ibid., p.8.
4. Ibid., p.45.
5. Ibid., p.46; *Works*, I.46 ff.
6. *Works*, I.47.
7. Ibid., 96.
8. Ibid., 117-18. For sources of this passage, see *Tale of a Tub*, ed. A. C. Guthkelch and D. Nichol Smith, 2nd edn (Oxford, 1958), p.185n., and John R. Clark, *Form and Frenzy in Swift's Tale of a Tub* (Ithaca and London, 1970), p.30.
9. Yeats, 'The Second Coming', *Collected Poems* (London, 1952), p.211.
10. Yeats, 'Byzantium', ibid., p.281.
11. See above, pp.72-4.

12. Even the elementary schematism in which the chapters of digression alternate with chapters of religious allegory is violated in the later sections of the *Tale*. Nor are the formally labelled digressions the only examples of actual digressiveness in the work.
13. Louis T. Milic, *A Quantitative Approach to the Style of Jonathan Swift* (The Hague and Paris, 1967), pp.102, 109-11. For other kinds of 'irregularity', see pp.104, 105, 107, 121.
14. W. B. Carnochan, *Lemuel Gulliver's Mirror for Man* (Berkeley and Los Angeles, 1968), p.61.
15. Leo Spitzer, '*Explication de Texte* applied to Walt Whitman's poem "Out of the Cradle Endlessly Rocking"', *ELH, A Journal of English Literary History*, xvi (1949), pp.245 n.10, 246.
16. Whitman, *Song of Myself*, no.51, in *Leaves of Grass*, ed. Gay Wilson Allen (New York, 1960), p.96.
17. Spitzer, '*Explication* ...', p.241.
18. Ibid., p.246.
19. Ibid., p.249, and Spitzer, *Linguistics and Literary History* (New York, 1962), pp.206-7.
20. Spitzer, *Linguistics and Literary History*, pp.207-8.
21. Spitzer, '*Explication* ...', pp.248-9; *Linguistics and Literary History*, p.206.
22. Spitzer, *Linguistics and Literary History*, p.206. On chaotic enumeration, see also Spitzer's *La Enumeración Caótica en la Poesía Moderna* (Buenos Aires, 1945).
23. Carnochan, p.61.
24. Ibid., pp.62-5.
25. Ralph Cohen, 'The Augustan Mode in English Poetry', in *Studies in the Eighteenth Century*, ed. R. F. Brissenden (Canberra, 1968), pp.174-6.
26. Ibid., p.174.
27. Ibid.
28. Ibid., pp.174, 191.
29. Ibid., pp.176, 177, 191, 192.
30. Byron, *Don Juan*, I.cc.
31. See E. R. Curtius, *European Literature and the Latin Middle Ages*, trs. W. R. Trask (London, 1953), pp.194-5, for a brief discussion, and for references to Ovid, Chaucer, Spenser, and others.
32. *Poems*, II.650.
33. See, with particular reference to catalogues in medieval authors, C. S. Lewis, *The Discarded Image. An Introduction to Medieval and Renaissance Literature* (Cambridge, 1964), pp.199-200.
34. Rosemond Tuve, *Elizabethan and Metaphysical Imagery* (Chicago, 1961), pp.119 ff.; George Puttenham, *The Arte of English Poesie*, ed. Gladys D. Willcock and Alice Walker (Cambridge, 1936), p.236.
35. See above, pp.46-7, 55.
36. Pope, *Epistle to Cobham*, l.179.
37. This is not to suggest that Erasmus merely confines himself to alternative phrasings in the narrowest sense. The section to which I referred in

ch.I, n.45 above, for example, discusses the accumulation of numerous non-identical details. But this accumulation is seen as a stylistic strategy in itself, one of the methods 'of amplifying, adorning, or pleasing', a variant on 'varying'.

38. *Joseph Andrews*, III.i.

39. *Works*, XI.296.

40. Swift has some briefer anthologies of 'polite' language, notably in several poems: 'Verses Wrote in a Lady's Ivory Table-Book', *Journal of a Modern Lady*, and *Verses on the Death of Dr. Swift*, ll.80 ff. (*Poems*, I.60-1; II.444 ff., 556 ff.) The last two are more extensive than Fielding's, the first a rather special case, a gay trifle lightly thrown off, yet charged with an unFieldinglike aggressive imagery of ill-breath, excrement, spittle. Fielding, for his part, has no compilations which remotely approach the length of Swift's larger pieces, the *Complete Collection* or (a somewhat different thing) the *Directions to Servants*.

41. The Introduction by 'Simon Wagstaff' facetiously insists 'that the Collection I now offer to the Publick, is full and compleat'. But he knows that carping critics will complain of omissions, and invites readers to inform him if he has left out 'the least Thing of Importance', for inclusion in the second edition (*Works*, IV.101; see also 107). Characteristically, we are made to feel that if the collection is complete, it is yet also incomplete as far as the actual conversation of present-day polite persons is concerned.

42. *Works*, IV.xxviii, 100-1, 124.

43. See *Works*, IV.115 for an amusing admission that some details are introduced only for the sake of eliciting certain phrases, even though the details might appear out of their proper context.

44. For a brief discussion by Simon Wagstaff of the characterization, see the Introduction, *Works*, IV.116-17.

45. Ibid., 215.

46. This is even true when Fielding makes gestures of not being able to account for a circumstance or phenomenon in his novels. See my discussion in *Henry Fielding and the Augustan Ideal Under Stress*, pp. 84, 129.

47. *Works*, IV.216.

48. Richard N. Coe, *Ionesco. A Study of his Plays*, rev. edn (London, 1971), p.67. See the whole chapter, which is entitled 'The apotheosis of the platitude'.

49. Eugène Ionesco, *Notes et Contre-Notes* (Paris, 1966), pp.247 ff.

50. Ibid., p.253.

51. Ibid., p.247, 252-3. See Coe, pp.64 ff., 67.

52. *Notes et Contre-Notes*, p.252.

53. *Works*, IV.114.

54. *Notes et Contre-Notes*, p.251.

55. Ibid. In the play (scene I), as printed in the first volume of Ionesco's *Théâtre* (Paris, 1954), p.24, this piece of nonsense occurs in a somewhat different form from that given by Ionesco in the *Notes*.

56. *La Cantatrice Chauve*, scenes VII, VIII, XI (*Théâtre*, I.37, 47, 53).

57. *Notes et Contre-Notes*, p.250. See also pp.257-8 for an account of how the title was hit upon.

58. Ibid., p.253.
59. Ibid., p.259; *Théâtre*, I.56.
60. *La Cantatrice Chauve*, scene IV (*Théâtre*, I.26 ff.).
61. Ibid., scenes V, I (*Théâtre*, I.31-2, 22 ff.).
62. *Notes et Contre-Notes*, p.252.
63. See Hugh Kenner, *Flaubert, Joyce and Beckett. The Stoic Comedians* (London, 1964), pp.24 ff. *et passim*.
64. René Girard, *Mensonge Romantique et Vérité Romanesque* (Paris, 1961), p.157.
65. Ibid., p.156. On Swift's paired arrangements, see above, p.68.
66. Kenner, pp.15, 23.
67. George P. Mayhew, *Rage or Raillery*, pp.152-3; D. Hamilton, 'Swift, Wagstaff, and the composition of *Polite Conversation*', *Huntington Library Quarterly*, xxx (1967), 281-95. Hamilton exaggerates the dissociation of Wagstaff from Swift. Herbert Davis suggests wrongly that Wagstaff first appeared only in the London edition, and not in the more authentic Dublin edition (both 1738), and that he might have been 'added by Mrs Barber or the London publisher' (*Works*, IV.xxix). Wagstaff does not appear on the Dublin title-page, but appears in the Dublin text (pp.iv, xxxiv), as well as in the London edition (see *Works*, IV.101, 124).
68. *Joseph Andrews*, II.xiii, II.v.
69. *Covent-Garden Journal*, ed. G. E. Jensen (New Haven, 1915), I.155-7.

CHAPTER V CATALOGUES, CORPSES AND CANNIBALS

1. Louis T. Milic, *A Quantitative Approach to the Style of Jonathan Swift* (The Hague and Paris, 1967), pp.87 ff.
2. Ibid., pp.104 ff.
3. Ibid., p.121.
4. *Works*, XI.296.
5. See above, pp.15-17, 50-2.
6. *Works*, XI.247.
7. Ibid., XII.114. For a distinction between the lists in *A Modest Proposal* and those in *Gulliver*, see E. P. J. Corbett, in *A Modest Proposal*, ed. Charles Beaumont (Columbus, 1969), p.83 and n.
8. For some good recent observations on Rabelais's lists, see Gabriel Josipovici, *The World and the Book* (London, 1971), pp.118 ff.
9. Rabelais, I.ix. The passage continues with a friendly, convivial address to the reader. Quotations are from *Oeuvres*, ed. Abel Lefranc *et al.* (Paris, 1912 onwards). Swift read Rabelais in French; see Harold Williams, *Dean Swift's Library* (Cambridge, 1932), p.50.
10. Rabelais, I.i. For other examples of such sets of contradictory epithets among sixteenth-century authors, see *ed.cit.*, I.23, n.37.
11. *Works*, XI.276-7.
12. Rabelais, I.lii. See also the whole of I.liv.
13. See Corbett, p.83, for a similar comment on Swift's 'displays of copia' in *A Modest Proposal*.

14. See André Breton's remark, disputing a comparison between Rabelais and Swift by Voltaire, in *Anthologie de l'Humour Noir* (Paris, 1966), p.25: 'De Rabelais il partage aussi peu que possible le goût de la plaisanterie lourde et innocente et la constante bonne humeur d'après-boire.'
15. Similarly, Rabelais's arithmetical fantasies and exaggerations tend to consist of huge abundances (long lists, large numbers, etc., for their own sake), as in I.xxxvii or I.xlvii (*ed.cit.*, II.320, 377-8). Swift, on the other hand, tends more towards arithmetical precision. His calculations are often very meticulously worked out, and carefully adjusted to exact satiric ironies. The *Modest Proposal* as a whole, or the ledger of Marlborough's cost to the nation in *Examiner*, no.16 (*Works*, III.23), are among the clearest examples. But the observation applies also to more expansive passages, like the computation about the 10,000 parsons and 200 young gentlemen in the *Argument Against Abolishing Christianity* (*Works*, II.30); or the crazy statistics of the first *Drapier's Letter* (*Works*, X.3 ff.), where the object is the precise and negative one of demonstrating the inconvenience and non-viability of Wood's project, rather than a delight in exaggeration *per se*.
16. Paradoxically, too, Pope did not admire Rabelais as much as Swift did. See Joseph Spence, *Observations, Anecdotes, and Characters*, ed. J. M. Osborn (Oxford, 1966), nos.133, 511-13. On the question of affirmations of 'order' in Rabelais and in Pope, it has been suggested to me by Mrs Jenny Mezciems that Rabelais's affirmations do not, like Pope's, reassert existing structures of order, but that they give a sense of pulling down and *rebuilding*. My point about Swift is that he pulls down or negates, without either reaffirming or rebuilding.
17. On Swift's language games, see George P. Mayhew, *Rage or Raillery* (San Marino, California, 1967), pp.131-55. See also articles by Mayhew, and by Irvin Ehrenpreis and James L. Clifford, in *Bulletin of the John Rylands Library*, xxxvi (1954), 413-48, and xxxvii (1955), 368-92. Even Swift's language-games often have a deliberate satiric significance or overtone.
18. *Dunciad*, I.22.
19. Coleridge, *Table Talk*, 15 June 1830: *anima Rabellaisii habitans in sicco*. The phrase goes back to Rabelais, I.v: 'Si je ne boy, je suys à sec, me voylà mort. Mon ame s'en fuyra en quelque grenoillere. En sec jamais l'ame ne habite'. For traditional notions about souls in dry places, see note to Rabelais, I.v, *ed.cit.*, I.55, n.33, and *Gargantua*, ed. Ruth Calder and M. A. Screech (Geneva, 1970), p.41n.
20. *Gulliver's Travels*, II.vii, and especially IV.v (*Works*, XII.134, 247). See above, pp.15-17, 50-2.
21. Eldridge Cleaver, *Soul on Ice* (London, 1971), p.145.
22. 'Prologue to a Long Novel', *Advertisements for Myself* (London [Panther Books], 1970), pp.438-9. Quotations are from this edition, which is unexpurgated, unless otherwise noted. For other Mailerian lists see for example *The Presidential Papers* (Harmondsworth, 1968), pp.18-19, 53, 131.
23. *Advertisements for Myself*, p.427.
24. Ibid., p.428.
25. Ibid., p.438.

26. A. B. England, 'World without order: some thoughts on the poetry of Swift', *Essays in Criticism*, xvi (1966), 39.
27. *Poems*, II.645.
28. *Beggar's Opera*, III.xvi.
29. Fielding, Preface to *Miscellanies, Complete Works*, ed. W. E. Henley (London, 1903), XII.243, *à propos* of *Jonathan Wild*.
30. For Fielding's views on the appropriateness of different attitudes towards the behaviour of the great and the humble, the rich and the poor, see, for example, *Complete Works*, XIII, 37 ff., 138-9, and some comments in my *Henry Fielding*, Profiles in Literature (London, 1968), p.120.
31. 'Advertisement from the Publisher to the Reader', prefixed to 1754 edition of *Jonathan Wild, Complete Works*, II.xv.
32. Fielding, *Covent-Garden Journal*, no.3, 11 January 1752, ed. G. E. Jensen (New Haven, 1915), I.150.
33. See Milic, ch.iv, *passim*.
34. Joyce, *Portrait of the Artist as a Young Man* (London, 1956), p.245.
35. Wyndham Lewis, *Blasting and Bombardiering*, Introduction (London, 1967), p.3.
36. See *Advertisements*, p.426, where Marion Faye is described as being one of those 'who are Napoleonic in their ambitions and wide as the Renaissance in their talents'. The allusion here seems to me no more than a verbal flourish: Renaissance versatility, whether evoked ironically or otherwise, plays no very deep or important part in Mailer's story. For a somewhat fuller ironic treatment of the ideal in an American comic novel, see Saul Bellow, *Adventures of Augie March*, ch.v.
37. Yeats, *Collected Poems* (London, 1952), p.150.
38. Frank Kermode, *Romantic Image* (London, 1961), p.38.
39. Yeats, *Collected Poems*, p.151.
40. Dryden, *Absalom and Achitophel*, I.550, 545-6.
41. T. S. Eliot, *Collected Poems 1909-1935* (London, 1951), p.80.
42. Keats, letter to Richard Woodhouse, 27 October 1818.
43. *Advertisements for Myself*, p.425. The Panther Books edition, from which I quote, gives 'motions' instead of 'emotions', and I give the latter reading from the version published by André Deutsch (London, 1961), p.429, which follows the reading of the American first edition, published by Putnam (New York, 1959), p.515. The Deutsch text, though expurgated, seems more authentic in some details. The question of whether Mailer's speaker is to be identified with Mailer himself is discussed later, pp. 130 ff.
44. In the *Battle of the Books*, the 'modern' Dryden is also mocked for failing in his attempt to achieve the epic sublimity of the ancient Virgil (*Works*, I.157-8).
45. *Works*, XII.247. See above, pp.15-17, 50-2.
46. Poirier, *Mailer*, p.34.
47. *Advertisements*, p.440.
48. Allen Ginsberg, *Howl and other Poems* (San Francisco, 1959), p.12.
49. *Rape of the Lock*, IV.54.
50. For the market-place or department-store as images evoked by poetic

catalogues or what Leo Spitzer, discussing Whitman, Claudel and others, has called the device of 'chaotic enumeration', see Spitzer, 'Interpretation of an Ode by Paul Claudel', *Linguistics and Literary History* (New York, 1962), p.206. And see Allen Ginsberg on Whitman, in 'A Supermarket in California': 'What thoughts I have of you tonight, Walt Whitman, for I walked down the sidestreets under the trees with a headache self-conscious looking at the full moon./In my hungry fatigue, and shopping for images, I went into the neon fruit supermarket, dreaming of your enumerations! ...' (*Howl and other Poems*, p.23).

For my image of the melting-pot, see Mailer's own image of a 'heat-forge' in *Advertisements*, p.437, where he talks of the party thrown by Cara Beauchamp, a Negro bawd of Marion Faye's, at which the guest-list was found: 'it had an artist's assortment of those contradictory and varied categories of people who made up the obdurate materials of new sociological alloy in the heat-forge of a ball at Cara Beauchamp's.'

51. For some analogues to Pope's passage, see the Twickenham commentary, *Rape of the Lock*, ed. Geoffrey Tillotson, 3rd edn (London and New Haven, 1962), p.188 n.54.

52. *Advertisements*, pp.438, 425.

53. Ibid., p.437.

54. Cited by David Lodge, 'Objections to William Burroughs', *Critical Quarterly*, viii (1966), 203. Comparisons of Burroughs to Swift are common, as in the quotation from *Playboy* about his 'Swiftian vision', on the cover of *The Ticket that Exploded*, Evergreen Black Cat Edition (New York, 1968). For some comments, see Lodge, pp.206-7.

55. *Advertisements*, pp.426, 427.

56. E.g. *Tale*, XI (*Works*, I.123-6).

57. Poirier, *Mailer*, pp.65-6, citing Peter Brooks.

58. This is very evident in Whitman, and also, in a different way, in the Claudel ode discussed by Spitzer, *Linguistics and Literary History*, pp.206-7 and 226 n.28, *et passim*.

59. *Advertisements*, p.426.

60. *The Deer Park* (London, 1967), p.309. For the notion of 'coming out the other side' in the psychology of R. D. Laing and of Sartre, see R. D. Laing and D. G. Cooper, *Reason and Violence. A Decade of Sartre's Philosophy 1950-1960* (London, 1964), p.74, and R. D. Laing, *The Politics of Experience and The Bird of Paradise* (Harmondsworth, 1967), pp.97 f., 104 ff.

61. *Advertisements*, p.286.

62. Ibid., pp.283, 409. For Mailer on Reich, see for example *Advertisements*, pp.347, 406; *Armies of the Night* (New York, 1968), p.34; Poirier, *Mailer*, pp.73, 77. For Reich's notions of God, see Charles Rycroft, *Reich* (London, 1971), pp.76-7, 89-91.

63. *The Prisoner of Sex* (London, 1971), p.87.

64. Ibid., p.196. Compare the mocking imagery of vision, fire, orgasm etc., in *Mechanical Operation of the Spirit* (*Works*, I.189). Anti-Puritan satire before Swift was also much given to noting the operation of a lustful or

visionary 'fire' in Puritan worship: see Clarence M. Webster, 'Swift and some earlier satirists of Puritan enthusiasm', *Publications of the Modern Language Association of America*, xlviii (1933), 1144 ff.
65. *Advertisements*, p.431.
66. See *Armies of the Night*, p.103; *Prisoner of Sex*, p.87. For related concepts, see Poirier, *Mailer*, pp.28, 69.
67. *Presidential Papers*, p.198. See above, p.68.
68. Yeats, 'Crazy Jane Talks with the Bishop', *Collected Poems*, p.294.
69. *Works*, I.103-4.
70. *Advertisements*, pp.404, 414; *An American Dream*, ch.ii (London, 1966), pp.46 ff.
71. *An American Dream*, pp.47 ff.
72. *Prisoner of Sex*, pp.117.
73. Ibid.
74. *Tale*, XI (*Works*, I.121).
75. *Works*, I.92.
76. *Prisoner of Sex*, p.110, citing Miller, *The World of Sex*, etc. (London, 1970), p.76.
77. The fullest accounts, and a bibliography, of the background to Swift's anti-Puritan satire are to be found in articles by Clarence M. Webster, especially those in *Publications of the Modern Language Association of America*, xlvii (1932), 171-8; xlviii (1933), 1141-53; l (1935), 210-23. See also W. P. Holden, *Anti-Puritan Satire 1572-1642* (New Haven, 1954), *passim*.
78. See Webster, *PMLA*, xlviii (1933), 1153; Susie I. Tucker, *Enthusiasm* (Cambridge, 1972), p.69: 'Swift is one of the earliest critics to recognise that Enthusiasm may be found elsewhere than in religion.' Cf. Phillip Harth, *Swift and Anglican Rationalism* (Chicago and London, 1969), pp.111-12.
79. Norman O. Brown, *Life Against Death. The Psychoanalytical Meaning of History* (London, 1968), 163-81. Against Brown: Irvin Ehrenpreis, *Swift: the Man, his Works, and the Age*, vol. I (London, 1962), pp.244-6; Martin Price, *To the Palace of Wisdom* (Garden City, New York, 1965), p.194. Swift, and other satirists, in fact conceded a kind of ghastly sincerity to Puritans. See Harth, pp.71 ff.
80. *Works*, I.104. For Louis's fistula, a common topic of satirists, see also Swift, *Poems*, I.10, and *Poems on Affairs of State*. Volume VI: *1697-1704*, ed. Frank H. Ellis (New Haven and London, 1970), p.10.
81. Sir Thomas Browne, *Pseudodoxia Epidemica*, II.iii, cited in *Tale of a Tub*, ed. A. C. Guthkelch and D. Nichol Smith, 2nd edn (Oxford, 1958), p.358.
82. Allen Ginsberg, *Kaddish and other Poems 1958-1960* (San Francisco, 1961), pp.92-4.
83. *Works*, I.102-3. On vapours, see Harth, pp.101 ff.
84. Ibid., 97.
85. Ibid., 100-1. At the end of section VI we had been told of the explicit connection between the Aeolists and Jack, whom they acknowledge 'for their Author and Founder' (*Works*, I.89). But the Aeolist chapter itself

(section VIII) is more generalized, avoiding reference to Jack until the end.
86. An exception should perhaps be made for extreme revolutionary sectarians like the Ranters, who were given to excremental notions about God, to open blasphemy, and to open sexual permissiveness. They were severely repressed in the middle of the seventeenth century, and had ceased to be a significant social force at the time Swift was writing. See A. L. Morton, *The World of the Ranters* (London, 1970), pp.70-114, esp. pp.76-7, 79 ff., 89 ff.; and Christopher Hill, *The World Turned Upside Down* (London, 1972), pp.252 ff., 273 ff.
87. *Advertisements*, p.425. Mailer's remarks may be compared with the Ranters' defiance of pharisaic accusations of blasphemy (Morton, op. cit, pp.79-80).
88. *Works*, I.26, 99.
89. See above, p.65.
90. *Tale*, ed. Guthkelch and Nichol Smith, pp.323, 326 etc.
91. *Works*, I.71 and n.
92. Ibid., XII.38 ff.; *Poems*, I.193 and III.807-8. On Swift's moods of contempt for other clergymen, and his ambiguous self-implication in this contempt, see Morris Golden, *The Self Observed: Swift, Johnson, Wordsworth* (Baltimore and London, 1972), pp.39 ff., 59-60.
93. *Works*, I.177.
94. Ibid., 178.
95. Ibid., 184.
96. *Tale*, ed. Guthkelch and Nichol Smith, p.326; Romans, VII.
97. *Armies of the Night*, p.36. On homosexuality, see also *Advertisements*, pp.187 ff.; *Prisoner of Sex*, pp.161-74.
98. *Armies of the Night*, pp.76-7.
99. *Works*, I.176. On the special sense of '*Corruption*', see *Tale*, ed. Guthkelch and Nichol Smith, p.269n.
100. Gestures of irony, or of partial self-dissociation, often show themselves when Mailer talks about hip and related topics, even at his most admiring. See Poirier, *Mailer*, 77 ff. for a good discussion, with some details of which it seems to me possible to disagree, but which conveys well the principal ambiguity. For the nasty reverse (or Square or Wasp version) of orgasmic and aggressive aspirations, see *Why Are We in Vietnam?*, *passim*. This novel even has specifically Swiftian quips about the phallic properties of ears (ch.vi (New York, 1968), p.97; cf. *Tale*, XI (*Works*, I.125, 129-30)). For Swift on religious violence, see *Tale*, XI (*Works*, I.123-6); and on orgies, ancient and modern, *Mechanical Operation* (*Works*, I.186).
101. *Tale*, ed. Guthkelch and Nichol Smith, pp.322, 326.
102. See Mailer's attack on existentialist atheism, *Advertisements*, p.274. The seventeenth-century Ranters also had views about the positive religious value of 'blasphemy' and oaths (Morton, op. cit., pp.79-80; Hill, op. cit., p.273).
103. See the passage in a tape-recorded interview where Mailer says 'God is no longer all-powerful' and then records, impishly, in square brackets: '[Here a phrase was lost to static in the tape]' (*Advertisements*, p.309). On *frissons*, and Mailer's interest in experiences evoked by that word, see the

reference to 'the microscopically sensuous and all but ineffable *frissons* of mental becoming' (*Advertisements*, p.274).
104. See Poirier, *Mailer*, pp.117-18. On the Manichaeism, see Richard G. Stern, cited by Mailer in *Advertisements*, p.306: 'Although centuries of epic theological and philosophical finagling seem to have passed him by, he is the most explicit "theologian" of all the writers [of a group which includes Bellow, Malamud, etc.], a kind of Manichaean whose overlooking of his "heretic" predecessors seems not only forgivable, but, considering the quality and urgency of his expression, indispensable.'
105. *Advertisements*, p.309.
106. *Prisoner of Sex*, p.234.
107. *Advertisements*, p.442. In the comparison of himself with God, and in the notions of pantheistic relationship which he shares with Ginsberg and others (including Whitman), Mailer may again be compared with the Ranters (see Morton, op. cit., pp.92, 70, 73-4; Hill, op. cit., pp.151, 160 ff., 165-6, 168, 176).
108. Eliot, *Waste Land*, l.243. *Collected Poems 1909-1935*, p.70.
109. *Works*, I.180. For Ranter versions of the deliberate confusion between good and evil, God and the Devil, see Morton, op. cit., pp.77, 92; Hill, op. cit., p.273.
110. *Works*, I.100.
111. Ibid., 105, 106.
112. Ibid., 108.
113. Ibid., IV.36.
114. Ibid., I.108.
115. Ibid., IV.49. See above, pp.57-8, 73-4, 80.
116. *Works*, IV.49.
117. *Advertisements*, p.231.
118. Ibid., p.313.
119. Swift sensed as closely as does Mailer the ways in which a free indulgence of thought and 'spirit' resolves itself also into an indulgence of the senses; that certain forms of worship stimulate the connection; and that the restraints of institutional (as distinct from a deeply 'inward') religion hold it in check. When Mailer repudiates 'the God of the churches' and puts in his place

> that God which every hipster believes is located in the senses of his body, that trapped, mutilated and nonetheless megalomaniacal God who is It, who is energy, life, sex, force, the Yoga's *prana*, the Reichian's orgone, Lawrence's 'blood', Hemingway's 'good', the Shavian life-force; 'It'; God; ... the unachievable whisper of mystery within the sex, the paradise of limitless energy and perception just beyond the next wave of the next orgasm (*Advertisements*, p.283),

he is setting up several connections which Swift too explores in his discussions of the Aeolists and the Mechanical Operators at 'the Height and *Orgasmus* of their Spiritual exercise' (*Works*, I.189): connections between 'limitless' aspiration and the provisional orgasmic 'leap', between spiritual quest and sexual release, between Yoga (cf. Swift on the '*Jauguis* . . . of *India*,' *Works*, I.178) and Reich. Mailer's example of Lawrence, the English Puritan turned apostle of sexual fulfilment, would have struck Swift as symbolically apt. And if Swift regarded these connections, albeit psychologically all too true, as at the same time blasphemous and obscene, and if he regarded sexual indulgence with a Pauline severity, it is of interest that Reich, the pundit of orgasmic regeneration (who believed, to boot, that man created God, and whose sexual gospel has been said to have a 'puritanical' solemnity of Lawrentian proportions), came at the end of his life 'to justify St. Paul's strictures on the Flesh' (see Charles Rycroft, *Reich* (London, 1971), pp.90, 32, 102).

120. Wotton, in *Tale*, ed. Guthkelch and Nichol Smith, p.323.
121. *Works*, IX.262.
122. See above, pp.51-2.
123. See above, pp.38-9.
124. *Works*, XI.296.
125. Ibid., 289-90. See above, p.27.
126. *Advertisements*, p.441.
127. Whitman, *Song of Myself*, no.20. My quotations are from *Leaves of Grass*, ed. Gay Wilson Allen (New York, 1960).
128. Ibid., nos.6-7, 49.
129. Ibid., no.15.
130. Ibid., no.8.
131. Ibid., no.49.
132. Ibid., no.24.
133. *Advertisements*, p.435. See above, p.71.
134. Howard M. Harper, Jr, *Desperate Faith. A Study of Bellow, Salinger, Mailer, Baldwin and Updike* (Chapel Hill, 1967), p.116.
135. *Advertisements*, pp.392-416.
136. *Presidential Papers*, p.144. For Mailer's autobiographical relationship with his narrators and characters, see Poirier, *Mailer*, pp.45-6, 125-6; Harper, *Desperate Faith*, p.113, etc.
137. *Advertisements*, p.391.
138. Ibid., p.305.
139. Ibid., p.269. The last seven words are quoted from the earlier English edition, published by André Deutsch (London, 1961), p.281, which agrees with the American first edition, published by Putnam (New York, 1959), p.336. The Panther text here reads 'nothing to do with me', which is clearly wrong from the context.
140. *Why Are We in Vietnam?*, p.27.
141. Ibid., p.22.
142. *Advertisements*, p.423.
143. Ibid., p.187.
144. Ibid.
145. Ibid., p.285.
146. *Works*, I.22.
147. *Advertisements*, p.286.

148 *Works*, I.132-3.
149. *Advertisements*, p.425.
150. Ibid., p.441.
151. Ibid., p.423.
152. Ibid., p.442.
153. Keats, letter to Richard Woodhouse, 27 October 1818.
154. *Works*, I.100.
155. Ibid., 243. For discussion of the passage in section VIII, see *Tale*, ed. Guthkelch and Nichol Smith, pp.159-60n. See also Pliny, *Natural History*, VIII.li, and Rabelais, v.xxx.
156. See Walter Jackson Bate, *From Classic to Romantic* (New York, 1961), pp.144, 146; also 132 ff., for some eighteenth-century precursors; and M. H. Abrams, *The Mirror and the Lamp* (London, 1960), pp.130, 245 ff., 347 n.77, etc.
157. Flaubert, *Madame Bovary*, ed. Édouard Maynial (Paris [n.d.]), Introduction, p.xxiv.
158. See Edgar Wind's chapter on 'Pan and Proteus' in *Pagan Mysteries in the Renaissance* (Harmondsworth, 1967), pp.191-217.
159. Pico della Mirandola, 'On the Dignity of Man', para.4, paras.3 ff., in *The Renaissance Philosophy of Man*, ed. E. Cassirer, P. O. Kristeller, and J. H. Randall, Jr (Chicago, 1956), pp.224 ff, 234. See also Wind, *Pagan Mysteries*, p.191 nn.1-2. For a satirical extension, in the transformations of Ben Jonson's Volpone and Mosca, see the discussion by Alvin Kernan, *The Plot of Satire* (New Haven and London, 1965), esp. pp.130 ff.
160. Poirier, *Mailer*, p.77.
161. *Works*, I.26-7.
162. *Dunciad*, I.20.
163. *Advertisements*, pp.203-4.
164. E.g. *A Fire on the Moon* (London, 1970), p.9: 'He has learned to live with questions. Of course, as always, he has little to do with the immediate spirit of the time. Which is why Norman on this occasion wonders if he may call himself Aquarius. Born January 31st, he is entitled to the name, but he thinks it a fine irony ... etc., etc. ...'
165. See Brigid Brophy's recent comment on *The Prisoner of Sex*, *Sunday Times Magazine*, 12 September 1971, p.53: 'Mr. Mailer writes in the third person, presumably because the pronoun "I" wouldn't remind the reader often enough that Mr. Mailer is a he. (I take it he's accumulating these references against the dread day when the world turns out to contain a Mr. Norman Mailest).'
166. 'A Letter from Capt. Gulliver, to his Cousin Sympson', *Works*, XI.6. Originally, Gulliver had thought the Yahoos of England 'utterly incapable of Amendment by Precepts or Examples' (XI.6) and was reluctant to publish. But on Sympson's encouragement, Gulliver allowed the book to be published, and 'firmly counted' on many reformations in the human race as a result (XI.6-7). His 'surprise', however, may be taken less as a change of view from his earlier scepticism, than as a Swiftian ironic turn meant to drive home the discredit of unmendability, just as the earlier scepticism

was an irony about the same unmendability. The change within Gulliver strikes us as rhetorical rather than characterological, and the shifts of irony take precedence over logic of argument or consistency of character, even if logic and consistency might be said to have been to some extent preserved.
167. *Advertisements*, pp.422-3. The word 'affectation', however, is taken from the edition published by Deutsch, p.426; the Panther text has 'affection'.
168. *Works*, I.109-110.
169. Ibid., 110.
170. Ibid., 140.
171. *Advertisements*, p.7.
172. See above, pp.2-3, 133 ff.
173. *Works*, I.81-2.
174. Poirier, *Mailer*, pp.59 f.; *Advertisements*, pp.17 ff.
175. *Works*, I.22, 102.
176. *Advertisements*, p.286.
177. Ibid., p.17.
178. Ibid., p.213.
179. *Armies of the Night*, p.68.
180. See Robert M. Adams, 'Jonathan Swift, Thomas Swift, and the authorship of *A Tale of a Tub*', *Modern Philology*, lxiv (1967), esp. 207 ff., 219 ff., 226.
181. *Armies of the Night*, p.68.
182. See Conrad, *A Personal Record* (London, 1925), 'A Familiar Preface', p.xix: 'I have always suspected in the effort to bring into play the extremities of emotions the debasing touch of insincerity.' On his distrust of 'absolute' modes of feeling, of 'fanaticism', etc., see pp.xxi-xxii. Cf. Peter Ure's interesting contrast between Yeats and Conrad, in which, despite important similarities, Conrad is said not to share Yeats's longing for an 'annulment of human intricacies' ('The Plays', in *An Honoured Guest. New Essays on W. B. Yeats*, ed. Denis Donoghue and J. R. Mulryne (London, 1965), p.149). On this topic, see also above, pp.66-8, 164-5 nn.35-6, 43.
183. Cf. Mailer's phrase about 'that uncharted journey into the rebellious imperatives of the self' which the hipster makes (*Advertisements*, p.271).
184. *Works*, I.109.
185. Ibid., 109-10.
186. Ibid., X.54.
187. Ibid., XII.25.
188. Ibid., 157-8.
189. Ibid., xxvii; *Poems*, III.794-801.
190. *Works*, XII.158.
191. *Poems*, III.830.
192. *Works*, XI.187, 190. See above, pp.21, 55.
193. The phrase is from Antonin Artaud, *Le Théâtre et son Double, Oeuvres Complètes*, vol. IV (Paris, 1964), p.103.
194. Ibid., IV.109.
195. *Advertisements*, p.425.
196. See above, pp.13-14, 35-6, 57.

197. Marshall McLuhan, *The Gutenberg Galaxy* (London, 1967), pp.255-6.
198. Ibid., p.259.
199. Ibid., p.255.
200. Ibid., pp.255 ff.
201. *The Village Voice*, 11 May 1961, p.14.
202. Ibid., pp.11-14.
203. *The Village Voice*, 18 May 1961, p.14.
204. Conrad, *Youth, Heart of Darkness, etc.* (London, 1956), pp.138, 144, 147, etc. See the apposite comment, made in another context by Diana Trilling, 'Norman Mailer', *Encounter*, November 1962, p.52: 'It is quite a long time now since Conrad asked us to choose between his Kurtz and his "Pilgrims", between an heroic principle of evil and a seedy, hypocritical bourgeoisie that lacks the courage of its essential malevolence.'
205. *Youth, Heart of Darkness, etc.*, p.151.
206. Ibid., pp.138, 147.
207. Ibid., p.144.
208. Cf. Artaud's 'liberté magique du songe' (*Oeuvres Complètes*, IV.103).
209. Ibid., 102-3, 109.
210. Conrad is not the only modern writer to have written about Africa as a land of inner self-discovery. Other examples are the African sections of Céline's *Voyage au Bout de la Nuit* (1932), and the whole of Graham Greene's *Journey Without Maps* (1936). In the latter, Greene comments on some tribal rites: 'One had the sensation of having come home, for here one was finding associations with a personal and a racial childhood, one was being scared by the same old witches ...' (Harmondsworth, 1971, p.93).
211. *Youth, Heart of Darkness, etc.*, p.150.
212. Ibid., p.151.
213. Ibid.
214. *Armies of the Night*, p.208. For various 'contradictions' in Mailer, see Diana Trilling, op. cit., pp.45-6.
215. *Armies of the Night*, pp.208-9.
216. Yeats, 'The Seven Sages', *Collected Poems*, p.272.
217. *Partisan Review*, XXXV (1968), 219.
218. *Works*, II.13.
219. Ibid., XII.41.
220. *Advertisements*, p.425.
221. Ibid., p.286.
222. George Orwell, 'Politics vs. Literature: An Examination of *Gulliver's Travels*', *Selected Essays* (Harmondsworth, 1957), p.132. Orwell notes the combination of totalitarian and anarchist elements.
223. See James A. Preu, *The Dean and the Anarchist* (Tallahassee, 1959), *passim*.
224. *Advertisements*, p.283.
225. Ibid., p.284.
226. Ibid., p.283.
227. Ibid., p.285.
228. *Partisan Review*, XXXV (1968), 219-20.

229. *Works*, XI.293.
230. Ibid., 293-4.
231. *Partisan Review*, xxxv (1968), p.221.
232. *Works*, XI.294.
233. *Partisan Review*, xxxv (1968), 219-20.
234. *Works*, XI.294.
235. *Partisan Review*, xxxv (1968), 219-20; *Works*, XI.273-4. The absence of literature or literacy, or the presence of a degree of hostility towards literature, are particularly recurrent items in the Utopian literature of the white man (see Robert C. Elliott, *The Shape of Utopia* (Chicago and London, 1970), pp.121-8).
236. McLuhan, *Gutenberg Galaxy*, pp.262, 256, 255; *Dunciad*, IV.630.
237. On the 'caste system' of the Houyhnhnms, 'which is racial in character', see Orwell, *Selected Essays*, p.131.
238. *Partisan Review*, xxxv (1968), 220.
239. See above, pp.67-8.
240. *Works*, I.115.
241. *The Village Voice*, 18 May 1961, p.14.

INDEX

The word 'cited' occurs in brackets against authors or titles quoted or alluded to in the text without actually being *named* in the place indicated.